Justification

in earlier

Medieval Theology

Charles P. Carlson, Jr.

MARTINUS NIJHOFF

THE HAGUE

JUSTIFICATION IN EARLIER MEDIEVAL THEOLOGY

To my mother and father

JUSTIFICATION IN EARLIER MEDIEVAL THEOLOGY

by

CHARLES P. CARLSON, JR.

MARTINUS NIJHOFF / THE HAGUE / 1975

ISBN 90 247 1709 4

TABLE OF CONTENTS

PREFACE

One of the pleasures and privileges of scholarship is the opportunity to express one's gratitude to friends and colleagues upon the occasion of a publication. As with many scholarly first books, this present work had its genesis as a doctoral dissertation, and hence my first and most profound acknowledgment must be to Professor S. Harrison Thomson of the University of Colorado, whom I am honored to be able to describe as my mentor. Only my fellow "Old Thomsonians" can appreciate the common debt we owe to this great medievalist who was also a magnificent teacher and counsellor. Presently in retirement, he continues to be our principal inspiration and model of scholarly distinction. I am also greatly indebted to another former mentor and now my senior colleague and chairman at the University of Denver, Professor Allen D. Breck, who, together with Deans Edward A. Lindell and Gerhard H. Mundinger, constantly encouraged and assisted my further progress and read the manuscript in its final stages, offering many valuable suggestions as to style and substance. My university provided me with generous support in the form of research funds and clerical services; I am grateful to those colleagues who made this assistance possible, as well as to friends at other institutions who shared their knowledge and frequently gave salutary advice. Finally, I thank my wife who, in addition to supplying the numerous and extraordinary forms of tender, loving care normally required of the academic spouse, successfully accomplished the formidable task of keeping two very lively preschool children out of my study during the critical periods of research and writing.

C.P.C.

LIST OF BIBLIOGRAPHIC ABBREVIATIONS

Affeldt W. Affeldt, "Verzeichnis der Römerbriefkommentare der lateinischen Kirche bis zu Nikolaus von Lyra", *Traditio* 13 (1957), pp. 396-406.

Bardenhewer O. Bardenhewer, *Geschichte der altkirchlichen Literatur*, 2d ed., 5 vols. (repr. Darmstadt : Wissenschaftliche Buchgesellschaft, 1962).

Clavis E. Dekkers and A. Gaar, *Clavis patrum latinorum*, rev. ed., *Sacris Erudiri* 3 (1961).

Denifle H. Denifle, *Die abendländischen Schriftausleger bis Luther über Justitia Dei (Rom. 1, 17) und Justificatio* (Mainz : Kirchheim, 1905).

DTC *Dictionnaire de théologie catholique*, 15 vols. (Paris : Letouzy et Ané, 1903-50).

McNally R. E. McNally, *The Bible in the Early Middle Ages* (Westminster, Md. : Newman, 1959), pp. 83-117.

Manitius M. Manitius, *Geschichte der lateinischen Literatur des Mittelalters*, 3 vols. (Munich : Beck, 1911-31).

MPL J. P. Migne, *Patrologiae cursus completus. Series latina*, 221 vols. (Paris, 1844-64).

Spicq C. Spicq, *Esquisse d'une histoire de l'exégèse au moyen âge* (Paris : J. Vrin, 1944).

Stegmüller F. Stegmüller, *Repertorium biblicum medii aevi*, 7 vols. (Barcelona : 1950-61).

WA Martin Luther, *D. Martin Luthers Werke : kritische Gesammtausgabe*, 1- vols. (Weimar : H. Behlau, 1883-). ("Weimar Ausgabe").

CHAPTER I

INTRODUCTION

The unique significance of the life and ministry of St. Paul has always been acknowledged, if variously interpreted, by teachers and scholars in all periods of the Church's history. This is no less true of the Latin Church in the Middle Ages. But the distinctive interpretations and emphases placed upon certain elements of Paul's teaching by medieval theologians, and the lack of emphasis upon others, present a number of special problems to the historian of Church doctrine and practice. This study concerns one of these problems, medieval interpretations of Paul's doctrine of justification. Before proceeding to this specific topic, however, a few general remarks concerning Pauline influence in the medieval period may serve to better introduce the subject within its historical context.

1. Preliminary Remarks : Paulinism in the Middle Ages

For the history of the early Church, the primary importance of St. Paul was as the "Apostle to the Gentiles", the missionary primarily responsible for the initial expansion of Christianity into the Graeco-Roman world, as chronicled in the New Testament book of Acts. But it is not this aspect of Paul's career which was to be of widest significance for the subsequent history of the Church. Indeed, it has been plausibly argued—especially since Paul did not initiate missionary activity among the Gentiles—that Christianity might have spread about the Mediterranean without him,[1] although one may conjecture, with considerable assurance, in a radically different form.

Rather, it was as an advocate of the Gospel and the most forceful interpreter of the Christian *kerygma* to the ancient world, adapting the

---

[1] H. Lietzmann, *A History of the Early Church*, trans. B. L. Woolf (New York : Meridian Books, 1961), vol. 1, p. 112.

Judaic thought-forms of the Gospel to the cultural environment of late Hellenism and in the process formulating his own distinctive Christian teaching, that St. Paul brought to fruition his incomparable influence upon the future of the Church. Lietzmann has essentially stated the case when he says of Paul, that "he gave the religion of Jesus the form in which it was capable of conquering the world ..."[2] Further, it is the Pauline teaching that has endured as the basic theological account of the work of Christ. One should note, with Harnack, the significance of the fact that Paul was both Apostle and theologian; this was "of the utmost importance", Harnack remarks, "for the legitimizing of the later development of Christianity as a system of doctrine ..."[3] And the circumstance that this first statement of a Christian theology—written by a man who was, in the first instance, a trained theologian of the Jewish faith—should be included in the New Testament canon assured the influence of his thought upon all subsequent development in Christian theology.

It has been a matter of particular interest to students of Christian thought that Paul's teaching has been prominently associated with both the most progressive and the most radical movements in Christian theology, indeed often acting as the dynamic influence upon their respective protagonists. A most prominent example is St. Augustine, who developed the Pauline concepts of grace, sin, predestination and free will into key doctrines of his vast dogmatic synthesis which has remained historically the principal source of orthodox doctrine for Western Christianity. One may also cite medieval figures such as the ninth-century bishop, Claudius of Turin, an exegete and controversialist, who defended a position of extreme iconoclasm which strongly anticipated Zwingli, basing his arguments on Paul's strictures against outward observances and ceremonialism; and also Claudius' supporter, the more prominent Agobard of Lyons.[4] A collateral influence can also be traced in two of

---

[2] Lietzmann, *loc. cit.* Of the extensive literature on this point, I might cite the brief but distinguished treatment by Werner Jaeger in his opening lecture on *Early Christianity and Greek Paideia* (Cambridge, Mass. : Harvard, 1961), pp. 3-12.

[3] A. Harnack, *History of Dogma*, trans. N. Buchanan, 3rd ed. (New York : Dover paperback ed., 1961), vol. 1, p. 133.

[4] Claudius' and Agobard's position is described in R. L. Poole, *Illustrations of the History of Medieval Thought and Learning* (New York : Dover paperback ed., 1960), pp. 25-44. Claudius is an interesting figure who deserves further investigation; of his writings, only his commentary on Galatians and some prefaces have been published (in *MPL* 104 and *Monumenta Germaniae Historica*, Epp. Kar. Aev. 2) and only scattered studies have appeared, although A. Cabaniss presents sections in English trans-

the important medieval writers on the Eucharist. Paschasius Radbertus, the ninthc—entury author of the first single work on the Eucharist and who taught an early form of the doctrine of Transubstantiation, twice quotes II Corinthians 5:7 ("for we walk by faith and not by sight") when discussing this sacrament in a technical sense as a mystery and figure.[5] Berengar of Tours, who precipitated another controversy on the Eucharist in the eleventh century, apparently following Radbertus' antagonist, Ratramnus of Corbie, quotes a similar passage from this same chapter several times (II Cor. 5:16 "And even though we have known Christ according the flesh yet now we know him no longer.")[6] but to opposite purposes as proponent of a theory of Spiritual Presence.

All these writers exhibit a common tendency in quoting and exploiting certain of the many passages in the Epistles which reflect the strong anti-materialistic strain in Paul's thought. In this connection, we might briefly note that a similar influence was manifested in much of medieval philosophy, as most directly illustrated in frequent citation of Romans 1:20, the *invisibilia Dei* passage, among philosophers of the Platonic-Augustinian tradition ("... His invisible attributes are clearly seen ... being understood through the things that are made."); this passage can be described as the Biblical charter of all medieval Platonisms. A lesser example of the influence of a Pauline text is the use of Ephesians 5:13 ("all that is made manifest is light"), along with the "Father of lights" text in James 1:17, for the theological and philosophical concept of illumination, as well as the "light metaphysics" of Erigena, Grosseteste, and others.

And at least two other theological progressives—indeed, theological rebels—of the medieval period should be cited : Peter Abelard, who

---

lation of the Galatians commentary and one of the writings on images, together with a useful biographic and bibliographic introduction in vol. IX of the Library of Christian Classics series : G. E. McCracken, ed., *Early Medieval Theology* (Philadelphia : Westminster, 1957), pp. 211 *et seq.* Cabaniss has also published a monograph on Agobard : *Agobard of Lyons : Churchman and Critic* (Syracuse, N. Y. : Syracuse, 1953), and some translated selections in the Library of Christian Classics volume cited, pp. 328 *et seq.*

[5] Paschasius Radbertus, *De corpore et sanguine Domini*, iii, 1 : iv, 3 (*MPL* 120, cols. 1275, 1279). I quote New Testament passages from the Confraternity of Christian Doctrine edition (New York : Doubleday Image Books, 1956), which is useful for the purposes of this study as a nearly literal translation of the Vulgate used by all medieval writers treated herein.

[6] Berengarius, *De sacra coena*, 45; 94; 200; cited by Poole, *Illustrations*, p. 30.

expounded much of his ethical thought and a startling new doctrine of
the Atonement in his Commentary on Romans; and John Wyclyf,
whose theologico-political writings abound in proof-texts from the Pauline
Epistles. But, in general, those progressives who show evidence of having
been influenced by a purely Biblical Paulinism and consequently set at
variance with some facet of Church tradition were extremely rare,
and, moreover, certainly not all of even this small group moved in the
direction of evangelical interpretations. It was not until the late fifteenth
and sixteenth centuries that a full recovery of the Pauline theology in
its textual integrity was begun and its peculiar dynamism realized in
a manner which had not occurred since the conversion and theological
career of St. Augustine. The process initiated among humanist scholars
of the Northern Renaissance—with such leaders as Colet, Lefevre, and
Erasmus—and immediately issued in proposals for Church reform,
rallying a substantial body of opinion which formed the so-called
humanist reform movement. The full revolutionary potential of this
recovery was manifested, of course, in the Reformation, and the ubi-
quity of Pauline theology in this latter movement has continued to be
a leading characteristic of Protestant thought. In particular, from Luther's
epochal "rediscovery" of the doctrine of justification, the Epistle to the
Romans has been a traditional starting-point or at least a touch-stone
in the careers of a distinguished line of theologians down to Karl Barth,
whose famous Romans commentary is a key work in twentieth-century
theology. Paulinism has been interjected into another context of controversy since the advent of the so-called "higher criticism" and the various
theses which have been propounded towards an interpretation of Paul
grounded on historical and philological methodology. Beginning with
the Hegelian interpretation of F. C. Baur and the Tübingen school
in the mid-nineteenth century, a vigorous debate has continued which
has involved some of the first names among present-day theologians
and produced a number of radical views, centering especially upon
questions concerning Paul's relationship to Jesus and to Judaic and
Hellenistic religious thought. Even in the post-Tridentine Roman
Church, minority voices have occasionally appeared as continuing
evidence of the power of Pauline concepts to exert a radicalizing influence, although the most important of these have centered on Augustine's
interpretation of the doctrine of grace; e.g., the Thomist-Molinist
controversy and Jansenism.

This brief sketch should sufficiently illustrate the frequent correlation
between revivals of Pauline theology on the one hand and spiritual

and institutional upheavals in the history of the Church on the other. There is, however, a distinct danger of overemphasizing and even universalizing this fact, and especially from a Protestant viewpoint, since the Reformation is the preeminent and classic example of precisely such an occurrence. Harnack is perhaps too much swayed by this viewpoint when he remarks and suggests :

Paulinism is a religious and Christocentric doctrine, more inward and more powerful than any other which has ever appeared in the Church. It stands in the clearest opposition to all merely natural moralism, all righteousness of works, all religious ceremonialism, all Christianity without Christ. It has therefore become the conscience of the Church, until the Catholic Church in Jansenism killed this her conscience. "The Pauline reactions describe the critical epochs of theology and the Church". One might write a history of dogma as a history of the Pauline reactions in the Church, and in doing so would touch on all the turning-points of the history. Marcion after the Apostolic Fathers; Irenaeus, Clement and Origen after the Apologists; Augustine after the Fathers of the Greek Church; the great Reformers of the middle ages from Agobard to Wessel in the bosom of the medieval Church; Luther after the Scholastics; Jansenism after the council of Trent : —everywhere it has been Paul, in these men, who produced the Reformation. Paulinism has proved to be a ferment in the history of dogma ... Just as it had that significance in Paul himself, with reference to Jewish Christianity, so it has continued to work through the history of the Church.[7]

A history on the framework suggested here has never appeared. It may very well be impossible to write such a work at this time. This is not only because further monographic research is needed, but, in addition, a better theoretical apparatus than presently available would be requisite to deal with the problems in the psychology and sociology of religion which would inevitably present themselves in such a survey. Yet, even if these desiderata were forthcoming, it is obvious from the results of over a half-century of study in medieval church history since Harnack published his great *History of Dogma* that he overstated the case, at least for the Middle Ages—medievalists have simply failed to uncover anything except scattered examples of "Pauline reactions", and these have been at best only tentative and imperfect anticipations of Reformation movements. Hence, any such history would have almost nothing to treat for a period covering nearly a thousand years of the Church's history.

However, it has been insufficiently stressed that, during the Middle Ages, Paulinism often served as an important vehicle for the exposition

[7] Harnack, *Hist. of Dogma*, vol. 1, pp. 35 f.

of orthodox theology in the traditional, conservative mainstream. As an immediate example, one may cite the obvious fact that the various categories of Pauline thought remained fundamental in the theological vocabulary, as found in the medieval doctrines of grace, baptism, predestination, and the concept of the Mystical Body in ecclesiology. But it should also be noted that, in tracing the influence of Paulinism as such in the medieval tradition, this circumstance is of a very qualified significance, since these and other distinctive Pauline concepts were received in the light of patristic interpretations and, further, underwent several centuries of dogmatic elaboration beyond the Church Fathers. The net result of this process was that, although the various elements of Paul's theology were incorporated as major categories within the structure and normative system of medieval theology, they tended to be treated in isolation from one another with little regard for their original contextual interconnections in Paul's own thought and writings. Pauline theology, as an integral whole, was thus progressively obscured by doctrinal accretions and its direct influence hence remained quite remote in most theological discussion throughout the medieval period. A remark of Erasmus, although made with a different reference, can be taken as an apt parable here : "You worship the bones of Paul hidden away in caskets, but not the spirit of Paul permeating his teaching. You make much of his body visible through a glass, but you think nothing of the whole mind of Paul resplendent in his words." [8]

Yet a Pauline influence was not totally dormant. The results of the researches of A. M. Landgraf have shown that, in the early scholastic period (i.e., through the twelfth century), commentaries on the Pauline epistles were of considerable significance in the earlier development of scholastic theology, and especially in the appearance of various schools of theology from the late eleventh century, whose development and distinguishing doctrinal emphases have been traced by Landgraf on the basis of Pauline commentaries produced by masters of the respective schools. [9] From this consideration, and the fact that Pauline texts

[8] *Enchiridion*, 14 (trans. R. Himelick [Bloomington : Indiana University Press, 1963], p. 112).

[9] Landgraf published several articles on this subject in *Biblica* and *Recherches de théologie ancienne et médiévale* which are difficult of access in this country. I have seen his "Untersuchungen zu den Paulinenkommentaren des 12. Jahrhunderts" in the latter journal (vol. 8 [1936], pp. 253-281, 345-368). For a statement of his basic conclusions, see remarks in his *Einführung in die Geschichte der theologischen Literatur der Frühscholastik unter dem Gesichtspunkte der Schulenbildung* (Regensburg : Gregorius-Verlag, 1948), pp. 29, 39 f.

are cited approximately as frequently as other Scripture by nearly all medieval theologians, it is apparent that there was no notable lack of attention given to Paul's writings during the Middle Ages. Rather, the main problem which presents itself to the historian of dogma is to explain why the key emphases and essential dynamic of Paul's thought did not manifest their latent power to any significant degree in the major movements of medieval theology after the time of St. Augustine, and in fact exhibited a peculiar quiescence throughout precisely that period in the history of the West which was dominated by theological categories of thought and was most productive in theology. And the obvious corollary problem is the remarkable and apparently sudden resurgence of Pauline influence among the Protestant reformers of the sixteenth century.

2. THE PROBLEM OF JUSTIFICATION IN MEDIEVAL THEOLOGY

This study does not purport to provide a definitive solution to these broad historical questions, but is intended as a contribution toward such a solution by treating a major topic implicit in any inquiry into this general area of research, St. Paul's doctrine of justification by faith. This topic is, of course, virtually dictated by its well-known importance in the events of the Reformation, beginning with Luther's critical experience of his discovery of a particular interpretation of that doctrine (justification "by faith alone") which he made the master-principle of his theology, the profound effect of that discovery in his own career as a reforming churchman, and the resolute emphasis upon salvation by faith so characteristic of all the other major figures of the Continental Reformation. And it is anticipated that the conclusions of this study will be of principal interest not to medievalists, but rather to students of Luther and of the Reformation and immediate pre-Reformation periods, specifically as it may be useful in illuminating certain aspects of medieval religious thought prior to the rise of the nominalist school in the fourteenth and fifteenth centuries—aspects which, in part, conditioned the theological environment in the critical years preceding the outbreak of the Reformation.

It should not be thought that the significance of the doctrine of justification is due merely to an historical contingency, i.e., the particular fact of its prominence in Luther's theological development and its subsequent reception into the Protestant tradition. Nor was it simply a theological invention on the part of Luther. One of the important results of the intensive scholarship in recent years on the pre-Reformation period has been to demonstrate that the term 'justification' was very current in the theological vocabulary of the later scholastics and that discussion of this and related matters concerning the role of faith, grace, and good works in the process of salvation was one of the major preoccupations of theological speculation in the two centuries preceding the Reformation. It is also well established that there were a number of more or less approximate anticipations of Luther's concept of justification from as early as the mid-fourteenth century,[10] on through very definite anticipations of Luther's exegesis of Romans among humanist commentators such as Lefèvre d'Étaples and John Colet on the very eve of the Reformation. And the matter can be argued on a purely logical plane that any careful study of the relevant Pauline texts, especially Romans and Galatians, should establish the centrality of the notion of justification as a controlling idea in Paul's thought; *prima facie*, it is a basic descriptive concept for his view of the human condition in relationship to God—a fundamental point in any higher religion—as well as expressing, in a specifically Christian doctrinal context, an essential mode or condition of the operation of divine grace in the human creature.

The fact is that medieval theologians had a significantly different and much more limited understanding of the concept of justification than Luther or, for that matter, all other theologians of either the late humanist or Reformation movements. One of the salient characteristics of discussions of justification among the later scholastics is that the subject was frequently treated in the context of discussions of the sacrament of penance. This elementary observation is one which has perhaps been inadequately stressed in most treatments of the background of the Reformation; it was surely no accident that Luther unwittingly precipitated the Reformation with a protest directed toward an abuse of the penitential practices of the late medieval Church. While it cannot be demonstrated that this can be directly connected with any dramatic turning point in Luther's thought such as his celebrated *Turmerlebnis*, Luther's preoccupation with the Church's teachings and administration of penance is well known from the biographical evidence of the spiritual crises of his earlier years, and can also be clearly documented in the gradual revision of the accepted theology of penance which begins to

---

[10] Probably the earliest being the English theologian Thomas Bradwardine (c. 1290-1349); see the studies by Gordon Leff, *Bradwardine and the Pelagians* (Cambridge : Cambridge University Press, 1957) and H. A. Oberman, *Archbishop Thomas Bradwardine : A Fourteenth Century Augustinian* (Utrecht : Kemink, 1957).

appear in his writings dating from several years before the indulgence controversy of 1517. In the very first thesis of the *95 Theses* ("Our Lord and Master Jesus Christ, in saying : 'Repent ye,' etc., intended that the whole life of believers should be penitent."), Luther was reacting not only to the indulgence issue but rejecting the entire orientation of late medieval teaching on justification which limited the concept primarily to a negative aspect, that is, as referring to forgiveness of sins—and for medieval Christians, this normally occurred through the sacrament of penance. The object of this study is to demonstrate that this particular orientation by which justification came to be associated with a sacramental observance did not originate among the later scholastics, but was rather gradually shaped by a much longer tradition of interpretation and a technical conception given the notion of justification which can be traced back as far as the ninth century.

The historical scope involved in a project of this nature is necessarily a very broad one, but the reader will find that the methodology adopted here is very straightforward. It consists of a survey of available theological sources from the patristic period through the thirteenth century, with an attempt in the concluding sections to elucidate the continuities and interconnections between these earlier sources and the works of major theologians of the late scholastic period in sufficient detail to substantiate the thesis just outlined. Some final remarks will suggest a few tentative conclusions concerning the significance of these findings as related to the Reformation era.

It is appropriate to conclude this introductory discussion with some bibliographic remarks. There has been much valuable discussion of the concept of justification in the later scholastic theologians in the numerous articles and books which have appeared in recent years in the field of late medieval studies. A rising interest in later scholasticism and the late medieval Church is undoubtedly the most notable contemporary trend in both medieval and Reformation studies. This scholarship is the product both of Luther specialists and other Reformation scholars interested in late scholasticism as the intellectual breeding-ground of the Reformation theologians and of a newer generation of medievalists specializing in the cultural and intellectual history of the later Middle Ages, an area of study pertaining to a critical era in the general history of European civilization which has hitherto been unduly neglected by the scholarly professions. Although the period is still incompletely explored and interpreted, it is now possible to discern at least the main lines of theological debate among the leading figures of the nominalist period to a degree

that was impossible only twenty years ago. Various works in this literature have been utilized and will be cited as relevant.[11]

But there has been no satisfactory systematic treatment of the topic
as conceived here, especially for the period of the early and high Middle
Ages. The closest approach to such a work is H. Denifle, *Die abendländischen Schriftausleger bis Luther über Justitia Dei (Rom. 1, 17)
und Justificatio*.[12] This volume is a comprehensive collection of excerpts
from patristic and medieval sources, principally commentaries on Scripture, commenting upon or glossing the key passages in Romans (1:17,
3:20 ff., 10:4, occasionally others) which Luther seized upon as "a real
gate to Paradise",[13] the basis for his doctrine of justification by faith.
Denifle, a Dominican scholar and eminent church historian, published
this source study as a supplement to his brilliant but highly unsympathetic
biography of Luther [14] (the work largely responsible for stimulating
the rise of critical Luther studies among modern Protestant scholars) as
a refutation of Luther's criticism of the medieval doctrine, specifically
as the Reformer expressed it in this assertion :

... I hated this word "the justice of God" which by the use and usage of all
the doctors I was taught to understand philosophically in terms of the so-called
formal or active justice with which God is just and punishes the sinners and
the unrighteous.[15]

Denifle's polemic purpose was to gather sufficient evidence to support
his contention that Luther was theologically ill-informed, and that,
from patristic times, commentators on Romans had unanimously taught
a "passive", forgiving justice of God which the penitent sinner obtains
by faith. Denifle's study does in fact demonstrate that the relevant pas-

---

[11] It would be impractical to provide even a selective listing of this vigorous and
expanding body of literature here; there is a good bibliography in H. A. Oberman,
Forerunners of the Reformation (New York : Holt, Rinehart and Winston, 1966),
pp. 319 *et seq.* A recent book edited by Steven E. Ozment, *The Reformation in Medieval
Perspective* (Chicago : Quadrangle Books, 1971), is a collection of articles which
provides an excellent overview of this emerging field, and can also provide much
bibliographic assistance.

[12] (Mainz : Kirchheim, 1905).

[13] Luther's preface to the Wittenberg Edition of his collected Latin works, 1545
(WA 54, 186 f.); excerpt in Eng. tr. in W. Pauck, tr., *Luther : Lectures on Romans,
Library of Christian Classics XV* (Philadelphia : Westminster, 1961), xxxvi f. This
is the most direct of Luther's biographical statement on his "Tower discovery" of
justification by faith in Rom. 1:17.

[14] *Luther und Luthertum* (Mainz : Kirchheim, 1904-07), 2 vols.

[15] Luther's preface, *loc. cit.*

sages in Romans were traditionally and consistently glossed in Augustinian and quasi-evangelical formulas by medieval commentators, including frequent use of the phrase *sola fide*. But Denifle's work suffers from the serious deficiency that his excerpts from the sources are too cursory and selective to indicate the full sense of the contexts he draws upon; hence the evidence he presents to support his argument against Luther is by no means conclusive. The inadequacy of Denifle's research is one reason why this study commences with a fresh examination of the Pauline commentaries.

Other treatments may be found in the articles on justification in the various encyclopedias of religion, but which give scant attention to the medieval period, except for the Thomist doctrine; an exception is the article by J. Rivière in the *Dictionnaire de théologie catholique*,[16] a discussion of monographic proportions marked by the usual scholarly excellence of contributors to that work, although avowedly anti-Protestant in viewpoint. Landgraf's monumental *Dogmengeschichte der Frühscholastik* has several relevant chapters which will be cited as appropriate.[17] The standard histories of dogma, especially those of Harnack[18] and Loofs,[19] provide valuable guidance on Augustine but contain few notices for the Middle Ages on the present subject. And in the older Reformation literature, the present author has seen no treatment of Luther's theology which devotes more than passing attention to the earlier medieval period in discussing justification. An example is the classic study of the Protestant doctrine of justification by A. Ritschl, where only a few pages are devoted to the medieval doctrine in his historical volume and the information presented is of but limited value.[20]

This paucity of literature, which is the principal justification of this inquiry into the problem, has made it necessary to place principal reliance upon a survey of the primary sources, and one or two observations should be made in this regard. The scholarly reader will quickly notice

---

[16] *DTC* 8, cols. 2042-2227. Other articles which may be consulted are : L. H. Imels in *Realencyclopädie für protestantische Theologie und Kirche* (3rd ed.) 16, pp. 482-515; J. G. Simpson in J. Hastings, *Encyclopedia of Religion and Ethics* 7, pp. 615-619; E. Vischer *et al.* in *Die Religion in Geschichte und Gegenwart* (2d. ed.) 4, cols. 1745-65.

[17] 4 vols. (Regensburg : Gregorius-Verlag, 1952-56).

[18] A. Harnack, *History of Dogma*, trans. N. Buchanan (several eds.).

[19] F. Loofs, *Leitfaden zum Studium der Dogmengeschichte*, 6th ed. rev. by K. Aland (Tübingen : Niemeyer, 1959).

[20] A. Ritschl, *The Christian Doctrine of Reconciliation and Justification*, vol. 1, *A Critical History*, trans. J. L. Black (Edinburgh : Edmunston and Douglas, 1872), pp. 73 *et seq.*

that Migne's *Patrologia latina* has been used as the major source of documents, which immediately imposes two restrictions : First, not all extant materials are included in *MPL*—obviously, for example, more recent discoveries since Migne completed his collection in 1855—but this series can still claim the great bulk of important writings in the period of its coverage (to the death of Innocent III, 1216). Secondly, many of the *MPL* texts are not of the standard of modern critical editions, although the resulting difficulties are not usually as acute for an inquiry in doctrinal history as may be encountered in areas of scholarship where a good text is essential, such as linguistics or manuscript studies. In several instances, however, more recent critical editions have been available and used here to obviate at least partially both these problems. A more drastic limitation is that a comprehensive examination of thirteenth century and later sources has not been possible, since there is no collection comparable to *MPL* for the later Middle Ages. Much of this enormous body of literature remains unpublished and, for practical reasons, no attempt has been made to survey manuscript sources. The printed sources are nevertheless sufficiently abundant to permit study of at least the most representative and authoritative thirteenth century theologians; and it is doubtful that a more detailed investigation including the host of lesser figures from this period would reveal any significant deviations from the main traditions. Definitive treatment of the fourteenth and fifteenth centuries is beyond the scope of this study, although selected sources have been utilized as necessary to complete the essential argument.

A final *caveat* is that numerous *loci* in the sources have undoubtedly been overlooked, due both to the inattention of the author and the imperfect critical apparatus available for a very large and variegated literature. However, it is believed that the weight, and, more especially, the pattern of the evidence presented is sufficient to demonstrate the emergence and dominance of a characteristic interpretation of the Pauline concept of justification which strongly linked it to the penitential theology and practices of the medieval Church in such a manner as to have disastrous consequences in the sixteenth century.

CHAPTER II

JUSTIFICATION IN THE PAULINE COMMENTARIES

As previously stated, the commentaries on the Pauline epistles served as important vehicles for the development and statement of theological views in the Middle Ages, especially before the appearance of the great *summae* of the thirteenth century. Among the authors were many of the most important theologians of the patristic and medieval periods, as may be illustrated by reviewing a partial list of commentators on Romans, the most important epistle for the doctrine of justification. Of the forty-nine extant commentaries on Romans to that of Nicholas of Lyra in the early fourteenth century, a list representative of the most prominent figures would include : For the patristic period—the earliest commentary of Origen, widely circulated in the Latin translation of Jerome's friend, Rufinus of Aquileia; Pelagius; Augustine; Cassiodorus; Bede. Among the Carolingians—Claudius of Turin; the *praeceptor Germaniae*, Rabanus Maurus; Sedulius Scotus. And among the scholastics—Lanfranc of Canterbury and his school; the authoritative *Glossa interlinearis* emanating from Anselm of Laon and his school; possibly the founder of the Carthusian Order, St. Bruno of Cologne (the authorship of the commentary is in question); Peter Abelard; Abelard's successor Robert of Melun; Gilbert de la Porrée; Peter Lombard; two commentaries of the Victorine school attributed to Hugh of St. Victor; Peter Cantor; the English archbishop Stephen Langton; St. Thomas Aquinas; the Spiritual Franciscan theologian Peter John Olivi; other later scholastics including Giles of Rome and Augustinus Triumphus. Peter Abelard and Giles of Rome are the only authors in this list who wrote on Romans as a single work; all others commented on Romans as part of works devoted to the Pauline epistles as a group. There are at least ten other writers for which there is evidence of having possibly written Pauline commentaries, including John of Salisbury, Matthew of Aquasparta, Peter Comestor, and Robert Grosseteste.[1] The names included here are admittedly an arbitrary selection from the entire roster, but any student of the period will agree that several are of first rank in historical importance; the list should also adequately indicate the diversity of schools and viewpoints represented.

It is likewise apparent that the Pauline commentaries represent a considerable body of theological materials. Unfortunately, this class of writings has received little scholarly attention from the viewpoint of doctrinal history, although there has been considerable technical study of the manuscripts, authorship, literary history, and other external criteria, and several excellent scholarly guides to the medieval Biblical commentaries greatly facilitate the study of these documents.[2]

There are two general characteristics of medieval Pauline exegesis which should be remarked upon before proceeding to an examination of specific texts.

The first comment concerns exegetical method. As part of the patristic legacy, the Middle Ages inherited a hermeneutic theory of multiple senses in interpretation of Scripture. The basic division in this theory was between the literal and spiritual meanings thought to be contained in Holy Writ. The concept was founded on the Pauline text : "... for

---

[1] Compiled from W. Affeldt, "Verzeichnis der Römerbriefkommentare der lateinischen Kirche bis zu Nikolaus von Lyra", *Traditio* 13 (1957), pp. 396-406.

[2] The basic guide to medieval Biblical commentaries is the exhaustive index of F. Stegmüller, *Repertorium biblicum medii aevi*, 7 vols. (Barcelona, 1950-61); the special purpose of this work is a comprehensive listing of MSS. Equally indispensable for Latin patristic literature is E. Dekkers and A. Gaar, *Clavis patrum latinorum*, rev. ed., *Sacris Erudiri* 3 (1961). The standard literary history of medieval Biblical commentaries is C. Spicq, *Esquisse d'une histoire de l'exégèse latine au moyen âge* (Paris : J. Vrin, 1944). Two recent brief aids are : R. E. McNally, *The Bible in the Early Middle Ages* (Westminster, Md. : Newman, 1959), pp. 83-117, which lists commentaries of the period 650-1000; the guide by Affeldt cited above, to commentaries on Romans. All of these give abundant references to editions and secondary literature. Two standard literary histories should be added here : O. Bardenhewer, *Geschichte der altkirchlichen Literatur*, 2nd ed., 5 vols. (Freiburg : Herder, 1932; repr. Dårmstadt : Wissenschaftliche Buchgesellschaft, 1962); for medieval Latin literature (to 1300), M. Manitius, *Geschichte der lateinischen Literatur des Mittelalters*, 3 vols. (München : C. H. Beck, 1931). When using *MPL* texts, the following has been consulted as a check on authorship attributions : P. Glorieux, *Pour revaloriser Migne : Tables rectificatives*, *Mélanges de science religieuse* 9 (1952), cahier supplémentaire. For a general introduction to this field, a basic work is Beryl Smalley, *The Study of the Bible in the Middle Ages*, 2d ed. (Oxford : Blackwell, 1952; also available in paperback, Universtity of Notre Dame Press, 1964).

the letter kills, but the spirit gives life (II Cor. 3:6)", but historically more directly reflects the twin streams of influence of the Alexandrian tradition of allegorical interpretation, epitomized in Origen, and the more literal Antiochene tradition as represented by Jerome. The spiritual sense was further divided so that among the patristic writers there was usually recognized, although in slightly differing schematizations, the four senses—literal, allegorical, anagogical, tropological—which were received in the medieval tradition of exegesis.[3] The method was most suited to Old Testament books, and one accordingly finds exegetical works, especially of the twelfth century when the vogue for literary studies was greatest, which painstakingly interpret the Biblical text phrase by phrase, often devoting a paragraph or more to each sense, neatly titling and setting down each of the senses of the text in order. In the case of the lengthier Old Testament books, the commentaries become vast. And, as one might expect, the greatest ingenuity in allegorical invention was necessarily devoted to the Song of Songs.

The Pauline commentaries, however, form a conspicuous exception to the usual four-fold method in following almost exclusively only the literal sense—or, because of their tendency toward theological elaboration, perhaps the method might more accurately be characterized by coining a new term, "literal-doctrinal" (strictly speaking, the literal sense was understood in terms of a purely mundane understanding of the text and to include two approaches : grammatical explication and what was sometimes referred to as the 'historical' sense; the doctrinal content in the Pauline commentaries considerably exceeds these limits). Thus, these works form a distinct class in medieval exegetical literature because of this characteristic, maintained traditionally from the earliest Latin commentaries of Ambrosiaster and Pelagius.[4] The operative

---

[3] The definitive history of this development is H. de Lubac, *Exégèse médiévale : les quatre sens de l'écriture*, 4 vols. (Paris : Aubier, 1959-64). For a good summary account, see McNally, *The Bible in the Early Middle ages*, pp. 53-61; this author quotes the familiar couplet of the schools :

Littera gesta docet, quid credas allegoria,

Moralia quid agas, quo tendas anagogia.

More extended discussion is in Smalley, *Study of the Bible*, pp. 1-36. Other useful summaries are articles on "History of Interpretation of the Bible" by R. M. Grant, "I. The Ancient Period", and J. T. McNeill, "II. Medieval and Reformation Period" in *The Interpreter's Bible*, vol. 1, pp. 106-114, 115-126.

[4] The importance of a Latin tradition, as opposed to the Greek patristic commentators on St. Paul (Origen, Theodore of Mopsuestia, John Chrysostom, *et al.*), is suggested by this comment on Pelagius :

factors here were, undoubtedly, both this tradition and the predominantly doctrinal character of the epistles themselves, in which the expository style of the Apostle's text scarcely lent itself to an allegorical approach. This imposed a special discipline upon the commentators in limiting their interpretation to doctrinal matters and thereby to produce a quantity of exegesis which is oriented more frequently and directly to hard-core theological issues than is usually found in commentaries on other Biblical books, encumbered by the artificialities of the four-fold method and an elaborate repertoire of conventional allegorical symbolism. The Pauline commentaries are therefore of considerable value as illustrative documents for the history of medieval theology.

A second characteristic is the close literary relationship prevailing through the successive commentaries—this largely works to nullify the advantage gained by adherence to the literal sense by limiting the originality of the commentators, and is but another exemplification of the strong sense of tradition in medieval religious thought. It is apparent that these authors were conscious of working in a distinct *genre*, as evidenced both by outright copying of whole passages from earlier works and from the fact that many specific *loci* in the Pauline texts were used by succeeding authors to elaborate on the same topic and often in the same patristic vein, even if the particular choice of words is original. As Miss Smalley aptly remarks, to study the outstanding names in this period is "simply to study their sources".[5] Some indication of the general lines of literary and doctrinal dependence will be indicated below for each author, and more will be elucidated from comparison of texts, tracing the specific sub-traditions, as it were, of exegesis on key passages relating to justification, especially the context of Romans 3:19-31. It should not compromise later conclusions to state here that this interdependence is a major factor in the predominant conservatism of medieval Paulinism which was to be completely broken only in the Reformation era.

The remainder of this chapter surveys twenty-two of the forty-nine extant commentaries on Romans, a selection which includes the bulk

---

Au point de vue de la forme, le commentaire de Pélage, sobre, dense, réaliste, s'attachant sans verbiage à l'explication littérale des textes, ne rappelle en aucune manière ces gloses de rapprochements bibliques, dont les Grecs, toujours prolixes, surchargeaient et parfois écrasaient le texte initial.

(G. de Plinval, *Pélage : ses écrits, sa vie, et sa réforme* [Lausanne : Librairie Payot, 1943], p. 132).

[5] Smalley, *Study of the Bible*, pp. 37 f.

of the more important commentaries,[6] together with occasional supplementary material. The presentation is in chronological order.

1. THE COMMENTARIES

(1) Ambrosiaster (fl. last half 4th cent.)

Commentaria in xiii epistolas Paulinas [7]

This commentary, which is dated from internal evidence as having been written during the pontificate of Damasus I, 366-384, is the earliest known Latin commentary on Paul's epistles. The author is unknown, although from Cassiodorus the work was long attributed to St. Ambrose and for this reason Erasmus coined the name 'Ambrosiaster' which remains in scholarly usage.[8]

The general character of Ambrosiaster's exegesis is literal, which he presents in succinct commentary notable for its brevity and clarity. An informed and alert writer, he makes reference to diverse topics of current interest, such as astrology (he is condemnatory), pagan religion, and miscellaneous heresies of the early Church; frequent illustrations derived from law have led to the suggestion that the author was a lawyer or public official before turning to theology. Souter remarks of him :

What chiefly attracts us is that Ambrosiaster had a real idea of historical method and of development. He affirms the original identity of bishop and presbyters. He recognizes the difference between the organization of the churches in his

---

[6] This includes all of the commentaries available in printed editions. Of the remaining twenty-seven, available only in MS., less than a half-dozen are by major authors (Augustinus Triumphus, Gilbert de la Porrée, Peter the Chanter, John Peter Olivi, and Stephen Langton); the secondary literature indicates that most are of marginal importance, although this should not exclude the possibility that some might repay further study.

[7] Edition : *MPL* 17, cols. 45-508 (in Ambrose's collected works with uncertain attribution). Literature : Denifle, pp. 1-3; Stegmüller nos. 1249-73 (vol. 2, 90); *Clavis* no. 184 (pp. 40 f.); Affeldt, pp. 372 f.; Bardenhewer III, 520-522; A. Souter, *The Earliest Latin Commentaries on the Epistles of St. Paul* (Oxford, 1927), esp. pp. 63-84.

[8] Sauter, *Earliest Latin Commentaries*, pp. 36 ff.; cf. H. J. Vogels, *Das Corpus Paulinum des Ambrosiaster, Bonner Biblische Beiträge* 13 (1957), pp. 7, 9. Stegmüller, *loc. cit.* : "Commentarius in epistolas Pauli [Rom.-Philem.] in latina lingua vetustissimus, compositus est tempore DAMASI papae [366/84] [cf. PL 17, 471]; c. 420 AUGUSTINUS locum quendam huius commentarii [PL 17, 12] affert [PL 44, 614] sub nomine SANCTI HILARII; temporibus CASSIODORI [Instit. div. litt. c. 8; c. 544] commentarius tribuitur AMBROSIO, quam attributionem sequuntur RABANUS, HAIMO, WALAFRIDUS STRABO, HINCMARUS, etc."

own time and that in apostolic times; he tells us more than once that there were not bishops in all places as yet in those times. He is also very suggestive on the early history of the Church of Rome. Probably no other commentator, Greek or Latin, realizes so clearly the attitude of the Jews to Paul and of Paul to the Jews : he is throughout alive to this aspect of St. Paul's teaching.[9]

Souter's last remark will be found significant in considering the following texts :

[Rom. 1:17 (*MPL* 17, cols. 58 f.)] "Justitia enim Dei revelatur in eo ex fide in fidem." Hoc dicit, quia in illo qui credit, sive Judaeus sit, sive Graecus, Justitia Dei revelatur. Justitiam Dei dicit, quia gratis justificat impium per fidem, sine operibus legis ... Ostenditur enim in eo veritas et justitia Dei, dum credit et profitetur : Justitia est Dei, quia quod promisit, dedit. Ideo credens hoc esse se consecutum, quod promiserat Deus per prophetas suos, justum Deum probat, et testis est justitia ejus. "Ex fide in fidem." Quid aliud est, "ex fide in fidem," nisi quia fides Dei est in eo, quod de se repromisit; et fides hominis, qui credit promittenti; ut ex fide Dei promittentis in fidem hominis credentis Dei justitia reveletur? In credente enim justus Deus apparet : in eo autem qui non credit, injustus videtur; negat enim veracem Deum, qui non credit Deum dedisse quod promisit. Hoc contra Judaeos loquitur, qui negant hunc esse Christum, quem promisit Deus. ...
[3:20 (col. 82)] "Quoniam quidem non justificabitur ex operibus legis omnis caro coram Deo." Non ideo minime justificatos homines asserit apud Deum; quia legem justitiae non servaverunt in praeceptis; sed quia sacramentum mysterii Dei, quod in Christo est, credere noluerunt. ... "Per legem enim cognitio peccati"; per fidem autem abolitio; ideo sequenda fides est. Quae est haec lex, per quam dicit cognitum esse peccatum, et cognitum quomodo? Videmus enim veteres non ignorasse peccatum; quia et Joseph in carcerem missus est, licet per calumniam (Gen. 39:20); et pincerna et pistor Pharaonis, causa peccati (Gen. 40:3). Quomodo ergo latebant peccata? Triplex quidem lex est; ita ut prima pars de sacramento divinitatis sit Dei : secunda autem quae congruit legi naturali, quae interdicit peccatum : tertia vero factorum, id est, Sabbati, noemeniae, circumcisionis, etc. Haec est ergo lex naturalis, quae per Moysen partim reformata, partim auctoritas ejus firmata in vitiis cohibendis, cognitum fecit peccatum; non quod lateret, sicut dixi : sed ostendit peccata quae fiunt, non impune future apud Deum; ne forte quis ad tempus evadens, legem illusisse putaretur. Hoc est quod lex ostendit.
[3:21 (cols. 82 f.)] "Nunc vero sine lege justitia Dei manifestata est, testimonium habens a lege et prophetis." Apertum est quia justitia dei sine lege apparuit, sed sine lege sabbati et circumcisionis et neomeniae et vindictae : non tamen sine sacramento divinitatis Dei : quippe cum justitia Dei de sacramento Dei sit. ...
[3:24 (col. 83)] "Justificati gratis per gratiam ipsius." Justificati sunt gratis, quia nihil operantes, neque vicem reddentes, sola fide justificati sunt dono Dei.
[3:28 (col. 84)] "Arbitramur enim justificari hominem per fidem sine operibus

[9] Souter, *Earliest Latin Commentaries*, pp. 64 f.

legis." Gentilem dicit hominem pro certo haberi, quod justificetur credens nulla faciens opera legis, id est, sine circumcisione aut neomeniis, aut veneratione Sabbati.

[8:4 (col. 124)] "Ut justificatio legis impleretur in nobis, qui non secundum carnem ambulamus, sed secundum spiritum." Ideo damnatum dicit peccatum, ut impleretur in nobis justificatio legis datae a Moyse; sublati enim de conditione legis, facti sumus amici ejusdem; justificati enim amici legis sunt. Quomodo autem impletur in nobis justificatio, nisi cum datur remissio omnium peccatorum, ut sublatis peccatis, justificatus appareat, mente serviens legi Dei? Hoc est non secundum carnem ambulare, sed secundum spiritum ...

On Romans 1:17 appears a somewhat shallow interpretation of the 'justice of God' as essentially a matter of God's keeping His promise—a legalistic, contractual relationship is posited between God and the believer.[10] This passage is not overly important for Ambrosiaster; note his "Hoc contra Judaeos loquitur ..."

Several points are worthy of notice in the comments on Romans 3:21-22 and 24 :

a) A concept of justification by faith is manifest in many passages; the commentary on the first five books of Romans is saturated with this terminology. But the concept is consistently stated in terms of a sharp antithesis between faith and law, specifically the Jewish ceremonial law. Hence freedom from the law is given a very specific, historical connotation in the Jewish background of the Christian faith (this is consistent with many other references to the Jews *passim*). There is consequently no hint of a more universalized interpretation of Pauline freedom as freedom from a law of works.

Another aspect of the historical framework within which Ambrosiaster develops this antithesis is in his distinction of a threefold law (above, v. 20 : *Triplex quidem lex* ...; this also occurs in the comment on Galatians 3:19). This section, while not of great significance in Ambrosiaster, will be seen to have been taken up by several medieval commentators.

b) An incipient connection appears between justification and sacramentalism (two *loci* in v. 20, one in v. 21), although it is not clear in this or other contexts whether a specific sacrament is meant—one would expect this to be baptism in this period, but there is no other context to bear this out in Ambrosiaster—or simply the general sense of *sacramentum* in classical Latin meaning any "mystery" or holy observance. Some support may perhaps be found in the comment on Romans 8:4, as well as a more precise definition of justification as following remis-

[10] Cf., for the same concept, Gal. 2:16.

sion of sins, this latter being a principal effect of baptism. But another comment, on Romans 3:5-6, gives a somewhat broader scope to the concept :

[(col. 78)] Hoc juxta sensum prophetae David dicit Apostolus : David autem quando peccaverat in cause Uriae Hethaei (II Reg. 11:4), sciens quia promissio peccatoribus dari non potest, exorat ut justificatio verborum Dei vincat judicium quo judicantur ii qui peccant (Psal. 50:6); et poenitentem reformet sanctificans, ut det ei quod justis se daturum promisit. ... Quia quamvis peccatores simus, reformamur tamen per poenitentiam : ut non jam peccatores, sed abluti promissionem mereamur accipere.

An indirect connection between penance and justification can be inferred from this context, and there is at least some anticipation of the later medieval interpretation which is treated in following sections of this chapter. It is likely that a more important influence resulted from the references to the word 'sacrament' in the exegesis noted above, when medieval readers would read this as a reference to a specific sacrament of the Church.

c) The comment on 3:24 is cited above to show that the phrase *sola fide*, so important for Luther and the translation of Romans 1:17 in his German Bible, was not without precedent, here in the earliest Latin commentary.[11]

A final observation is that Ambrosiaster has only a very rudimentary theory of grace; the term is sparingly used throughout his commentary, and is necessarily a limiting factor in his concept of justification, otherwise very prominent in his theology.

(2) St. Augustine (354-430)

The exegetical work of St. Augustine is uneven in quality. He wrote the most important treatise on hermeneutics produced in the patristic period in his *De doctrina christiana*, which is interesting for the liberal and scientific approach to Biblical texts advocated therein, anticipating modern critical methods on several points. He also produced large collections of homilies and some other occasional works on various Biblical

---

[11] Souter states (*Earliest Latin Commentaries*, p. 80) : "When he uses the expression *sola fides*, he, like other early writers, refers merely to the forgiveness of sin offered at baptism." Souter follows here and cites Loofs, *Leitfaden* (6th ed., pp. 309 f.). From the passages given immediately above, the matter does not seem so categorical. But one can easily agree when Souter states, in a good discussion of Ambrosiaster's theology (*op. cit.*, pp. 78-84), that Ambrosiaster "does not penetrate deeply" into the Pauline theory of grace.

books, much of it magnificent devotional literature but of no scientific value, and only two systematic works which can properly be considered as commentaries. One is the literal commentary on Genesis, the second his *Epistolae ad Galatas expositio*, a complete commentary on that epistle. He also wrote two works on Romans : *Expositio quarundam propositionum ex epistola ad Romanos*, which is a collection of answers to questions on selected passages and a forerunner of the medieval *quaestiones* form; and the beginnings of a full commentary on Romans which he was unable to continue during his very busy career, now usually titled *Epistolae ad Romanos inchoata expositio* (he completed vv. 1-7, 14-23 of the first chapter).[12]

All of these works date from about 394 during the earlier years of his clerical career and do not reflect his fully developed views; they are also unimportant from the standpoint of influence upon later writers. For Augustine's systematic and mature interpretation of St. Paul, it is necessary to turn to other works, of which the *De spiritu et littera* gives the most extensive treatment of the Pauline epistles, especially Romans. Accordingly, it is unnecessary to give any analysis of these commentaries in this study, and discussion of Augustine's theology of grace and justification is reserved for an assessment of his influence on medieval commentators at the conclusion of this chapter.

(3) Pelagius (*ca.* 350-*ca.* 425)

Expositiones xiii epistularum Pauli [13]

Pelagius wrote his expositions of the Pauline epistles in the period 406-409 at Rome. [14] This commentary by the well-known heresiarch

---

[12] Editions : These three works appear, respectively, in *MPL* 35, col. 2105-2148; cols. 2063-2088; cols. 2087-2106. Literature : Denifle, pp. 8 f.; Stegmüller nos. 1472-75 (vol. 2, 142 f.); *Clavis* nos. 280-282 (p. 73); Affeldt, p. 375; Bardenhewer IV, 486; E. Portalié, *A Guide to the Thought of St. Augustine*, tr. R. J. Bastien (Chicago : Henry Regnery, 1960), pp. 60, 63; cf. pp. 123 f. For a descriptive account of the character and method of these three works, see Souter, *Earliest Latin Commentaries*, pp. 182-199.

[13] Editions : A. Souter, *Pelagius' Expositions of Thirteen Epistles of St. Paul*, Cambridge Texts and Studies IX, no. 2; Text (1926); now reprinted in *MPL Supplementum* 1, cols. 1110 *et seq.* The edition in *MPL* 30, cols. 645-902 is pseudo-Jerome. Literature : Denifle, pp. 8 f.; Stegmuller nos. 3439-52 (vol. 3, 80); *Clavis* no. 728 (p. 166); Affeldt, pp. 392 ff.; Bardenhewer IV, 514 f.; J. Ferguson, *Pelagius* (Cambridge: Jeffer, 1956), pp. 116-143; de Plinval, *Pélage*, pp. 121-166; A. Souter, *Pelagius' Expositions*, TS IX, no. 1 : Introduction (1922), and no. 3; Pseudo-Jerome Interpolations (1931); *idem*, *Earliest Latin Commentaries*, pp. 205-225.

[14] Stegmüller (nos. 6355-67) states that Pelagius used as sources Ambrosiaster,

and opponent of St. Augustine is of particular importance because it was frequently utilized by medieval exegetes, as will be seen presently. But this writer has found no evidence that any overtly heretical views were propagated by this means, and certainly no case can be built asserting that medieval semi-Pelagianism resulted from this influence. This is partly explained by the circumstances of its circulation. One version was transmitted through Irish channels, appearing on the Continent in the ninth century, and Carolingian commentators were well aware of the reputation of the author and used this work with due caution. Another version, which had been interpolated and hence "sanitized" by an unknown hand, circulated under the name of St. Jerome. Erasmus suspected this mixed authorship, but the pseudo-Jerome version continued to be printed among Jerome's works up to and including the *MPL* edition. The original text was rediscovered only in the early twentieth century, in two MS examples, by Alexander Souter. The Pelagian prologues were often transcribed or adapted as introductions to commentaries from the ninth to twelfth centuries.

The principal theme of this commentary is moral exhortation; Souter has stressed this aspect in his writings, e.g., "The writer is constantly alluding to the influence of example on conduct, particularly the example of the Apostle on the lives of his converts ..."[15] This emphasis upon moral purpose is not unexpected in view of Pelagius' general theological position which has made his name a by-word for the heresy of works over free grace, but it may be somewhat surprising to find statements of impeccable orthodoxy on justification by faith. The main exceptionable feature of the commentary on Romans is a denial of original sin, which does not impinge upon the texts which relate to justification. The most interesting of these are as follows :

[Rom. 1:17 (MPL Suppl. 1, col. 1116)] "justitia enim dei in eo revelatur." Sive : Quod iustum fuerit ut, quo modo Abraham credens ex gentibus per solam primum fidem saluatus est, ita ceteri credentes saluarentur. Sive : Quod illud testamentum quod per legem deus verax promiserat, debuerit exhiberi. "Ex fide in fidem." Sive : Quod ex fide iustificatur Iudaeus et in fide gentilis, et ideo ["ex" et] "in" posuerit, ut tautologiae vitium declinaret. "Sicut scriptum est : iustus autem ex fide vivit." "Non ex operibus legis [Gal. 2:16]."

Jerome, Augustine, Origen, John Chrysostom, and Theodore of Mopsuestia. This does not derogate from the originality and personal viewpoint displayed throughout this work.

[15] Souter, *Earliest Latin Commentaries*, p. 216; cf. quote from Souter in Ferguson, *Pelagius*, p. 128.

A pseudo-Jerome interpolation is indicated by brackets in this next passage (another interpolation, not of significance, occurs on v. 21 and is omitted) :

[3:20-24 Col. 1128)] "Quoniam nos justificabitur omnis caro ex operibus legis coram illo." Modo non iustificabitur. Sive : Opera legis circumcisionem dicit sabbatum et ceteras caerimonias, quae non tam ad iustitiam quam ad carnis laetitiam pertinebant. [(MPL 30, col. 660) Item non contraria sibi dicit Apostolus, superius dicens : Qui ostendunt opus legis in cordibus suis. Et nunc dicit, ex operibus legis non justificari omnem carnem. Carnem accusat, cujus providentia legi Dei subjicere non potest. Lex enim ostendere novit peccatum : non tamen ostendit, qualiter debeat observari : et iterum punire noxia, non dans veniam poenitenti : Christus autem remissionem peccatorum donat credentibus, et docet quomodo debeant carnis vitia vitari, atque prudentia resecari.] "Per legem enim cognitio peccati." Non remissio, nec peccatum, sed cognitio. ... [21] "Nunc autem sine lege iustitia dei manifestata est." Sine lege litterae iustitia manifestata, quae nobis gratis a deo donata est, non nostro labore quaesita, et apertius per exempla Christi euidentiora patefacta, quae latebant in lege. "Testificata per legem et prophetas." Sive : Iustitia haec praedicata est a lege et prophetis in nouissimis temporibus esse uentura. ... [22] "Iustitia autem dei per fidem Christi Iesu in omnes et super omnes qui credunt in eum." Qua creditur Christo. "Non enim est distinctio." Inter Iudaeum et gentilem. [23] "Omnes enim peccaverunt et egent gloria dei." Quia non habent suam. [24] "Iustificati gratis per gratiam ipsius." Sine legis operibus per baptismum, quo omnibus non merentibus gratis peccata donavit. [3:28 (Cols. 1129 f.)] "Arbitramur enim iustificari hominem per fidem sine operibus legis." "Certi sumus" vel "iudicamus". Abutuntur quidam hoc loco ad destructionem operum iustitiae, solam fidem baptizato posse sufficere adfirmantes, cum idem alibi dicat apostolus : "et si habuero omnem fidem, ita ut montes transferam, caritatem autem non habeam, nihil mihi prodest [1 Cor. 13:2]", in qua caritate alio loco legis adserit plenitudinem contineri, dicens : "plenitudo legis est caritas [Rom. 13:10]". Quod si haec eorum sensui uidentur esse contraria, sine quibus operibus legis apostolus iustificari hominem per fidem dixisse credendus est? scilicet circumcisionis vel sabbati et ceterorum huiuscemodi, non absque iustitiae operibus, de quibus beatus Iacobus dicit : "fides sine operibus mortua est [Jac. 2:26]". hic autem de illo dicit, qui ad Christum veniens sola, cum primum credit, fide salutatur. addendo autem "operibus legis", ostendit esse etiam gratiae operam, quae debent facere baptizati.

Denifle interjects the following comment on Pelagius' gloss of Romans 1:17 : "Er sieht in die *justitia Dei* die *justificatio*."[16] But this needs qualification; Ferguson, in a penetrating discussion of the theology of the commentary, states :

---

[16] Denifle, p. 9.

... [Pelagius] states emphatically that we are all alike saved not by our own merits but by the free grace of God. So too it is by the will of God, not by his own merit that Paul is called to be an apostle. Those in Rome who are called to be saints are so by God's calling of them, not by their own deserts. A long list of passages demonstrates that we are saved and justified "gratis," by the free gift of God. But when we come to examine these passages more closely, it is generally clear what Paul means, but it is by no means so clear what Pelagius means. Romans iii.21 is an illuminating example. Justice comes to man by the free gift of God, not because he pursues it. This might suggest that the virtues we possess are implanted in us by God, and are in no sense our responsibility. But Pelagius does not mean this : he means that God gives us a pattern of justice which we are to follow. The pattern is perfectly clearly revealed in Christ; the responsibility for emulation is ours. Several of the passages deal with forgiveness of sins. Here again it should be remembered that Pelagius never denied that having sinned we stood in full need of free forgiveness, nor did he deny that we do sin; all he denied was that such sin was inevitable.[17]

It is patent that Pelagius continues the literalistic emphasis of Ambrosiaster in his interpretation of Romans 3:20 and 28 by also identifying works of the law with Jewish ceremonials. Plinval asserts that the theme and intention of Pelagius' commentary on the entire context of the earlier chapters of Romans (II-VIII) is a negative critique of Judaism, and this biographer of Pelagius does not consider these sections as having any doctrinal importance beyond this polemic purpose.[18] Certain theological nuances are nevertheless evident. Especially important is the exegesis of 3:28, where Pelagius makes the distinction concerning the ceremonial law explicit by specifically denying that the Apostle included 'works of justice' in his censure. Here the author uses as a corroboratory proof-text what is perhaps the most incisive statement of what most modern commentators consider an anti-Pauline polemic in the Epistle of James (2:26; "faith without works is dead"). This citation of James is regularly drawn into the exegesis at this point in the text by medieval commentators —so precise a point of correspondence is unmistakable evidence of direct or transmitted influence. "... this must be the starting-point for anyone who desires to understand the history of the Pauline doctrine of justification in the following centuries."[19] In general, however, the

---

[17] Ferguson, *Pelagius*, pp. 132 f.

[18] Plinval, *Pélage*, pp. 147 *et seq.* Plinval believes, however, that Pelagius is at his best and most faithful to the Apostle's thought on this portion of Romans; this author does not discuss Pelagius' treatment of justification.

[19] R. Seeberg, *Text-book of the History of Doctrines*, tr. C. E. Hay (Philadelphia : Lutheran Publication Society, 1905), I, 49. See also Landgraf, *Dogmengesch.*, I/2, pp. 17-24 for a number of examples of adjustments of the James passage to St. Paul on the faithworks question; some of these will be noted *infra*.

phrase in 3:21 *per exempla Christi* may be noted as the only overtly "Pelagian" emphasis in the sections quoted here.

In 3:24 and 28, Pelagius gives a strongly sacramental interpretation of justification in baptism which is not found in Ambrosiaster; it is not surprising to find this interpretation in Pelagius since it was the prevalent opinion on justification before Augustine, and was retained to some degree by the latter doctor.[20]

In this commentary one may also observe a pre-Lutheran use of the phrase *sola fide* in frequent *loci*.[21]

(4) Cassiodorus (*ca.* 485-583)

Expositio S. Pauli epistulae ad Romanos, una cum comple-xionibus in xii sequentes S. Pauli epistulas a quodam Cassiodori discipulo anonymo concinnatis [22]

This commentary was long attributed to Primasius of Hadrumentum (*fl. ca.* 550) due to an early editorial error and is printed in *MPL* under his name; since the critical work of Souter, the authorship of Cassiodorus and his students, *ca.* 540, is generally accepted for all of the text except the commentary on Hebrews.[23] The basis of this work is Pelagius' commentary, but purged and amplified with materials from orthodox Fathers. This is easily seen in the text, where a sentence or two of Pelagius is often retained unaltered or lightly paraphrased on individual verses but with more additional comment; my texts illustrate an example.

Cassiodorus was also the author of a *Complexiones in epistulas Apostolorum*,[24] a brief work glossing only a random selection of verses which, however, was not known in the Middle Ages. It contains nothing of interest for the present subject.

---

[20] Loofs, *Leitfaden*, pp. 309 f. This is discussed at the conclusion of this chapter.

[21] E.g., on Rom. 4:5 (the phrase occurs twice), 8:29, 10:3, Gal. 3:6, 3:11.

[22] Edition : *MPL* 68, cols. 415-686. Literature : Denifle, pp. 9-11; Stegmüller nos. 6989-7001 (vol. 4, 482; cf. vol. 2, 233); *Clavis* no. 902 (p. 200); Affeldt, p. 384; Bardenhewer V, 275.

[23] Souter, *Pelagius' Expositions*, no. 1, pp. 318-326. Stegmüller, *loc. cit.* : "E. PELAGII commentario ad Rom., quem attributum novit, CASSIODORUS c. 540 Pelagianum haeresim amovit, et questiones ex AUGUSTINO, De div. quaest. ad Simplicianum sumptas inseruit, quod, ut etiam in commentaria I Cor.-Philem. facerent, sequentes admonuit. ... in editione SMARAGDI, Expositio libri comitis, 1536, confundibatur sigillum P (Pelagius) cum sigillo PR (Primasius). Unde motus JOHANNES GAGNAEUS 1537 hunc commentarium attribuit Primasio."

[24] *MPL* 70, cols. 1321-1380; Manitius, vol. 9, p. 50.

Selected texts from the *Expositio* follow :

[Rom. 1:5 (MPL 68, col. 417)] "per quem accepimus gratiam et apostolatum ad obediendum fidei in omnibus gentibus." Gratiam, ut credamus et baptizemur, et quia gratis et jam ipse justificatus est nullis meritis suis.
[3:4 (col. 427)] "Ut justificeris", inquit, "in sermonibus tuis, et vincas cum judicaris." Videamus quomodo sibi hoc loco Apostoli sermo consentiat cum testimonio quod ex propheta, sermonem suum confirmaturus, assumpsit. Sententiam hac evidenter illo sensu Apostolus ponit, quo dudum David sub poenitentiae voce protulerat ...
[3:19-20 (col. 430)] "Et subditus fiat omnis mundus Deo." Ut sciat se sine gratia Dei salvum esse non posse : vel certe in confessione peccati speret misericordiam, cognoscens se esse in peccatis. "Quia ex operibus legis." Hoc contra Pelagianos facit, qui dicunt quod lex justificet. Opera autem legis circumcisonem dicit, et sabbatum, et reliqua. [20] "Non justificabitur omnis." Non justificabitur, quia nihil ad perfectum lex adduxit. Hinc contra eos incipit disputare, magno diuturnoque conflictu, qui gloriabantur in lege, et per legem se justificari credebant, et non per gratiam : docens per ordinem legem non potuisse auferre, sed potius auxisse peccatum, quod aufert gratia, quia lex jubere novit, cui succumbit infirmitas, sicut gratia juvare, qua infunditur charitas. Non dicimus nos justificatos eos fuisse qui fuerunt legi obedientes, sed nisi justificarentur, non essent obedientes.
[3:24 (col. 431)] "Justificati gratis." Sine ullis praecedentibus meritis, per baptismum justificati. Cum omnibus non merentibus gratis peccata donavit, audi gratis, et tace de meritis.
[3:28 (col. 432)] "Arbitramur enim justificari hominem per fidem." Definimus, certi sumus, hoc judicamus. "Sine operibus legis." Addendo legis, ostendit esse et fidei opera. Quomodo ergo Jacobus ait : Fides sine operibus mortua est? Sed Paulus de operibus legis dicit, Jacobus autem de operibus quae fidelem hominem esse probant, sicut ipse in sequentibus exponit : Ostende mihi ex operibus fidem tuam. Opera sunt per quae fides agnoscitur.

The following text is edited to illustrate the author's method of compilation; borrowings from Pelagius are in parentheses and a passage from Jerome's commentary on Galatians is bracketed :

Ga[. 2:16-17 (col. 588 f.)] "Scientes autem quod non justificatur homo ex operibus legis." Legis, non justitie operibus. (Opera) autem (legis circumcisio, sabbatum, dies festi,) baptismata, et cetera, (quae non propter justitiam,) sed occupandi populi gratia sunt mandata. "Nisi per fidem Jesu Christi : et nos in Christo Jesu credimus, ut justificemur ex fide Christi, et non ex operibus legis," id est, fidem a Christo donatam. "Propter quod ex operibus legis non justificabitur omnis caro." (Hoc tempore.) [Juxta simplicem (Hier. : humiliorem) intellectum justificabantur quondam ex lege, non omnis caro, sed hi tantum justificabantur quondam ex lege, non omnis caro, sed hi tantum homines qui in Palaestina erant. Nunc autem ex fide Jesu Christi justificatur omnis caro, dum Ecclesia ejus in toto orbe fundatur.] "Quod si quaerentes justificari in

Christo, inventi sumus et ipsi peccatores." (Si enim gentes fides sola non salva-
vit, nec nox, quia ex operibus nemo justificabitur. ...)

Cassiodorus on Romans 1:5 is quoted here for the orthodox interpretation of justification in baptism; it is based on the Pelagian gloss
("Gratiam in baptismo, apostolatum, quando ab spiritu sancto directus
est ..." [25]) but expands it to include a specific use of the term 'justification'.
Similarly, the comment on Romans 3:24 is significant for this connection,
but which introduces the Augustinian concept of merit—the phrase
sine praecedentibus meritis is Augustinian,[26] and frequently taken up
by medieval commentators.

On Romans 3:19, comparison should also be made with Pelagius :
" 'Et subditis fiat omnis mundus deo.' In confessione peccati."[27] There
is in Cassiodorus a slightly greater emphasis on confession, but in this
period the term did not have a sacramental connotation. On 3:4, however,
the author refers the interpretation to David's repentance—or penance?
the Latin *poenitentia* is ambiguous—in the same manner as Ambrosiaster.
Both of these *loci* will be followed in later authors.

On 3:20, the gloss is explicitly anti-Pelagian, but in the following
sentence the phrase *Opera autem legis ... et sabbatum* is taken directly
out of Pelagius (!); the context immediately following (not reproduced
here) also had Pelagian phrases.

The comment on Galatians, heavily dependent on Pelagius, is given
here as an illustration of the literalism with which Cassiodorus also
interprets Paul to stress the antithesis between Jew and Gentile and,
correspondingly, between law and faith. The author adds, however,
an emphasis upon the Church which is missing in Pelagius or Ambrosiaster; it is, instead, taken directly from Jerome's authentic commentary
on Galatians.[28] This is only of incidental significance in this context,
but may be interpreted as reflecting the growing significance of the
Church as a visible institution in the century of Gregory the Great.

Two further incidental observations : Cassiodorus also uses Pelagius
verbatim for his gloss on Romans 1:17; the phrase *sola fide* occurs, as
with Pelagius, on Romans 4:5 and in other places.

---

[25] *MPL Suppl.* 1, col. 1114.
[26] E.g., *De spiritu et littera*, c. 10, n. 16. The phrase on v. 20 *quo infunditur charitas*
is also typically Augustinian.
[27] *MPL Suppl.* 1, col. 1128.
[28] *MPL.* 26, col. 369C.

(5) Rabanus Maurus (776 or 784-856)

Enarrationum in epistolas Beati Pauli libri triginta [29]

Rabanus' immense commentary on Paul was composed *ca.* 836-842. It is nothing more than a *catena*, i.e., 'chain', of excerpts from patristic sources, a testimony of the famous teacher's industry, if not his originality, and a monument to the two characteristics with which Grabmann sums up this century in theological studies with its enormous respect for patristic *auctoritas* : ultra-conservatism and receptivity.[30]

Rabanus' exegetical method is directly traceable to the influence of the Venerable Bede, who originated the method of arranging excerpts from the Fathers to gloss Biblical texts. Rabanus was trained under Alcuin at Tours, whose own exegetical work preserved the tradition of the great English scholar, and Rabanus himself therefore may be considered a direct academic descendant of Bede. But Rabanus' method differs from that of Bede in that he adhered to a strict rule of using only direct quotations from the Fathers, resulting in a kind of mechanistic method, whereas Bede frequently adapted or paraphrased his sources and occasionally and with a great spirit of modesty added comments *"ex nostro labore."*[31]

Rabanus' exegetical work is easily criticized for its consequent lack of originality, a charge which is frequently brought to bear against the scholarship of the Carolingian Renaissance in general, but Rabanus' work should be seen in the perspective of his practical objective, which was simply to provide suitable handbooks or dossiers of patristic texts to monastic institutions, especially the pioneer cloisters in the Germanic frontier regions of the Frankish Empire which were gravely lacking in literary resources. The role of Rabanus' commentaries and others of a similar type in making patristic authors more accessible and familiar to the literate class of the period—thereby transmitting and increasing the influence of classical culture of a kind—should not be underestimated.[32]

---

[29] Edition : *MPL* 111, cols. 1273-1616; 112, cols. 9-834. Literature : Denifle, pp. 15 f.; Stegmüller nos. 7064-77 (vol. 5,32); Affeldt, p. 399; McNally, pp. 110 *et seq.*; Spicq, pp. 38-44; Manitius I, pp. 288-302; J. B. Hablitzel, *Hrabanus Maurus; Ein Beitrag zur Geschichte der Mittelalterlichen Exegese, Biblische Studien*, Bd. 11, Heft 3 (Freiburg : Herder, 1906), *passim.*

[30] M. Grabmann, *Geschichte der scholastischen Methode* I, pp. 178 *et seq.*

[31] Hablitzel, *Hrabanus*, pp. 8, 17 f.

[32] *Ibid.*, pp. 102 ff.

Reproduction of many sample passages would be superfluous here. With one exception, it will suffice to note his sources for the sections of Romans and Galatians of principal interest for the present study. On Romans 1:17, Rabanus uses Ambrosiaster's gloss. On 3:19-28, the author strings together passages from Ambrosiaster's and Origen-Rufinus' commentaries, with passages from Augustine (he does not use Pelagius in this work, although his prologue is a condensed version of Pelagius'). He retains the three important elements of Ambrosiaster's commentary on 3:20-21 : the sacramental concept of justification ("justitia Dei de sacramento Dei sit"), the three-fold law, and the literalistic antithesis between Jewish law and faith. On Galatians 2:16 he follows Ambrosiaster with the addition of some context from the genuine Jerome commentary on Galatians.

One element of Augustinian doctrine makes its appearance which becomes important in later commentators, the concept of 'faith working through love' :

[Rom. 3:28 (MPL 111, col. 1344)] "Arbitramur enim justificati hominem per fidem sine operibus legis." ... (Aug.) Nam erant quidem in lege qui de operibus legis gloriabantur, quae fortasse non dilectione, sed timore faciebant, et volebant se justos videri, et praeponi gentibus quae opus legis non fecerant. Apostolus autem praedicans fidem gentibus, cum eos qui accedebant ad Dominum videret justificatos ex fide, ut jam quia crediderant, bene operarentur, non quia bene operati sunt, credere mererentur, exclamavit securus, et ait : Quia potest justificari homo ex fide, sine operibus legis, ut illi magis non fuerint justi, qui quod faciebant, timore faciebant, cum fides per dilectionem operetur in corde, etiamsi foris non exit opere.

This gloss is taken from a sermon of Augustine, but it is a favorite Augustinian theme and found frequently in other works;[33] it had a considerable importance in scholastic theology and will be examined in some detail in following sections.

(6) Sedulius Scotus (*ob. post* 858)

Collectanea in omnes B. Pauli epistolas [34]

Sedulius Scotus, one of the many Irish scholars who migrated to the Carolingian Empire in the ninth century, wrote several commentaries

[33] Sermo 2, c. 8 (*MPL* 38, col. 32). Cf. *De spir. et litt.* c. 36, n. 56; Sermo 53, c. 10 f.
[34] Edition : *MPL* 103, cols. 9-270. Literature : Denifle, pp. 11 f.; Stegmüller no. 7064 (vol. 5, 28); Affeldt, p. 399; McNally, pp. 110 *et seq.* : Spicq, p. 45; Manitius I, pp. 315-318.

on Christian authors, as well as short commentaries on the Gospels and a major work on the Pauline epistles. His scholarship is characteristic of the Carolingian Renaissance; the commentary exemplifies the type of patch-work of patristic sources which was accepted procedure in exegesis during this period of conservatism and conservation of ancient sources in doctrine.[35] The work was composed *ca.* 848-858.[36] The excerpts below will graphically illustrate the nature of the doctrinal synthesis underway in all Biblical scholarship in this century which provided the foundations of medieval orthodoxy.

Selected texts are presented with authors indicated in the left margin; this is a modification of marginal symbols which appear in the Zürich and Bamberg MSS and are very likely Sedulius' own notations.[37] Brackets show the text divisions; in five places, parentheses indicate editorial additions by the present author where Sedulius failed to show his sources :

[Rom. 1:17 (MPL 103, cols. 18 f.)]

"Justitia enim Dei revelatur in eo, ex fide in fidem."

Ambrose   [Justitia Dei est, quia quod promisit, dedit. "Judaeo." Credenti quod ei promisit Deus prophetas suos. Justum Dominus probat "ex fide" Dei promittentis, "in fidem" hominis credentis. "Justitia Dei revelatur." Qui credit veracem Deum dedisse quod promisit, hoc contra Judaeos loquitur qui negant esse Christum quem promisit. "Sicut scriptum est." In Habacuc videlicet. "Justus ex fide", id est, non ex operibus legis, "Vivit" (Habac. II), hoc est, praesentem vitam ducit, vel vitam

Pelagius   aeternam acquirit. [Aliter secundum Pil. "Justitia Dei est." Quod justum fuerat, ut quo modo Abraham credens ex gentibus, per solam fidem justificatus est, ita caeteri fidem ejus imitantes, salvarentur. "Ex fide" Abraham : "In fidem" hominis credentis; sive "ex fide" Judaei, "in fide" gentilis :

---

[35] H. J. Frede, *Pelagius, der Irische Paulustext, Sedulius Scotus* (Freiburg : Herder, 1961), p. 89 : "Sedulius bietet einen praktischen, katenenartigen Handkommentar, der den in den antiken Pauluskommentaren gesammelten exegetischen Schatz ausschöpft und dem Benutzer die bislang gefundenen Erklärungsmöglichkeiten aufzeigt."

[36] Stegmüller no 6367, 7 (vol. 4, 208) : "PELAGIO tamquam fonte principali usus est SEDULIUS, qui adhibet etiam ALCUINUM, *Hebr*; AMBROSIASTRUM, *Rom* : *I. Cor*; *Quaest. nov. test.*; THEODORUM DE MOPSUESTE, *Gal*; *Eph*; *Tit*; CASSIODORUM (PS. PRIMASIUM) sub nomine ISIDORI; ORIGENEM, *Rom.* interprete RUFINO; JUNILIUM; non adhibet PS. HIERONYMUM, *Rom-Philem*." Cf., for use of Pelagius, Souter, *Pelagius' Expositions*, no. 1, pp. 336-339.

[37] Reconstructed here according to information provided in an article by A. Souter, "The Sources of Sedulius Scotus' *Collectaneum* on the Epistles of St. Paul", *Journal of Theological Studies* 18 (1917), pp. 184-228.

Origen- Rufinus	ideo autem "ex" et "in" posuit, ut tautologiae vitium decli-
	naret. [Justitia Dei in evangelio revelatur, per id quod ad
	salutem nullus excipitur venire, sive Judaeus, sive Graecus,
	sive barbarus; nam omnibus dicit Salvator : "Venite ad me,
	omnes qui laboratis, et ego reficiam vox" (Matt. XI) (Reve-
(? — prob.	latur justitia Dei, quae obtecta prius velabatur in lege; reve-
Augustine)	latur enim in his qui ex fide Veteris Testamenti ad fidem
	novi Evangelii veniunt; et cum in Evangelium veniunt, ex
	fide legis, in fidem Christi diriguntur. Justus autem meus
INPMASP (?)	ex fide vivit, id est, Veteris et Novi Testamenti : [nam alterum
	sine altero integritatem vitae non habet. Aliter "ex fide"
	praedicantium, "in fidem" credentium. Sive ut Augustinus
Augustine	exponit, "ex fide" [verborum quibus nunc credimus quod
	nondum videmus, "in fidem" rerum, qua in aeternum quod
Jerome	nunc credimus, obtinebimus. [Quare non homo vel vir ex
	fide vivere dixit, ideo ne reprobaret opera dum hucusque
	fidem et gratiam commendavit, hic vero opus ostenditur,
	dicens : Justus est, fide vivet; quia justum indicat, bona opera
	habentem.
	[3:19-20 (col. 41)]
Ambrosiaster	"Et subditis fiat omnis mundus Deo." [Dum omnes indigent
	misericordia Dei, tam Judaei, quam Graeci. Aut subditus
	sit omnis mundus Deo, humili scilicet confessione pecca-
Pelagius	torum. ["Quia non justificabitur ex operibus legis omnis
Pelagius	caro coram ipso." [Opera legis, dicit circumcisionem, et sabba-
	tum, et caeteras caeremonias, quae non tam ad justitiam,
(Ambrosiaster)	quam ad carnis laetitiam pertinebant : (quia per fidem decrevit
	Deus justificare homines, non per legem : (si qui enim in
	veteri lege justi erant, non nisi per gratiam justificati sunt.
Ambrosiaster	[Omnem carnem, omnem hominem dixit, ut est illud; "Et
	videbit omnis caro salutare Dei" (Luc. III). Sed et hoc quod
Origen-	addidit, "coram ipso", [non otiose accipiendum, quia aliud
Rufinus	est justificari coram Deo, aliud coram hominibus, hoc est,
	ad comparationem aliorum hominum, potest qui emendatius
	vixerit, justus videri; ad comparationem autem Dei, non
	solum homo non justificabitur, sed sicut Job dicit : "Stellae
	autem non sunt mundae coram ipso" (Job XXV), quae utique
	coram nobis mundae sunt, hoc est, ad comparationem homi-
	num mundae habentur. "Per legem enim cognitio peccati."
Pelagius	[Non remissio, nec ablatio peccatorum, sed cognitio.
	Ideo enim per legem quid sit peccatum agnoscitur, quia
	in oblivionem ierat lex naturae : ante autem legem, leviora
	quaeque non cognoscebantur esse peccata, id est, quae aliis
	non nocebant, ut concupiscentia, et ebrietas, et caetera
Augustine	hujusmodi. [Sollicite satis haec legenda sunt, ut neque lex
	ab apostolis improbata videatur, neque eorum liberum arbi-
	trium sit ablatum. Itaque quatuor istos gradus hominis
	distinguamus : ante legem, sub lege, sub gratia, sub pace ...

Ambrosiaster [Joseph in carcerem missus est, licet per calumniam, et pin-
(paraphrased) cerna, et pastor Pharaonis causa peccati in carcere trusi
sunt, quomodo ergo latebant peccata? Triplex quidem est
lex, ita ut prima pars de sacramento divinitatis Dei sit; secunda
autem quae congruit legi naturali, quae interdicit : tertia
vero lex factorum id est, sabbata, neomeniae, circumcisio, etc.
[3:21-24, (Col. 42)]

"Nunc autem sine lege justitia Dei manifesta est." [Justitia
Pelagius   Dei est sanctificatio per fidem, et remissio peccatorum.
Ambrosiaster   "Sine lege." [Sabbati scilicet, et circumcisionis, et neomeniae,
et vindictae : non tamen sine sacramento divinitatis Dei,
quippe cum justitia Dei de sacramento Dei sit. "Testificati
per legem et prophetas." Ideo hoc addidit ne indulgentia
peccatorum contra legem videatur, quippe quae olim in lege
Ambrosiaster   promissa futura esse per adventum Salvatoris. [Ideo autem
justitia Dei dicta est, quae videtur esse misericordia, quia
de promissione habet originem : et promissio Dei, cum
redditur justitia, Dei dicitur ... "Per legem enim manifestatio
peccati, nunc sine lege justitia Dei cognita est." [Ad quod
Origen-   dicendum, quia "omne quod manifestatur lux est." Peccatum,
Rufinus   quia lux non est, non manifestatur, sed agnoscitur : idcirco
et in superioribus agnitionem peccati aptius dixerit. "Omnes
(? — prob.   enim peccaverunt." (Supple originaliter in Adam, et propriae
Augustine)   voluntatis praevaricantia. "Et egent gloria Dei. [Id est,
Pelagius (?)   gratia Dei, qui non habent suam (gloriam, qui creati sunt.
(Cassiodorus,   "Justificati gratis." (Hoc est, sine ullis operibus praecedenti-
slightly   bus, per haptismum gratis peccata donavit. ...
condensed)

[3:28 (cols. 44 f.)]
"Arbitramur enim justificari hominem per fidem," etc. [Sine
Pelagius   quibus operibus legis Apostolus justificari hominem per
fidem dixisse credendus est? scilicet circumcisionis, et sabbati,
et caeterorum hujusmodi, non absque justitiae operibus,
de quibus beatus Jacobus dixit : "Fides sine operibus mortua
est" : Hic autem de illo dicit, quia ad Christum veniens,
sola, cum credit, fide salvatur. Addendo autem, sine quibus
mortua est fides. [Quomodo justificatur homo sine operibus
legis? Credit aliquis, percipit fidei sacramenta, et mortuus
Augustine   est : defuit illi operandi tempus, plane dicimus justificatum,
"credentum in eum qui justificat impium" : ergo iste justificatus, et operatus non est. Impletur sententia Apostoli,
dicentis : "Arbitramur justificari hominem per fidem sine
operibus legis", ut latro, qui cum Christo crucifixus credidit,
et justificatus est. Potest ergo homo justificari ex fide sine
operibus legis, cum fides per dilectionem operetur in corde,
etiamsi foris non exit in opere. ...

The eclectic nature of this treatment should be obvious to the reader at a glance, and is even more synthetic than the *catena* method of Rabanus. As with Rabanus, the most important feature historically in this work is the incorporation of Augustinian elements into the doctrinal synthesis. On Romans 1:17, for example, is an Augustinian tag which makes frequent appearances in later commentators.[38]

On 3:19, Sedulius also follows Pelagius on confession. On 3:20, the basis of the interpretation is Pelagian, but the author continues with a reference to free will, again an Augustinian *motif*, but then proceeds with an analysis which anticipates scholastic methodology : In this is incorporated first a four-fold distinction of the stages of the Christian's life from Augustine [39] (not reproduced above), then Ambrosiaster's three-fold law concept *verbatim*. A quotation from Origen intervenes between this and a further quotation of Ambrosiaster; thus is combined the element of the literal, historical interpretation of Pauline freedom with a sacramental interpretation. The doctrinal development is completed in a paraphrase of Cassiodorus in this place (although not indicated in the MSS) which identifies baptism as the justifying sacrament. The gloss immediately preceding, on 3:23—a reference to original sin—is noted as further evidence of the basically Augustinian outlook of the author.

3:28 again follows Pelagius and Cassiodorus in glossing this with James 2:26, but follows this with the Augustinian concept of 'faith working through love'. Here he quotes from the same context of Augustine as Rabanus (however, comparison of other portions of the two commentaries shows that Sedulius was not dependent on Rabanus).

(7) Florus of Lyons (*ob. ca.* 860)

Expositio in epistolas beati Pauli [40]

This author was a prominent Carolingian ecclesiastical personage. He was deacon to Bishop Agobard of Lyons and a leading conservative

---

[38] I have not found the precise reference in Augustine, but cf. *De Spir. et litt.* c. 15, n. 27 : "Haec gratia in veteri testamento velata latitabit, quae in Christi Evangelio revelata est." See Denifle, pp. 3 f., and Portalié, *Guide*, p. 124, for further examples.

[39] *Enchir.* c. 118.

[40] Edition : *MPL* 119, cols. 279-420; this is not a text, but rather a list of references to the Augustinian passages compiled by Florus. Literature : Stegmüller nos. 2279-90 (vol. 2, 311); Affeldt, pp. 378 f.; Spicq, pp. 45 f.; Manitius I, p. 564; C. Charlier, "La compilation augustinienne de Florus sur l'Apôtre", *Revue Benedictine* 57 (1947), pp. 132-186.

writer and church politician. Among his work are polemic writings against the three major progressive figures in ninth century theology, the Neo-Platonist philosopher John Scotus Erigena, the predestinarian theologian Gottschalk, and the liturgical reformer Amalarius of Metz.[41]

Florus compiled two *catena* type commentaries on the Pauline epistles. The first, collected from twelve Church Fathers, has not been edited or printed. The second, which is treated here, is composed exclusively of excerpts from St. Augustine's writings.[42] This latter commentary exists in many MS examples, and frequent traces of its influence can be found in later writers. William of St. Thierry used it as the basis of his commentary in the twelfth century.

Because of the unreliability of the *MPL* text,[43] no detailed analysis will be attempted here. Two passages should be cited because they were received into the *Glossa ordinaria*, the standard medieval reference work on the Biblical text.

The following is that portion of *De spiritu et littera* in Florus which is used to gloss Romans 3:24 in the *Glossa* :

Nam itaque justificati per legem, non justificati per propriam voluntatem : sed "justificati per gratiam ipsius"; non quod sine voluntate nostra fiat, sed voluntas nostra ostenditur infirma per legem, ut sanet gratia voluntatem, et sanata voluntas impleat legem, non constituta sub lege, nec indigens lege.[44]

This is an interesting example of the manner in which Augustine, as well as St. Paul, was interpreted; this statement, out of context —indeed,

---

[41] Biographical sketch by A. Cabaniss, "Florus of Lyons", *Classica et Medievalia* 19 (1958), pp. 212-32. Other treatments are in E. S. Duckett, *Carolingian Portraits* (Ann Arbor : Univ. of Michigan Press, 1962), esp. pp. 110-118; A. Cabaniss, *Agobard of Lyons* (Syracuse : Syracuse Univ. Press, 1953); *idem, Amalarius of Metz* (Amsterdam: North Holland Publishing Co., 1954); also consult the index in McCracken, *Early Medieval Theology*, for various remarks on Florus by Cabaniss in his introductions to the Carolingian selections.

[42] Charlier (*op. cit.*, pp. 168-186) gives an index to the Augustinian extracts compiled from the earliest MSS. I have compiled the following statistics from this index : Florus extracted from 56 letters, 127 sermons, and 69 of Augustine's 102 separate works.

[43] Affeldt, *loc. cit.*; Charlier, *loc. cit.* The *MPL* edition, since it is only a list of references, is difficult to use and in several instances I was unable to locate passages from the references given, apparently due to inaccuracies. Charlier's index cannot be used as an aid to correcting the *MPL* edition since it does not include precise textual references.

[44] *De spir. et litt.* c. 9, n. 15 (*MPL* 44, cols. 209 f.); in Florus *MPL* 119, cols. 287 f.; *Glossa Ord., MPL* 114, col. 480B. I have found this also in Hervaeus' commentary (see section below), *MPL* 181, col. 639A.

it is the only such reference in a lengthy context in Augustine—exaggerates the role of human will in justification and could be construed in something quite other than an evangelical sense.

A second passage which should be noted is the comment on Romans 3:28. Here Florus quotes the same Augustinian sermon as Rabanus and Sedulius, only giving more of the context. These three authorities together firmly fixed Augustine's concept of "faith working through love" as the standard interpretation of this verse in the *Glossa ordinaria* and elsewhere.[45]

(8) Ps.-Haymo of Halberstadt (probably Haimo of Auxerre, *fl.* 840-860)

Expositio in Divi Pauli epistolas [46]

This commentary, of uncertain authorship, composed *ca.* 840-860, emanated from the important ninth-century monastic school at Auxerre.[47] The work is of significance as the first commentary in the tradition written as an original composition with an independent viewpoint—it is not merely a synthesis of patristic quotations. It is further important because it was widely reproduced and read from the tenth to twelfth centuries; many MSS survive from these centuries. It was used as a major source by the later important commentator Lanfranc of Bec.

The author's method is interesting in that it reveals a spirit of independence and personal investigation. Although dependent on earlier interpretations, these are handled with intelligence and judgment, and the author often gives a choice of alternate interpretations of authorities, ranging from Origen to Claudius of Turin. He also occasionally makes his comments in a question-and-answer form, which marks the work as an early example of the scholastic *quaestio* method. Also of interest are occasional references to pagan philosophers, as well as etymological notes on key words in the text where he often cites a Greek equivalent.

---

[45] Florus, *MPL* 119, col. 286; *Glossa ord.*, *MPL* 114, col. 481. William of St. Thierry also follows Florus here (*MPL* 180, col. 581A). The same theme is further extended in Florus : cf. Rom. 4:4-6 (col. 287).

[46] Edition : *MPL* 117, cols. 361-938. Literature : Denifle, pp. 18-22, Stegmüller nos. 3101-3114 (vol. 3, 16); Affeldt, pp. 382, f.; McNally, pp. 110 *et seq.*; Spicq, pp. 50 f.; Manitius I, pp. 516 f.; Glorieux, *Pour revaloriser Migne*, p. 57.

[47] L. Maître, *Les écoles épiscopales et monastiques en Occident avant les universités* (768-1180) (Paris, 1924), states that under Heiric, a disciple of Haymo of Auxerre, this school had some two thousand students and six hundred religious.

The commentary thus has relevance to the perennial question of the extent of a knowledge of Greek in the ninth century. A possible hypothesis is that the author had some personal connection with John Scotus Erigena, who definitely knew Greek (Spicq states that a gloss in Haymo's commentary on First Corinthians is due to Erigena's influence [48]), but an examination of several of these *loci* indicates that the author need have had no more knowledge of Greek than other Carolingian scholars who knew the alphabet and a few Biblical terms.

Miss Smalley characterizes this work by remarking that: "Haimo stands on the line that divides the compiler of select extracts from the author of a commentary" and also adds that Haymo, with other contemporary Biblical commentators of the mid-ninth century, "prove that theological discussion was becoming a normal part of exegesis."[49] The work also has a strong flavor of classroom lecturing and protoscholastic *liberaliter disputare*. Langdraf has especially stressed the importance of this work in the development of the medieval schools.[50]

Selected excerpts follow :

[Rom. 1:5 (MPL 117, col. 368)] "Per quem accepimus gratiam et apostolatum ad obediendum fidei in omnibus gentibus pro nomine ejus." Gratia dicitur gratis data. Et gratiam hic debemus intelligere fidem et remissionem peccatorum ...
[3:4 (col. 385)] "Sicut scriptus est : Ut justificeris in sermonibus tuis, et vincas cum judicaris." ... Justificeris indulgentiam peccati dando ad te conversis sicut promittis, et vincas remittendo peccata dum judicaris non posse dimittere.
[3:21, 23-24 (cols. 390 f.)] "Hunc autem", id est in Domini adventu, et in praesenti tempore "justitia Dei manifestata est sine lege". Justitia Dei in praesenti

---

[48] Spicq, pp. 51 f.; cf. pp. 15 f.
[49] Smalley, *Study of the Bible*, p. 40.
[50] Landgraf, *Einführung*, pp. 11 f. :

In dem unter dem Namen Haimos von Halberstadt gedruckten, einem Haimo von Auxerre oder auch dem Remigius von Auxerre zugeschriebenen, jedenfalls aber dem 9. Jahrhundert angehörigen Paulinenkommentar finden wir nun verschiedene auf die Schule jener Zeit sich beziehende Vermerke. Einer derselben besagt, dass derjenige die Glaubenswahrheiten scholastisch vorträgt, der sie philosophisch, d.h. dialektisch zu erörtern versteht. Zudem wird hier das einfache Disputieren von dem streng scholastischen, das identisch ist mit dem liberaliter disputare, unterschieden. Das zweite vermag nur der in den artes liberales Geschulte.

Somit wird nach der Ansicht eines Autors des 9. Jahrhunderts eine Frage dann scholastisch behandelt, wenn sie nach der Methode der Philosophie—Philosophie verstanden in Sinne der Zeit—erörtert wird. Und wiederum nach den Worten dieses gleichen Autors war die Methode der Philosophie damals die dialektische. Obendrein erfahren wir aus den gleichen Texten, dass bereits im 9. Jahrhundert von dieser Methode Gebrauch gemacht wurde.

tempore sine lege manifestata est : non ea solummodo quo ipse justitia est, sed qua induit impium, quando misericorditer de infideli facit fidelem de adultero et fornicatore facit castum et continentem, de injusto et peccatore facit justum et amatorem virtutum. Quae justitia in Christo est revelata, et data "sine lege", id est sine observatione legali, quia nulli lex secundum myste- ria et sacrificia traditur jam observanda; sed dicit : "Qui crediderit et baptizatus fuerit, salvus erit (Marc. XVI)". Hoc est justus erit. Possumus etiam ipsam justitiam Dei Patris, id est Filium intelligere a quo et per quem justificamur, quia sine observatione legis per opera deitatis manifestatus est Filius Dei esse.

"Testificata a lege et prophetis." Justitia baptismatis, qua justificamur, per legem testificatur, dum dicitur : In novissimis diebus circumcidet Dominus cor tuum, id est auferet peccata tua : et justificabit te per baptismum (Deut. XXX). Testificatur et per prophetas, dum dicitur : Ipse iniquitates nostras protabit, et peccata nostra ipse tollet (Isa. LIII).

[23] "Omnes enim peccaverunt et egent gloria Dei". id est indulgentia et vania peccatorum indigent omnes, tam Judaei quam gentiles : pro qua glorificandus est Deus.

[24] "Justificati gratis per gratiam ipsius : per redemptionem, quae est in Christo Jesu". "Gratias" dicit, id est sine ullis praecedentibus meritis. Verbi gratia. Qui ad baptismum venit, nihil unquam boni fecit, baptizatur, statimque justificatur. Ecce gratis justificatur per gratiam, id est per donum Dei : et hoc "per redemptionem quae est in Christo Jesu", non in operibus legis. Redemp- tio nostra qua sumus redempti, et per quam justificamus, passio Christi est quae juncta baptismo, justificat hominem per fidem : et postmodum per poenitentiam. Ita enim illa duo mutuo sunt conjuncta, ut unum sine altero hominem non possit justificare. Nam neque fides Dominicae passionis sine aqua baptismatis hominem mundat, nisi forte in martyrio quod pro baptismate accipitur : neque aquam baptismi bine fide Dominicae passionis purificare hominem valet. Jungantur ergo simul sicque praestabunt perfectam redemp- tionem, perfectamque mundationem. Itaque neque Judaeus, neque gentilis suis justificatur operibus, cum uterque sit praevaricator suae legis : Judaeus videlicet naturalis et scriptae; gentilis autem naturalis. Sed redemptione qua Christus nos redemit suo sanguine et fide : et aqua baptismatis, qua quisque renatus, si statim obierit, salvabitur in vita : si autem vixerit, debet ornare fidem operibus, "Quia fides sine operibus mortua est". ...

[10:4 (col. 449)] "Finis enim Legis, Christus est, ad justitiam omni credenti." ... Quod qui credit et confitetur justificatur, si tamen opera digna fide fecerit. ...

The texts given make one fundamental point clear : for Haymo, grace and justification is but an equivalent of remission of sins—this narrow interpretation is the principal feature of his concept of justi- fication.

It should be further remarked that justification is most often connected with baptism, in many other *loci* in this commentary, in which the author develops his views according to a sharp distinction between "carnal observances" and baptism, specifically in terms of the antithesis of

Jewish ceremonialism vs. Christian baptism [51]—here also is the usual historical literalism, but with a much stronger emphasis upon sacramentalism.

Of special interest is that Haymo also includes the other sacrament pertaining to remission of sins, i.e., penance. The gloss of Romans 3:4 indicates this; Haymo follows Ambrosiaster in referring the verse to David's repentance. Most interesting is the statement on baptism and penance on 3:24 ("Ita enim illa duo mutuo sunt conjuncta, ut unum sine altero hominem non possit justificare") which establishes a virtual economy of sacramental justification.

The gloss on Romans 10:4 is given for an instance of Haymo's adjustment of works to justification, which indicates his agreement with James 2:26 (he uses this text to gloss Romans 1:17 also).

(9) Hatto (Atto) of Vercelli (*ca.* 885-961)

Expositio epistolarum D. Pauli [52]

This commentary, by a tenth century Lombard bishop, is dated by Stegmüller from between 924 and 940; Hatto's own work appears probably only in the commentaries on Romans and I and II Corinthians.[53] Like Haymo, this is a strongly didactic work but also shows a wider horizon of secular learning—the author occasionally uses pagan writers.[54] He is also fond of fanciful etymologizing. There is a marked tendency in this commentary to break up the sentences of the Pauline text and perform elaborate exegesis on individual phrases. This makes the commentary quite lengthy and detailed, but has a definite and

---

[51] Cf. on Rom. 1:6-7, immediately following the gloss on 1:5 which I give, where occur three further statements on baptism; also Rom. 3:19-20 (for justification under OT law), Rom. 3:28 and esp. Gal. 2:16 (for justification in baptism against the OT background).

[52] Edition : MPL 134, cols. 125-834. Literature : Denifle, pp. 25-27; Stegmüller nos. 3126-93 (vol. 3, 20); Affeldt, p. 383; McNally, pp. 110 *et seq.*; Spicq, p. 54; Manitius II, pp. 28 f., 32.

[53] Stegmüller, *loc. cit.* : "*Epp. Pauli* compositus c. 924-940; multum dependet a CLAUDIO TAURINENSI"; *idem*, no. 6367, 5 (vol. 4, 208) : "Claudio Taurinensi necnon Pelagio usus est ..." Affeldt, *loc. cit.* : "Also Eigentum Hattos können nur die Kommentare Rom.—2 Cor., vielleicht noch der zum Galaterbrief angesprochen werden. Zu Eph. und Phil. bietet Hatto nur eine kürzere Fassung der Kommentare des Claudius von Turin identisch. Die Kommentare 1 Thess.—2 Tim. des Claudius und Hatto sind identisch mit denen des Ambrosiaster."

[54] E.G., a line from Virgil is quoted on Rom. 1:2.

unfortunate effect of disintegrating the text, and, with it, the essential meaning of the Apostle's thought.

Selected texts follow :

[Rom. 1:17 (MPL 134, cols. 137 f.)] Sequitur : "Justitia enim Dei in eo revelatur ex fide in fidem." Justitia dicitur, quasi juris status. Justitia ergo est, cum unicuique proprium ejus tribuitur : unde et justus dicitur, eo quod jus custodiat. Justitia autem Dei Christus est, quae revelatur in eo, id est per illud, scilicet per Evangelium. Quod vero dicit, "ex fide in fidem", tale est, quale et illud, quod alibi ait : "Nos autem revelata facie speculantes gloriam Dei, transformamur in eamdem imaginem a gloria in gloriam, tanquam a Domini Spiritu (II Cor. III, 18). A gloria dicit Evangelii ad gloriam aeternae remunerationis. Similiter et hic, ex fide legis in fidem Evangelii, vel ex fide verborum et operum, in fidem aeternae retributionis, sive ex fide hominis in fidem Dei. Et ut suam narrationem prophetico testimonio comprobaret, adjecit : "Sicut scriptum est : Justus autem ex fide vivit." Quod dicit, "ex fide", non illa est intelligenda, quae verbo tenus tenetur, sed quae operibus adimpletur, quia fides sine operibus mortua est in semetipsa.

[3:4 (cols. 155 f.)] David autem, quia peccavit, cum esset rex, aiebat : "Tibi soli peccaveri," etc. Ac si deceret : Tu, Domine, promisisti te sine personarum acceptione vindicaturum in peccatores. Dum ergo mihi peccatum dimittis, homines tuam patientiam judicant esse mendacium. Me tamen confitente et satisfaciente, ideo peccatum dimittis, ut justificeris et vincas eos qui te judicant esse mentitum, qui non judicas bis in idipsum. Tuae quippe pietatis miseratio te ostendit non esse ementitum. Aliter : Erant nonnulli, sicut Epicurei, qui dicebant, Deum non habere curam hominum, quemadmodum et bestiarum ...

[3:28 (col. 163)] "Arbitramur justificari hominem per fidem sine operibus legis." Arbitramur hoc loco non dubitative dictum intelligendum est, sed affirmative. Ac si diceret : Firmissime credimus quia ex fide justificatur homo sine operibus legis. Magnum igitur est meritum fidei, nam praeterita peccata relaxat, et praesentia absolvit et futura praecavere facit possessoremque suum ad futura bona peragenda fortiorem reddit. Sed quid est quod ait, justificari hominem sola fide, cum alibi dicat; "Fides est quae per dilectionem operatur;" (Gal. V, 6). Et coapostolus ejus Jacobus : "Fides sine operibus mortua est" (Jac. II, 20). Non igitur sibi hae apostolicae sententiae contrariae sunt. Quia Apostolus, non ideo ait hominem sola fide justificari, ut, si post acceptam fidem male vixerit, justus sit, sed, quia, si contigerit ut accepta fide statim moriatur, sola fide justificabitur, etiamsi non sit ei operandi tempus concessum. Non enim apostolus Paulus de illis loquitur operibus quae fidem sequuntur, sed, ut Jacobus, quae fidem praecedunt, per quae nemo justificari potest, quia "sine fide impossibile Deo placere" (Hebr. X, 6).

The gloss on Romans 1:17 is interesting for its legalistic conception of the justice of God. The peculiar etymological derivation "justitia quasi iuris status" is borrowed from Isidore of Seville's famous encyclopedia, the *Etymologiae* [55] (early 7th century). This is the closest approach

---

[55] Isidore, *Etymol.* XVIII, c. 15, n. 2 (*MPL* 82, col. 560B). The only commentator

in the commentaries to making a connection between justification and secular law; the limited application made here, however, is only to clarify the language of the epistle and not for theological purposes. The medieval concept of justification is always basically forensic, but given only a theological, and not legal, interpretation. The reference to James at the end of this section probably follows Haymo. The comment on 3:28 attempts a more thoroughgoing adjustment between Paul and James, and shows again that the problem was regarded with seriousness by theologians of this period.

A portion of Romans 3:4 is given as an example of Hatto's classical scholarship, as well as to show that justification has some relationship to remission of sin, although this author is free of the strident sacerdotalism and sacramentalism of Haymo; for example, he prefers to regard baptism in a genuine Pauline *motif* as a 'death with Christ' and a resurrection into a new life.[56] There are other points of interest in this commentary which reflect an ability to recognize problems in the text and attempt discussion and solution in some depth. On Romans 3:20, he states that *Hic locus cautere legendus est* lest it seems that the Apostle destroys free will; the solution is based on the same Augustinian fourfold distinction of the law which Sedulius and Florus quote in this place.[57] The exegesis on Romans chapters 4 and 5 is, however, notable for a sound and informed Augustinianism which approaches an evangelical quality in some of its emphases, e.g., an interesting interpretation of 5:11 beginning : "Reconciliationem dicit justificationem, quae facta est in sanguine ipsius" which shows an appreciation of the Atonement for remission of sins. Also interesting is the comment on Romans 5:1-2 ("Justificati igitur ex fide, pacem habeamus ... per quem et accessum habemus fide in gratiam istam in qua stamus ...") where *in gratiam istam* is glossed : "Gratiam vocat adoptionem filiorum ..."

This author possessed a considerable theological sophistication and is noteworthy for his personal advance beyond the narrow sacerdotalism of most of his contemporaries, especially in his understanding of the Augustinian theory of grace. But he retains much of the theoretical content of traditional exegesis, with the usual literalistic interpretation

---

who follows this peculiar etymological interpretation is a contemporary Benedictine named Thietlandus (ob. 964), who wrote a Pauline commentary strongly dependent on Hatto; Denifle, pp. 27 f., prints portions; listed by Affeldt, pp. 404 f.

[56] On Rom. 4:25.

[57] Sedulius, as quoted above; Florus, *MPL* 119, col. 286.

of Romans 3:19-31 against the Judaic background and a peculiarly legalistic interpretation of his own on *justitia Dei*.

(10) Lanfranc of Bec (of Canterbury) (*ca.* 1003-1089)

In omnes Pauli epistolas commentarii cum glossula interjecta [58]

Lanfranc's commentary is of principal importance as an example of the important gloss type of exegesis which ultimately issued in the standard medieval reference work on the Bible, the *Glossa ordinaria*, in which many of Lanfranc's glosses were received. The history of the gloss is obscure before Lanfranc, and, although we are on fairly firm ground with his Pauline collection, there are numerous critical difficulties barring a precise determination of his own text since there was much inter-borrowing of individual glosses. The *MPL* edition is one of many redactions and is used here without assurance of being the actual Lanfrancian text, although it preserves the main lines of Lanfranc's methods and interpretations.[59]

The general character of this work is summarized by Lanfranc's modern biographer :

While at Bec and Caen he wrote his lengthy commentaries on the Epistles of S. Paul, and left them behind when he came to England. ...

The work consists of simple exegesis, together with explanatory footnotes, which contain ample quotations form the Latin fathers. The greater proportion of the quotations are taken from Augustine. ...

The commentaries were written for elementary students of the Bible. The explanation of the text was the main object. Doctrinal questions are seldom discussed. No opportunity for emphasizing 'proof texts' for the monastic life was allowed to pass by. Celibacy, the tonsure and asceticism generally are supported by quotations from S. Paul.[60]

One may add to these remarks the observation that the commentary was regarded by contemporaries as exhibiting the essence of the dialec-

---

[58] Edition : *MPL* 150, cols. 101-406. Literature : Denifle, pp. 28-30; Stegmüller nos. 5370-83 (vol. 3, 519); Affeldt, p. 387; Spicq, p. 54; Manitius III, p. 81 f.

[59] Stegmüller, *loc. cit.* : "Editio PL 150 nititur codice Redonense ... et commentarium Lanfranci non exhibet integruum." Cf. Affeldt, *loc. cit.* There is considerable technical literature on the difficult critical problems concerning the origins and inter-relationships of the gloss, as well as on this work; the best introductory discussion and summary of the problem is Smalley, *Study of the Bible*, pp. 46 *et seq.*

[60] A. J. MacDonald, *Lanfranc : A Study of his Life, Work and Writing* (Oxford, 1926), pp. 58 f. Cf. R. W. Southern, "Lanfranc of Bec and Berengar of Tours", *Studies in Medieval History Presented to F. M. Powicke* (Oxford, 1948), pp. 36 f.

tical method.[61] Because of the authoritative status of the work, it is valuable as evidence for interpretations which were considered standard and widely taught and otherwise disseminated in glossed copies of Scripture.

The glossing is both interlinear and marginal, and the selections are reproduced here with the two forms shown in parallel columns; the marginal commentary is composed of brief excerpts from Ambrosiaster, Augustine, and Lanfranc's own glosses (all glosses in the following selections are Lanfrancian).

TEXT (Lanfranc's glosses italicized):

MARGINAL COMMENTARY:

(MPL 150, cols. 107 ff.)

[Rom. 1:5]
7. ... per quem accepimus gratiam *remissione peccatorum* et apostolatum ...

[1:7]
9. ... gratia *remissio peccatorum* vobis et, 10, 11. pax a Deo, *reconciliatio apud Deum*, Patre nostro, et Domino Jesus Christo.

9. "Gratia", remissio peccatorum.

[3:4]
5,6. Ut justificeris *verax appereas* in sermonibus tuis.

5. "Ut justiceris", David peccavit in causa Uriae, sciens quia promissio peccatoribus non prodest. Orat ut Deus judicium quo judicatur peccatoribus nihil dare, vincat; et se poenitentem sanctificet, ut dans sibi quod justis daturum se promisit, justificetur in sermonibus suis.

[3:26-27]
21, 22. ad ostensionem justitiae suae.
23. Propter remissionem praecedentium delictorum, in sustentione Dei,

---

[61] Southern, *loc. cit.*, states:
The peculiarity of Lanfranc's work was marked by Sigebert of Gembloux: "Lanfrancus dialecticus ... Paulum apostolum exposuit et ubicumque opportunitas locorum occurrit secundum leges dialectice proponit, assumit, concludit." That is to say—if we understand him rightly—he explained the argument, disentangled its branches, and put into proper logical form what the Apostle had left to be inferred from a few rapid sentences. 'The order of the argument is as follows ... This is a proof of the preceding verse. ... This is an argument *a simili ... a causa ... a contrario*. ... Here, by disproving one alternative, the Apostle proves, as his manner is, the other': these are phrases which often recur in Lanfranc's commentary.

ad ostensionem justitiae ejus in hoc tempore, ut sit ipse justus, 24, et justificans eum qui est ex fide Jesu Christi. Ubi est ergo gloriatio tua? Exclusa est. Per quam legem? 25. factorum? Non, sed 26. per legam fidei.

22. "Ad ostensionem". Ad hoc Deus filium suum mundo praedicari fecit, ut ostenderet quod per fidem ejus justificantur peccatores. 23. "Propter remissionem praecedentium delictorum in sustentatione Dei. Patienter enim Deus sustinuit praecedentia delicta mundi, ut ostenderet qui vera justificatio est in hoc tempore, id est, in fide Jesu Christi. Si enim omnes peccatores puniisset, non esset qui in hoc tempore justificari posset. 24. "Justus et justificans," id est, verax, complens ea quae promisit. 25. "Factorum", id est, an alia lex prolata est, habens alia observationes, per quas observationes tuae annihilentur. 26. "Per legem fidei." Legem fidei vocat legem Christi, in quo asseritur salvari hominem per solam fidem dum dicitur : "Qui crediderit, et baptizatus fuerit, salvus erit."

[5:16]
21. gratia autem ex multis delictis in justificationem.

21. "Gratia autem ex multis." Ordo est : Gratia autem in justificationem ex multis delictis.

[5:18]
24. per unius justitiam in omnes homines in justificationem vitae. *Ita misericordia Dei per unius justitiam in omnes homines processit.*

24. "Per unius justitiam." Per justitiam et obedientiam Christi, vita omnium credentium justificata est. Quia inde factus est hostia acceptabilis Deo pro peccatis omnium, quia justus et immaculatus sine peccat, et obediens fuit usque ad mortem.

[6:7]
13. Qui enim mortuus est, justificatus est a peccato.

13. "Qui enim mortuus est." Ratio cur non serviendum sit peccato. Peccato enim justificatio perit.

The glosses given here are all that could be gathered with any relevance to Lanfranc's concept of justification. Although on Romans 3:27 he uses the *sola fide* formula, the only firm doctrine on grace and justification seems to be as these are synonymous with remission of sins. It is again noted that this conclusion cannot be regarded as definitive in view of the uncertainty of the text.[62]

---

[62] Denifle, pp. 28 f., prints excerpts from a considerably different version, but I see nothing in these, at least, to change my conclusion here.

(11) *Glossa ordinaria* [63]

Selections from the MPL version of the *Glossa ordinaria* are given here with even greater misgivings than those from Lanfranc. The work is printed under the name of the ninth-century German theologian Walafrid Strabo, but this traditional attribution is accepted by no modern researcher, and, indeed, the original *Glossa ordinaria*, if there ever was such a single exemplar, cannot be determined with presently available evidence. The most that can be claimed for the unsatisfactory *MPL* edition is that it contains material emanating from the school of St. Anselm of Laon (*ca.* 1050-1117), from whence it is now believed that the gloss form originated. Most of the material incorporated is from patristic sources.

There is little of interest in the interpretation of Romans 3:19 ff., and it is not reproduced here. 'Works of law' are again understood as Judaic ceremonies and "figures" of Christian sacraments; the concept is Augustinian here, as is most of the context—e.g., 3:24 is glossed from *De spiritu et littera* (c. 9, n. 15) probably following Florus of Lyons, as noted when discussing Florus' commentary. 3:28 is of interest in combining the conventional reference to James 2:26 with the Augustinian concept of *fides quae per dilectionem operatur*. This is done in much the same manner as Sedulius, which may very well be the source for the teaching, if not the precise text (as with Sedulius, Rabanus, and Florus, a quotation from Augustine's Sermo 2 is used, but the *Glossa* adds an additional quotation embodying the same concept from the *Enchiridion*, c. 107).

However, Romans 4:1-4 is interesting for approaching a somewhat systematic definition of justification :

[Rom. 4:1-4 (MPL 114, cols. 481 f.)]
1. "Secundum carmen." Id est ex operibus legis. Quasi dicat : Dicemus quod fuit justus ex eis? non, quia si ex carnali observatione est justus, habet gloriam aeternam quae ex justitia sequitur : sed a se habet eam, non a Deo. Vel, haec justificatio est in opinione hominum, et non apud Deum. Ad Deum autem habet gloriam : non ergo ex operibus justificatus est, unde justificatus est? Sequitur et dicit unde, etc.

[63] Edition : *MPL* 114, cols. 469-670. Literature : Denifle, pp. 16-18; Stegmüller nos. 112-117, 351-354, 356 (vol. 2); Affeldt, pp. 373 f.; Spicq, pp. 110-113; Manitius III, 238 f. For an introduction to the technical problems and literature, Smalley, *Study of the Bible*, pp. 46 *et seq.* is again recommended; an account of the state of research on the *Glossa ordinaria* to 1948 is in J. de Ghellinck, *Le mouvement théologique du XIIe siècle*, 2nd ed. (Bruges : Éditions "De Tempel", 1948), pp. 104-112.

3. "Credidit." Credere, sufficiens causa fuit ei justitiae, et est aliis, sed tamen qui habet tempus operandi, ei non dabitur merces secundum gratiam tantum, sed secundum debitum operationis suae; sed ei qui non habet tempus operandi, si credit, sola fides sufficit ad justitiam, et ita ad salutem secundum gratiam propositam omnibus, vel secundum quod Deus legem ante posuit.

4. "Ei autem," etc. Quasi dicat : Abraham est justus ex fide : sed ei qui operatur illa carnalia, vel aliqua bona ut gratiam mereatur, si merces est ei, non est ex gratia, sed ex meriti sui debito. Illi vero qui non facit haec carnalia vel aliqua bona, sed tantum credit, fides sufficit ad justitiam, et ita attribuit aliis quod dixit Abraham, scilicet quod si est justus ex operibus, habet gloriam, sed non apud Deum, et ideo ex fide.

"Secundum gratiam." Si gratia est, gratis datur seu gratis constat. Nihil boni fecisti, et datur tibi remissio peccatorum. Attenduntur opera tua et inveniuntur omnia mala.

But, as with Lanfranc, the concluding gloss *Secundum gratiam* seems to place the concept of justifying grace in the context of remission of sins. Additional evidence is on Galatians 3:6 (col. 575) :

"Sicut Abraham credidit Deo, et reputatum est ei ad justitiam." Justitiam vocat hic peccatorum remissionem et bonae vitae observantium.

(12) St. Bruno of Cologne (1032-1101)

Expositiones in omnes epistolas Pauli [64]

This commentary is usually attributed to the founder of the Carthusian Order and thought to have been written during Bruno's period as *scholasticus* of the important cathedral school of Rheims, prior to his retirement from teaching and founding of the Order in 1084.[65] His scholastic career and writings have been little studied, although it has been noticed that his Pauline commentary is partially dependent upon St. John Chrysostom and is thus of interest for literary history as evidence of Greek influence in the West during this period. In form, this work is counter to the prevailing trend toward glossing in that it is a running commentary upon the text, in which the author makes an effort to get at the meaning of the whole context.

Selected texts follow :

[Rom. 1:6 (MPL 153, col. 21)] "Per quem" Jesum Christum "accipemus gratiam", id est remissionem.

---

[64] Edition : *MPL* 153, cols. 11-566. Literature : Denifle pp. 34-36; Stegmüller nos. 1817-30 (vol. 1, 219); Affeldt, pp. 376 f.; Spicq, p. 55; Glorieux, *Pour revaloriser Migne*, p. 61.

[65] See Affeldt, *loc. cit.* Glorieux lists the work as anonymous, end of 11th century.

[3:4-5 (cols. 37 f.)] Praeterea notandum est quod cum David, nullum praeten-
dens meritum, ex sola gratia confidat se salvandum, seque in peccatis confitea-
tur, quo nemo sanctior vixit in lege, neminem ex merito posse salvari, sed per
solam gratiam. ... Per hoc apparet quod "iniquitas nostra commendat"
justitiam Dei, id est commendabilem facit Deum, per solam gratiam justificantem homines a peccatis; et hoc utique verum est, quia quanto gratia ejus
copiosior est in remissionem peccatorum, tanto procul dubio commendabilior
est Deus.

[4:25 (col. 48)] ... "traditus est ad mortem, et resurrexit propter justificationem ... propter delicta nostra", id est, ut nos mundaret a delictis nostris,
qui etiam "resurrexit propter justificationem nostram", id est, ut nos mundatos
a delictis nostris, per positionem virtutum justos efficeret. Non ideo, ait,
mortuus est propter delicta nostra, resurrexit propter justificationem, quin
mors ejus causa sit nostrae justitiae, et resurrectio causa remissionis peccatorum. Sed ideo ait resurrexit, propter justificationem, ut ostenderet resurrec-
tionem ejus sic esse causam nostrae justificationis, ut esset signum rei futurae
in nobis : duplicis scilicet resurrectionis. Prima est, qua in baptismo a morte
peccati resurgimus, ad vivendum in justitia. Haec autem resurrectio animae,
quae prius mortua in peccatis, nunc autem confortato libero arbitrio potest
obniti omni malae suggestioni, Deumque cognoscit. Secunda resurrectio est
futura secundum corpus : quando, impassibilitate et immortalitate resumpta,
conregnabimus Christo, si prima resurrectio integre fuerit custodita ...

[5:15 (col. 53)] ... si, inquit, per unum delictum unius, "multi mortui sunt,
multo magis" secundum dignitatem personae Christi et causae, abundavit
"gratia Dei", id est remissio peccatorum.

[5:20 (col. 55)] "Ubicunque" enim "abundavit delictum", vel sub lege vel
extra legem, "ibi gratia abundavit super" delictum : quia non solum remisit
peccata, sed et juste operari concessit. Quia iterum aliqui errabant ex eo
quod dictum est gratiam superabundasse ubi fuit delictum, dicentes se impune
opportune etiam peccare, quia gratia Dei omnia dimitteret, et quanto plura,
tanto gloriosior esset, determinat quidem Paulus gratiam Dei, quotquot
peccata sint, in baptismo omnia dimittere, sed postquam justificati sunt, si
iterum peccant, non sicut prius ex gratia, sed merito poenitentiae dimittentur
peccata. ...

The argument proceeds in orderly and connected fashion in this
commentary. The exegesis on Romans 3:19 ff. (not reproduced here)
seeks to demonstrate that justification is not by works of law and occurs
without human merit. Romans chapter 4 is devoted to a conclusive
interpretation that, from Abraham, justification is *sola gratia Dei* and
ex fide—and that *sola fides* suffices for justification; here the thought
is largely Augustinian. The comment on 4:25, given above, gives Bruno's
general theory of justification through the Atonement. In these sections,
Bruno manifests his independence from tradition by ignoring the question of faith vs. works usually treated in these *loci*.

The exegesis of 3:4 is interesting for its perceptive interpretation of confession in the Evangelical sense of 'confessing that all are saved only by the grace of God', and not as confession in penance. However, his concept of grace and justification takes the narrow interpretation : in 1:6 and 5:15, grace is defined as remission of sin, and his frequent phrase, 'justification *from sin*' as in 3:5 above,[66] gives sufficient indication of his essential concept.

Bruno concludes his systematic theological treatment of justification on chapters 3-5 with a practical note in his comment on 5:20—a clear statement of the sacramental economy of grace, attributing a theory of penance and merit to the Apostle.

(13) Peter Abelard (1079-1142)

Commentarius in epistolam ad Romanos [67]

Book II of this commentary, on Romans 3:19 ff., is of major importance in the history of dogma as the *locus* of Abelard's doctrine of the Atonement, contained in a *quaestio* and *solutio* interposed in the commentary itself. This is his so-called "exemplarist" theory in which Christ's death is considered as effective primarily through its exemplary value as a manifestation of divine love which, in turn, evokes a response of in the sinner. By this concept, Abelard reduces redemption to a single principle,[68] and his concept of justification is accordingly entirely conditioned by it and the consequent view of the relationship of God and man as highly personal, working through a bond of *charitas*. Doctrinally, it marks a complete break with tradition (it can be compared with no other commentary treated in this chapter), although its general origin seems to be Augustinian; it can be critically regarded as a development of the general Augustinian love-ethic of 'faith working through love', but radically carried forward to the exclusion of all forensic or sacra-

---

[66] Cf. Rom. 3:20, 22; 10:10; and the concept is explicit and founded on Paul's text in 6:8 (col. 57) : "Nam" ille "qui mortuus est" in baptismo, a peccato liberatus est. Nec hoc solum, sed etiam "justificatus a peccato".

[67] Edition : *MPL* 178, cols. 783-978. Literature : Denifle, pp. 49-52; Stegmüller no. 6378 (vol. 4, 218 f.); Affeldt, pp. 365 f.; Spicq, pp. 118 f.

[68] Loofs, *Leitfaden*, pp. 416 f.; cf. R. S. Franks, *The Work of Christ* (London : Nelson, 1962), pp. 146 *et seq.* For a comprehensive theological treatment, see J. G. Sikes, *Peter Abailard* (Cambridge, 1932), pp. 204 *et seq.*; and Harnack, *Hist. of Dogma*, vol. 6, p. 79 f. Abelard's theory of the Atonement has found a modern champion—see the controversial 1925 Bampton Lectures by the noted historian of medieval universities : H. Rashdall, *The Idea of Atonement in Christian Theology* (London : Macmillan, 1920), esp. pp. 360 *et seq.*

mental considerations. Abelard's theology in this commentary has been criticized for its subjectivity [69]—not unjustly, for his style of argument is affirmation of personal convictions rather than carefully reasoned exposition of doctrine. But this work is further proof of the fact that Abelard was the most original and creative of medieval theologians,[70] and one of the most passionate in his beliefs.

Since this commentary stands so completely outside the exegetical tradition which is being traced here, it would be superfluous to reproduce any of the text; the interested reader is referred either to the *MPL* text or a conveniently available English translation of the important second book.[71]

(14) William of St. Thierry (ob. 1148)

Expositio in epistolam ad Romanos [72]

The author of this work is remembered as a friend and biographer of St. Bernard of Clairvaux. William also wrote two other commentaries, both on the Song of Songs, one consisting entirely of excerpts from the works of Gregory the Great. All of these commentaries are undistinguished, the interpretations collected out of patristic and other sources in much the same patch-work fashion as the earlier Carolingian exegetes. Spicq describes the commentary on Romans thus : "... Guillaume exploite largement le commentaire de Florus de Lyon (IXe siècle) et élimine toutes les questions débattues : 'Epistolam Pauli ad Romanos ... suscepimus ... suppressis, quae in ea sunt quaestionum molestiis'."[73] The result is a work which is singularly uninteresting.

On Romans 3:19 ff., the general interpretation is made up largely of Augustinian excerpts, much of which is appropriated from Florus' compilation. Only one excerpt is given here, from the comment on 3:27, which appears to be the author's own interpolation—the statement

---

[69] Notably by Harnack, *loc. cit.*

[70] Rashdall, *Idea of Atonement*, p. 363 : "Abelard's Commentary on the Epistle to the Romans is by far the most philosophical and original of the medieval commentaries."

[71] E. R. Fairweather, ed., *A Scholastic Miscellany* : *Anselm to Ockham, Library of Christian Classics X* (Philadelphia : Westminster, 1956), pp. 276-287.

[72] Edition : *MPL* 180, cols. 547-694. Literature : Denifle, pp. 53 f.; Stegmüller no. 3031 (vol. 2, 436); Spicq, pp. 122 f.; Manitius III, p. 124.

[73] Spicq, *loc. cit.*, quoting William's preface to his Romans commentary (col. 547).

follows from a context adapted from *De spiritu et littera* which Florus gives, with some material which cannot be immediately identified as to source.[74] It is the only such gloss on the Pauline phrase *lex fidei* encountered in this study, but does follow the defined tradition of emphasis upon the sacraments :

[Rom. 3:27 (MPL 180, col. 580)] Lex vero factorum, est lex sancta, et mandatum sanctum, et justum, et bonum [cf. Rom. 7:12] : sed per cujus bonum peccatum operatur mortem, prohibens et faciens omnem concupiscentiam; imperans et non adjuvans, puniens nec liberans. Habet autem lex fidei instituta quaedam in sacramentis Ecclesiae, legis factorum sacramentis actu faciliora, utilitate meliora, virtute majora, numero pauciora; tanquam justitia fidei revelata, et in libertatem vocatis filiis Dei, et jugo servitutis ablato, quod duro et carni dedito populo congruebat. ...

(15) Hervaeus Burgidolensis (*ca.* 1080-1150)

Commentaria in epistolas divi Pauli [75]

Spicq describes the Benedictine author of this commentary as manifesting "une grande curiosité théologique",[76] although the general conservatism of the early twelfth century prevails through most of the work, with the principal indebtedness for source-material again to Augustine. Hervaeus does seem to prefer sharp definition in his concepts, however, in contrast to most compilers. The commentary is very literal and historical, as in contexts where the antithesis between the Old and New Testaments is emphasized, as on Romans 1:17 : "Vere Evangelium est virtus Dei, 'nam justitia Dei revelatur in eo', quae velata fuerat in Veteri Testamento."[77] Also, on 3:20 ("quia ex operibus legis non justificabitur omnis caro") : "Et notandum, quia nunc legem quinque libros Moysi nominat."

The most significant feature of the commentary is a treatment of the concept of justification by faith. On 3:28 Hervaeus conventionally quotes James 2:26, as has frequently been observed in exegesis on this verse since Pelagius, but in chapter 4 the author applies some close

[74] It is, at least, apparently not Augustinian (based on my search through the *MPL* index to Augustine's works, tom. 45).

[75] Edition : *MPL* 181, cols. 591-1692. Literature : Denifle, pp. 54-56; Stegmüller nos. 3276-89 (vol. 3, 50 f.)—notes some dispute as to authorship; Affeldt, pp. 383 f.; Spicq, pp. 109 f., 123.

[76] Spicq, p. 123.

[77] Based on an Augustinian phrase in *De spir. et litt.* c. 11, n. 18, frequently echoed in medieval writers: Florus also used it specifically to gloss Rom. 1:17 (*MPL* 119, col. 281).

reasoning to the matter of Abraham's justification by faith. The critical
portions of his argument are as follows :

[Rom. 4:3 (MPL 181, cols. 644 f.)] Nam qui prius ex fide justificatus est in
conspectu Dei, postea et ex operibus est justificatus etiam in conspectu hominum. Unde et Jacobus apostolus in epistola sua contra eos qui nolebant bene
operari, sed de sola fide praesumebant, ipsius Abrahae opera commendavit,
dicens : Vis autem scire, o homo inanis, quoniam fides sine operibus otiosa
est? Abraham pater noster nonne ex operibus justificatus est, offerens Isaac
filium suum super altare? Nec est Jacobus in hac sententia contrarius Paulo
dicenti, quia si Abraham ex operibus justificatus est, habet gloriam, sed non
apud Deum, ac per hoc asserenti quia non ex operibus est justificatus. Uterque
enim verum dicit. Paulus quippe, commendans justitiam quippe, commendans
justitiam quae ex fide est, adversus eos qui fidem negligentes, gloriabantur de
justitia quae est ex operibus, dixit Abraham non esse justificatum ex operibus,
sed quae fidem praecederent. Jacobus autem, ut dictum est, adversus illos
qui percepta fide torpebant otio, et putabant se per eamdem fidem, utpote
justificatos, posse salvari, etiam si bona opera non haberent, dixit Abraham
ex operibus esse justificatum, sed quae fidem secuta sunt. Unde ut ostenderet,
se non dissentire a Paulo, sed potius concordare, protinus addidit : Vides
quoniam fides cooperabatur operibus illius, ut ex operibus fides consummata
est, et suppleta est Scriptura, dicens : "Credidit Abraham Deo, et reputatum
est illi ad justitiam (Gen. XV)", et amicus Dei appellatus est. Et adhuc subjecit :
Videtis quoniam ex operibus justificatur homo, et non ex fide tantum? Manifestum est enim, eum loqui de operibus quae fidem subsequuntur. Quia Paulus
sine praecedentibus operibus dixit, hominem solo fide posse justificari. ...
[4:4 (col. 645)] Dixi, quia Abraham justus est ex fide. ... Sed qui sic justificatus
est, non debet deinceps a bonis operibus torpere. Nam ei, qui post fidem quam
gratis acceperit, operatur opera bona, "non imputatur merces", id est secundum
fidem tantum, sed "secundum debitum" operationis suae. Ita fit ei, qui post
acceptam fidem vivit et bene operatur : non enim aliter a Domino mercedem
percipit. Sed "ei qui non operatur", id est qui postquam baptizatus est, non
habet tempus operandi, vel propter infirmitatem non potest operari, quanquam
velit, sed absque opere de hac vita rapitur cum fide et bona voluntate, huic
nihil operanti, sed tantummodo "credenti in eum qui justificat impium",
id est sola fides sufficit ei ad justitiam ...

The result of Hervaeus' redefinition of justification by faith is to
sharply limit the justifying effects of faith to little more than the conversion experience or baptism, and is something of value principally to
the dying or infirm who are unable to perform meritorious acts and
hence attain a righteousness of works. The author here is using the James
text in the most destructive manner possible to negate Pauline justification and leave the widest possible scope to works; this is the most
overtly semi-Pelagian interpretation of the subject to be found in the
commentaries treated in this study.

(16) Peter Lombard (*ca.* 1100-1160)

Collectanea in omnes divi Pauli epistolas [78]

This commentary, by the author of the famous *Sentences*, is of importance for its later influence : it largely displaced earlier glosses on the Pauline epistles and was commonly known in the schools as the *Magna Glossatura* (the title *Collectanea* is not in the MS tradition). The work is another *catena* with an occasional *quaestio* or connecting comment by the author;[79] an example of what appears to be the latter is given below, on Romans 3:25-26.

This commentary does not approach the quality or clarity of the later *Sentences*. Lombard presents a collection of the conventional formulas which passed into the glossing tradition, but with no success at integrating the material; hence, no distinct line of doctrine emerges from the mass of detailed exegesis. For the quality of the Lombard's theologizing in this work, the reader is referred to the substantial extracts which Denifle printed after thorough editing.[80] Presented here are excerpts which, while it is impossible to determine the Lombard's views on justification without reference to the *Sentences*, at least indicate points of emphasis which are consonant with the general theological points which have been elucidated in previous commentators.

[Rom. 3:19 (MPL 191, col. 1359)] ... [Haymo, Ambrosiaster]. Decrevit enim Deus per sacramentum mysterii fidei, quod in Christo est, hominem justificari, non per legem, quia lex non justificat apud Deum, sed fides. De lege

---

[78] Edition : *MPL* 191, cols. 1297-1696; 192, cols. 9-520. Literature : Denifle, pp. 56-64; Stegmüller nos. 6654-68 (vol. 4, 336-338); Affeldt, pp. 397 f.; Spicq, pp. 125-127; Manitius III, p. 153; Smalley, *Study of the Bible*, pp. 64, 73-76.

[79] Manitius, *loc. cit.*, gives a succinct description :
Die Erklärung selbst besteht in einer katenenartigen Zusammenstellung von Sätzen der Kommentare aus den Vätern und aus späteren Kirchenlehrern. Petrus kommentiert beinahe Wort für Wort, er bevorzugt aber die Heraushebung des mystischen Schriftgehaltes vor der Deutung des Wortsinnes, streut allerdings zuweilen methodische Grundsätze und eigne Deutungsversuche ein. Seine Hauptquellen sind die Glossa ordinaria Walahfrids und die Glossa interlinearis Anselms von Laon und es treten besonders Augustin, Ambrosius, Hilarius [i.e., Ambrosiaster] und Haimo hervor, von den Griechen Origenes und Johannes Damascenus. Auch dieses Werk ist von besonderer Bedeutung, da es der späteren Zeit als die eigentliche Glosse zu Paulus galt. Daher wurde es frühzeitig mit Erklärungen versehen, zunächst von Petrus de Corbolio, dann von Späteren, die sich auf dessen Erläuterungen stützen.

[80] Denifle, *loc. cit.*

autem loquimur secundum caeremonialia, ut dictum est, non secundum moralia, quae utique justificant, et in Evangelio consummantur.

[3:25-26 (col. 1363)] Solet autem quaeri utrum antiquis justis qui in inferno tenebantur peccata essent remissa per fidem et poenitentiam, quem eos vere habuisse constat; et si remissa erant omnia, qua de causa apud inferos detinebantur. Ad quod dicimus, quod omnia erant eis dimissa per fidem et poenitentiam ...

[3:27 (col. 1364)] ... "justificari per fidem sine operibus legis", carnalibus, [Ambrosiaster] id est sine circumcisione, aut neomeniis, aut veneratione Sabbati, vel sine operibus legis quibuslibet etiam moralibus. [Augustinus, De fide et operibus] Sed hoc intelligendum est de operibus praecedentibus fidem, non sequentibus, sine quibus inanis est fides, ut ait Jacobus : "Fides sine operibus mortua est (Jac. II)". Et ipse Paulus ait : "Si habuero omnem fidem, charitatem autem non habuero, nihil sum (I Cor. XIII)". Bene igitur Apostolus fidem praedicans gentibus, ut ostenderet non merito bonorum operum perveniri ad fidem, sed fidem sequi bona opera, dicit hominem justificari per fidem sine operibus legis ...

(17) Robert of Melun (*ca.* 1100-1167)

Questiones de epistolis Pauli [81]

Robert of Melun was an important scholastic theologian of the first half of the twelfth century. An Englishman by birth, he was one of the earlier of the series of scholars of that nation who distinguished themselves at Paris and subsequently had important careers in scholastic learning during the high Middle Ages. Robert was Abelard's successor at the school of St. Geneviève and later directed a school at Melun. Among his pupils were John of Salisbury and Thomas Becket.

Robert's set of *Questiones* is an example of the fully developed scholastic literary form as it was applied to exegesis, as opposed to the continuous commentary. It is dated by Robert's modern editor between 1145 and 1155.[82] The work presents certain problems for the present subject since, as Denifle notes,[83] Robert does not comment on Romans 1:17 or address himself directly to the problem of justification in the traditional manner on other key texts. However, as Denifle illustrates

---

[81] Edition : R. M. Martin, ed., *Oeuvres de Robert de Melun*, t. II : *Questiones theologice de epistolis Pauli*, Spicilegium Sacrum Lovaniense 18 (Louvain, 1938). Literature : The above edition contains a comprehensive introduction and critical apparatus. Also, Denifle, pp. 75-83; Stegmüller nos. 7499-76 (vol. 5, 157-160); Affeldt, p. 401; Spicq, pp. 131 f.; Manitius III, p. 149 f.; Landgraf, *Einführung*, pp. 69-72; Smalley, *Study of the Bible*, pp. 73 f., 215-219, 228-230.

[82] See Martin's introduction to the edition cited, pp. lvi-lviii.

[83] Denifle, p. 75.

with the question on Romans 11:6, Robert consistently maintains that, in justification, "... totum ex gratia Dei est, non ex operibus."[84] To this may be added several other passages where the same position is expressed, a total dependence upon grace for good works and salvation, e.g. : "Est quidem totum ex gratia, aliquid vero ex merito, sed per gratiam. Homo enim nichil boni per se potest. ..."[85] Substantial portions of the commentary on Romans 3:19 ff. are devoted to a demonstration, in fairly traditional fashion, that the law and good works do not suffice for justification and deals with the problem of the salvation of Abraham and the Old Testament patriarchs. Justification is by faith in Christ, and this is explained in two ways, developing Romans 3:20 and 22. First, this faith is manifested in the Gospel :

In Evangelio enim manifeste omnia que ad fidem Christi necessaria sunt predicantur et docentur; "ex qua fide dilectio est" que inustos facit. ... Et ideo, quia verba Legis nichil de fide Christi sonant, dicimus quia fides Christi per Legem non docetur. Quod quia fit per Evangelium, merito ei iustificacio asscribitur, et non Legi.

Vel ideo, quia tanta virtus inest verbis Evangelii, ut etiam ipsa audita gratiam qua iustificantur audientes conferant. Quod, quia verba Legis non habent, nec ipsa ad perfectum ducere possunt.[86]

Secondly, Robert interprets faith in accordance with the Augustinian concept of faith working through love (the emphasis upon *dilectio* in this work is probably due to Abelardian influence). This excerpt is an excellent example of the scholastic flavor of this commentary :

[Rom. 3:22] "Iustitia autem est per fidem Ihesu Christi."

Hic iterum queritur, de qua fide loquatur Apostolus. Sed manifestum est quia de fide Christi.

De qua queritur, utrum possit haberi a bonis et malis.

Et dicunt quidam, quia fides Christi est "fides operans per dilectionem", que a nullo nisi a bono haberi potest.

Sed potest queri ab his, quid intelligant per fidem operantem per dilectionem, an unum an duo, id est, an fidem tantum, an fidem cum dilectione. Sunt autem duo fides et dilectio. Dilectio enim nascitur ex fide. Quod autem duo sint, manifestat Apostolus dicens : "Nunc autem manent fides, spes, caritas, tria hec, maior autem his est caritas."

Ipsi tamen, similitudine inducta, hoc confirmant, quod fides operans per dilectionem nichil aliud est quam fides. ...[87]

---

[84] Denifle, p. 83 n. 3; *Quest.*, pp. 140 f.
[85] *Quest.*, p. 73 (on Rom. 4:4): cf. pp. 71, 125.
[86] *Quest.*, p. 57.
[87] *Quest.*, pp. 58 f.

But does this concept of faith exclude works? Robert's position is stated in his interpretation of Romans 4:4 :

Glossa : "Sed ei qui habet tempus operandi." Unde, quia non excluditur hic quin et quidam habentes tempus operandi et non facultatem, ex sola fide salvantur, id est, sine operibus misericordie. Nam quod alibi [dicitur quod] fides sine operibus [non] mereatur, ad terrorem est dictum; vel de interiore opere [est] intelligendum, sine quo nemo adultus salvatur.

[Rom. 4:4] "Ei autem, qui operatur," etc.

Hic ostenditur quia valent opera ad merendum. Sed queritur de quibus operibus hic agat, an de interioribus, an de exterioribus. Sunt quidem exteriora, ut vestire pauperes, vagos et egenos inducere in domum suam, visitare infirmos et huiusmodi. Quod si agat de huiusmodi operibus, tunc multi sunt qui habent tempus operandi et non operantur, ut sunt viri contemplativi qui tantum vacant contemplationi. Unde et ipsi meriti minoris erunt quam illi qui fidem habentes huiusmodi operantur. Item, si de opere interiore agat, quod est amore, orare et huiusmodi, cum unusquisque iustificatus per fidem opera huiusmodi habeat, quomodo dicit hos per solam fidem iustificari, qui non habentes tempus operandi exeunt sine operibus. Est autem opus fidei dilectio, sine qua nemo potest exire et salvari.

Agit autem de his qui possunt in exterioribus operari; quibus, si aliqua necessitate preventi fuerint se huiusmodi opera faciant, "sola fides sufficit ad iustitiam."[88]

Here it is patent that Robert follows Hervaeus Burgidolensis in the latter's radical limitation of justification by faith,[89] Robert extending the interpretation to include the case of contemplatives who do not perform 'exterior' works. But his concept of justification retains a somewhat dynamic aspect in that he does not confine it to remission of sins; in at least two other places, the author gives his concept further scope and precision in distinguishing theologically between *kinds* of grace :

---

[88] *Quest.*, pp. 70 f.

[89] It is certain that Robert had Hervaeus before him; the editor of this edition indicates four places where Robert refers to Hervaeus (pp. 101, 147, 171, 204). This passage does not explicitly quote Hervaeus and hence does not prove conclusively that Robert took this teaching exclusively from this source. Another possible relationship can be deduced from information in one of the editor's critical notes (p. 70); in the copy of the *Glossa* which Robert used there is a marginal interpolation which, I note, in part paraphrases Hervaeus on this point (see Hervaeus, *MPL* 181, cols. 645D-646A). Hence, either one or both works would account for the source of this doctrinal point in Robert (an alternate explanation is that Hervaeus and Robert shared a common source). This is not unusual, since Robert used most of the standard patristic and medieval commentaries (see Martin's introduction, pp. xxxi-xli), but always with independence and often qualifying or amplifying an earlier interpreter.

[Rom. 5:15] ...

"Non solum ignoscit, sed iustificet [Ambrosiaster]."

Videtur quod nulla hic facienda sit distinctio, cum remittere peccata sit iustificare : in hoc enim quod remittit Deus peccatum iustificat.

Sed est sensus, non tantum per [pre]venientem gratiam contritionem inspirat, sed per subsequentem in bono conservat.[90]

[Rom. 8:30] "Quos vocavit hos iustificavit."

Cum vocando iustificet Deus, non videtur convenienter Apostolus ista distinguere, vocare et iustificare.

Sed dicimus, hanc convenientem distinctionem factam, quia per vocationem intellexit Apostolus gratiam qua primo caritate admittuntur; per iustificationem, gratiam qua in caritate conservantur.

"Quod minus." *Glossa.*

Hoc dictum est, quia iustificatio sine merito nostro in presenti vita est, sed per merita nostra salvamur in alia. Unde illud "maius", hoc "minus" appellatur.[91]

It should be noted parenthetically by way of explanation that Robert stands toward the beginnings of this scholastic tendency in the treatment of grace. Reviving the Augustinian distinction between prevenient and cooperating grace, the scholastic theologians continued to distinguish more and more categories of grace in individual systems of progressively greater elaboration and complexity to a point which, to modern students, approaches literal incredibility. It is already acting as an outside influence affecting this commentator's exegesis and is symptomatic of a general decline of the bibliocentric approach to theology of the early Middle ages with the rise of scholasticism.

In sum, Robert unequivocally teaches a justification by grace alone, but not necessarily by faith alone. This fundamental position is important in describing the farthest theoretical advance in medieval theology generally towards an evangelical interpretation of Paul's doctrine.

(18) Richard of St. Victor (*ob.* 1173)

Aliquot loci difficiles Apostoli [92]

---

[90] *Quest.*, p. 90 (cf. Ambrosiaster, *MPL* 17, col. 102).

[91] *Quest.*, pp. 115 f.

[92] Edition : *MPL* 196, cols. 665-684. Literature : Stegmüller no. 7342 (vol. 5, 113); Spicq, pp. 127-130; Manitius III, p. 119.

(19), (20) Ps.-Hugh of St. Victor

Quaestiones et decisiones in epistolas D. Pauli [93]
Allegoriae in Novum Testamentum [94]

Comparable excerpts from three works are given as representative of the Victorine school. So far as is known, none of the Victorines wrote a formal commentary on the Pauline epistles. Richard's work is, as the title implies, a random treatment of passages which seem difficult or contradictory. The style is informal, using first and second person to establish a *rapport* with his reader, but the style of argument is closely-reasoned scholastic *Sprachlogik*.

Richard's argument with regard to his concept of justification is based on the Old Testament definition of law. Why, then, asks Richard, does the Apostle make such a point of it? *Propter ... legis zelatores.* The author then continues with an explanation of why this law cannot justify, and proceeds to a discussion of justification and works :

[Rom. 3:24 (MPL 196, Cols. 669 f.)] "Justificati gratis per gratiam ipsius." Ipse est enim "qui justificat circumcisionem ex fide, et praeputium per fidem." Ecce ex his aperte cognoscitur unde homo justificatur. Procul dubio per fidem, non autem per legem. "Justitia" enim "Dei per fidem Jesu Christi." Ecce aperte habes quod ex fide est justitia.

Sed restat quaerendum utrum semper ex fide sola, an aliquando ex sola fide sine operibus, et aliquando ex fide simul et operibus. Quaeramus, si placet, super hoc ipsum ipsius Apostoli testimonium : "Arbitramur", inquit, "justificari hominem per fidem sine operibus legis." Ecce iterum habes aperte quod possit homo aliquando justificari ex sola fide absque legis opere. Sed nunquid semper ex sola fide, et sine omni legis opere? Minime. Nam si tempus operandi habet, "fides sine operibus mortua est (Jac. II)". Non enim auditores legis, sed factores justificabuntur. Absque dubio quandiu homini tempus operandi conceditur, ab eo, nec immerito, divinitus exegitur fides quae per dilectionem operetur. Ex prolatis itaque testimoniis manifeste colligitur quod homo quidem justificetur quandoque ex sola fide, quandoque ex fide simul et legis opere, nunquam vero ex sola lege. Ex his itaque, ut arbitror, perpendi potest quod Apostolus in suis dictis sibi contrarius non est. In eo siquidem quod dicit uno loco, quoniam ex operibus legis non justificabitur omnis caro,

---

[93] Edition : *MPL* 175, cols. 431-634. Literature : Denifle, pp. 65-74; Stegmüller nos. 3831-44 (vol. 3, 184 f.); Glorieux, *Pour revaloriser Migne*, p. 67. The author is probably the same as that of the Ps.-Richard *Exceptiones*, identical with the Ps.-Hugh *Allegoriae*, lib. V-VIII.

[94] Edition : *MPL* 175, cols. 875-924. Literature : Stegmüller nos. 3847-48 (vol. 3, 187); Glorieux, *Pour revaloriser Migne*, p. 68; Affeldt, p. 385; Spicq, p. 121.

aperte dat intelligere quod humanae industriae omnino non sufficit sola legis doctrina sine fide Christi et gratia ...

His definition of justification is also a straightforward piece of scholastic logic :

[Gal. 2:16 (cols. 673 f.)] "Ex operibus legis non justificabitur omnis caro." Aliud est esse justum et aliud est esse justificatum. Siquidem Deus est justus, nec tamen justificatus. Constat autem quoniam peccatum facit hominem injustum. Quid itaque est peccatorum justificari, nisi a peccato liberari?[95]

The pseudo-Hugh *Quaestiones*—of which Denifle prints a number which are entirely traditional and not very enlightening—are actually short paragraphs of comment, i.e., *scholia*, on phrases extracted from the text of the Pauline epistles. The form and part of the content manifest the influence of Robert of Melun's *Questiones* [96] (although the excerpts given below are not dependent on Robert). The random form of these *quaestiones* makes it difficult to find consistent interpretations of specific doctrinal points. Two of these, neither given by Denifle, are all that seem to bear upon justification by faith, and are give here for comparison with Richard's comments :

[Rom. 1:17 (MPL 175, col. 881D)] "Justitia Dei in ea revelatur ex fide in fidem." Fides dicitur eo quod operibus impleatur.
[2:13 (col. 883)] "Non enim auditores legis justi sunt", etc. Auditores legis dicuntur, qui legem habent, nec eam etiam secundum litteram observant. Auditores etiam legis dicuntur, qui eam secundum litteram observant, nec aliud in ea attendunt. Item dicitur opus legis, quod ipsa secundum litterae superficiem docet facere. Opus etiam legis dicitur illud, propter quod instituta est, hoc est, opus fidei : quod opus legis quicunque faciunt justificantur. "Hic est finis legis in Christum credere, et ei per dilectionem adhaerere."

One gloss from the *Allegoriae*, probably by the same author as the *Quaestiones*, is an especially succinct statement of the Augustinian "faith working through love" :

[Rom. 10:4 (MPL 175, co. 884D)] "Omni credenti ad justitiam." Est qui credit non ad justitiam; qui scilicet habet fidem per dilectionem non operantem, et ideo per fidem non justificatur.

---

[95] Cf. col. 674D : "Hominis justificatio idem est quod ejus liberatio a peccato."
[96] See Martin's introduction in Robert of Melun, *Quest.*, pp. xlvi f.; this is followed by Smalley, *Study of the Bible*, p. 74, and Spicq, p. 121.

(19) St. Thomas Aquinas (*ca.* 1225-1274)

Lectura in omnes epistolas Pauli [97]

St. Thomas' commentaries on the Pauline epistles are based upon lectures which he revised for publication at Naples in 1272-73, shortly before his death. In format, they consist of a series of lecture-length discussions, each covering a pericope or section of a half-dozen or so lines of the Pauline text. St. Thomas shows an immense Biblical learning in his liberal use of scriptural quotations; he consistently attempts to elucidate the meaning of passages by comparison with other Biblical texts. However, scholastic method is paramount as Thomas meticulously dissects the text, phrase by phrase, subjecting it to a constant process of division and sub-division into a series of logical distinctions and syllogisms. To a person trained in more modern traditions of scholarship, such methods seem hardly scientific for a truly critical study of an historical and literary document. One can readily understand how this style of exegesis can be accounted as one factor in the decline of Biblical studies in the later Middle Ages; it was not a suitable vehicle for the characteristic forms of theological inquiry favored by the later scholastics.[98]

The Pauline commentaries are not considered among Thomas' more important works and do not contain his definitive teaching on justification (which is rather to be found in the *Summa theologiae,* to be discussed in a following chapter). In the Romans commentary, one does not find a single definition or a logically-connected doctrine as such, although there are a sufficient number of references both in this and the Galatians commentary to discern at least the kernel of his thought on the subject. The excerpts given below do not completely reproduce his argument, but seem most illustrative of essential points. In general, it can be stated that Thomas' commentaries do not mark any notable advance over previous exegesis, but one does find traditional interpretations translated

---

[97] Edition : S. E. Fretté, ed., *Opera omnia* (Paris : Vivès, 1876), vols. 20-21. Literature : Denifle, pp. 135-144; Stegmüller, no. 8051 (vol. 5, pp. 322 ff.); Affeldt, pp. 403 ff.; Spicq, pp. 298-316.

[98] Cf. remarks by J. Pieper, *Guide to Thomas Aquinas* (New York : Pantheon Books, 1962), p. 98 : "... nevertheless I am compelled to say that there are works in which the weakness of scholastic method is revealed. ... We do not take kindly to finding the fourteen epistles of St. Paul presented as a clearly arranged nexus of theses which are linked to one another logically rather than historically." Cf. M.-D. Chenu, O.P., *Toward Understanding St. Thomas,* trans. A.-M. Landry and D. Hughes (Chicago: Henry Regnery, 1964), pp. 250-253.

into the technical language characteristic of Thomas' writing and of high scholasticism generally.

For example, on Romans 2:13 ("Non enim auditores legis justiabunt apud Deum, sed factores legis justificabuntur"), Thomas opposes a Pelagian interpretation with an argument that concludes as follows :

Sic autem non intelligitur hic quod factores legis justificentur, quasi per opera legis justitiam acquirant. Hoc quidem esse non potest neque quantum ad opera caeremonialia, quae gratiam justificantem non conferebant, neque etiam quantum ad moralia, ex quibus habitus justitiae non acquiritur; sed potius per habitum justitiae infusum hujusmodii opera facimus.[99]

Here one must have reference to Thomas' general philosophy and the scholastic concepts of *habitus* and infused virtues to fully explicate his meaning,[100] although his basic theological thrust is clear—throughout this commentary, St. Thomas is at pains to show, in very orthodox fashion, that it is not "works of the Law" that justify, but rather faith.

It is perhaps more pertinent to explore his notion of faith. On the critical Romans 1:17 text, Thomas defines the faith necessary for justification as follows :

Actus autem fidei, qui est credere, dependet ex intellectu et voluntate movente intellectum ad assensum. Unde actus fidei erit perfectus, si voluntas perficiatur per habitum caritatis, et intellectus per habitum fidei; non autem si habitus caritatis desit : et ideo fides formata caritate est virtus, non autem fides informis.[101]

This passage is a further example of a technical elaboration given a traditional concept by the thirteenth century scholastics. Thomas gives the definition of justifying faith that was common among thirteenth century theologians, of "faith formed by love"; it is essentially the Augustinian "faith working through love" recast in terms of scholastic psychology.[102]

---

[99] *ad Rom.* ii, 3 (vol. 20, p. 417); cf. *ad Gal.* iii, 4 (vol. 21, p. 208) for a similar statement.

[100] *Habitus* or 'habit' in scholastic philosophy refers to any quality which disposes a rational being to perform definite types of acts; virtues and vices in an operative sense are habits inclining a person to good or bad acts, and, like purely physical habits, may be reinforced by repetition. As opposed to natural habits (what St. Thomas implies here by *opera moralia*, acts resulting from natural virtues innate in mankind, i.e., the cardinal virtues of ancient philosophy), an 'infused' habit is of supernatural origin, bestowed or poured into the soul by the grace of God. *Justitia* in the sense of righteousness is, for St. Thomas and other scholastics, one of the infused moral virtues.

[101] *ad Rom.* i, 6 (vol. 20, p. 397); cf. *ad Gal.* iii, 4 (vol. 21, p. 207).

[102] I.e., 'formed' or 'perfect' faith is that faith which has been informed by the

A more extended context is found in a section on Romans 3:22 ("Iustitia autem Dei per fidem Jesu Christi, super omnes qui credunt") :

Dicitur autem justitia Dei esse per fidem Jesu Christi, non quasi per fidem mere-amur justificari, quasi ipsa fides ex nobis existat, et per eam mereamur Dei justitiam, sicut Pelagiani dixerunt : sed quia in ipsa justificatione qua justi-ficamur a Deo, primus motus mentis in Deum est per fidem : "Accedentum enim ad Deum oportet credere" ut dicitur Hebr. 1,6 : Unde et ipsa fides, quasi prima pars justitiae, est nobis a Deo. Ephes. II, 3 : "Gratia estis salvati per fidem, et hoc non ex vobis; Dei enim donum est." Haec autem fides ex qua est justitia, non est fides informis, de qua dicitur Jac. 11, 6 : "Fides sine operibus mortua est"; sed est fides per caritatem formata, de qua dicitur Gal. V,6 : "Nam in Christo Jesu neque circumcisio aliquid valet" sine fide, per quam in nobis habitat Christus. Ephes. III, 17 : "Habitare Christum per fidem in cordibus vestris" : quod sine caritate non fit. ... Addit autem, "Qui credunt in eum"; quod pertinet ad fidem formatam, per quam homo justi-ficatur, ut dictum est.[103]

One notes that St. Thomas also felt it necessary to deal with the James 2:26 passage. And, in another place, on Romans 3:28 ("Arbitramur enim, justificari hominem per fidem sine operibus legis"), Thomas similarly qualifies his view of the role of faith in justification by noting that justification does not exclude subsequent works :

... ita tamen quod hoc intelligat sine operibus praecedentibus justitiam, non autem sine operibus consequentibus : quia, ut dicitur Jac. II, 26 : "fides sine operibus" scilicet subsequentibus "est mortua", et ideo justificare non potest.[104]

Finally, it can be shown that Thomas also links justification to remis-sion of sin, although this is by no means a prominent emphasis. In one place, he refers to such a justification taking place in baptism,[105] but the following passage, on Romans 2:26, better typifies this negative aspect of justification :

---

habitus of love, which is also one of the three theological virtues and, as such, a super-natural or 'infused' virtue. This is opposed to 'unformed' faith, which is faith in the sense of intellectual assent or mere belief. This passage has an indirect significance for Luther; as will be explained below, it was the source for Nicholas of Lyra's gloss on Rom. 1:17, which Luther cites and refutes in his Lectures on Romans.

[103] ad Rom. iii, 3 (vol. 20, p. 431).

[104] ad Rom. iii, 4 (vol. 20, p. 434). In a reference to Romans 1:13 in a similar context in his Galatians commentary, Thomas makes it clear that justification by faith also does not exclude the sacraments of the Church (ad Gal. ii, 4 [vol. 21, p. 196]).

[105] ad Rom. iv, 2 (vol. 20, p. 464); such a reference is not surprising, since theolo-gians from at least the time of Peter Lombard frequently referred to baptism as a so-called "first justification".

... ostendit quod per remissionem peccatorum Dei, justitia ostendatur : sive accipiatur Dei justitia qua ipse est justus, sive qua alios justificat : unde subdit : "Ut sit ipse justus"; idest ut per remissionem peccatorum Deus appareat sicut promiserat, tum quia ad justitiam Dei pertinet quod peccata destruat, homines ad justititiam Dei reducendo : Psal. X, 8 : "Justus Dominus, et justitias dilexit" : et etiam ut "sit justificans eum qui est ex fide Jesu Christi", ed est qui per fidem Jesu Christi accedit ad Deum. "Accedentem enim ad Deum oportet credere" : Hebr. XI, 6.[106]

(20) Giles of Rome (*ca.* 1247-1316)

In epistolam Pauli Apostoli ad Romanos commentaria [107]

Giles of Rome (Aegidius Romanus), born into the famous Colonna family, entered the Order of Augustinian Hermits during his teens and was sent to the University of Paris to complete his education. A student of St. Thomas Aquinas, he came to the defense of his master during the doctrinal controversies generated by the teachings of Siger of Brabant and the Latin Averroists during the 1270's and was forced to leave Paris after the condemnation of 1277. For this reason, he has frequently and erroneously been treated as a disciple of St. Thomas. In fact, Giles later established himself as an avowed defender of the Augustinian tradition and a leading conservative among the generations of theologians which flourished after St. Thomas and St. Bonaventure during the closing years of the thirteenth century. A prolific writer, he himself was a regent master at Paris from 1285 until 1291, when he was elected general of his order. He was subsequently (1294) appointed archbishop of Bourges. He is perhaps best known for his role as a pro-papal polemicist in the quarrel between Pope Boniface VIII and Philip IV of France; his treatise *De ecclesiastica potestatae* underlay the famous bull *Unam sanctam* of 1302.

Giles' Romans commentary manifests to a greater degree the scholastic tendencies observed in St. Thomas' commentary. Like St. Thomas, he organizes his material in the form of lectures, each covering several lines of the text of the epistle. He proceeds first with a minute logical dissection of the text, reducing Paul's words to a series of propositions. He then follows with the characteristic scholastic device of positing and solving one or more hypothetical objections which might be raised against these propositions. Often, his major concern seems to be merely

---

[106] *ad Rom.* iii, 3 (vol. 20, p. 433); cf. *ad Gal.* iii, 3 (vol. 21, p. 205).

[107] Edition : *Opera*, tom. I (Rome : Antonius Bladus, 1555). Literature : Denifle, pp. 173-179; Stegmüller, no. 913 (vol. 2, pp. 20-23); Spicq, p. 320; Affeldt, pp. 370 f.

to clear up possible verbal ambiguities in the text. The result is an extremely conservative and curiously limited exegetical approach, especially from a theological standpoint. The theological content of this commentary is, in general, kept at the level of elementary common-places. And, although Giles reflects the theological climate of his time in his willingness to make occasional references to Aristotle and other philosophical sources, his primary authorities aie always St. Augustine and Peter Lombard. This work clearly exemplifies the fact that, by the later thirteenth century, Biblical commentaries no longer served as vehicles for advanced theological speculation.

Indicative of Giles' very literal concept of exegesis is his narrowly historical interpretation of the first several chapters of Romans. He views these as essentially a polemic directed by Paul against the Judaism of his time. Giles' comment on 1:17 may be taken as an example, where he gives the traditional Augustinian interpretation of the phrase, "ex fide in fidem", as referring to the Old and New Testaments :

... Haec iustitia in veteri testamento figurabatur occulte, sed in evangelio revelatur aperte. Bene ergo dictum est, quod evangelium est virtus Dei, (cum iustitia dei revelatur in ipso) et hoc (ex fide in fidem) hoc est, ex fide dei promit-tentis in fidem hominis credentis, ex qua fide, supple, homo vivet, et saluatur per fidem, quae videlicet est in evangelio revelata.[108]

Giles then gives seven senses in which "ex fide in fidem" may be taken, most of them little more than pious trivialities; e.g., from faith in one God to faith in the Triune God, from faith in the First Coming to faith in the Second Coming, etc.

Giles' literalism is also illustrated by an objection he posits to 2:13 ("non enim auditores legis iusti sunt apud Deum, sed factores legis iustificabuntur") : Does this mean that Paul asserts that 'doers of the law' are justified by their own works? Giles then presents a standard anti-Pelagian solution. Although the full text is too lengthy to be reproduced here, the argument can be conveniently summarized. The proposition is not true in a direct sense; man cannot, of his own efforts, merit the "first grace" of justification. But, in an indirect sense, the proposition can be considered true, since a man already in a state of grace may, of his free will, merit an increase of grace and justice "per opera in gratia facta".[109] In effect, Giles reads into this passage a semi-Pelagian compromise.

---

[108] *ad Rom.*, fol. 10v. As previously noted, this gloss, based on *De spir. et litt.* c. 11, no. 18, can be traced back as early as Florus of Lyons.

[109] *ad Rom.*, fol. 17v.

Giles' treatment of the third chapter of Romans is especially typical of his method. Taking the context of 3:20-31 as a single passage, he interprets Paul as giving a series of seven reasons in support of the proposition stated at the opening of the passage (3:20) : "... quia ex operibus legis non iustificabitur omnis caro coram illo." Repetition of his argument would be unnecessarily tedious; his theology is quite traditional. One passage might be quoted to illustrate his traditionalism in his use of the Augustinian "faith working through love"; here on 3:28 ("Arbitramur enim hominem iustificari per fidem sine operibus legis") :

Per fidem ergo, quae per dilectionem operatur, est iustificatio nostra : non autem per legis operationem : immo si volumus magis proprie loqui, cum lex illa fuerit lex timoris et lex fidei sit lex amoris, dicemus quod opera sequentia iustificationem, sunt magis opera fidei, quae operatur per dilectionem et per amorem : sed opera praecedentia sunt magis opera legis, quae operatur per comminationem, et per timorem. Unde et glosa dicit, hoc esse intelligendum de operibus praecedentibus, non sequentibus. Formetur ergo sic ratio. Ex operibus praecedentibus iustificationem nullus iustificatur : sed opera legis sunt huiusmodi; ergo per legis opera nullus iustificatur. [110]

(21) Peter Aureoli (*ca.* 1280-1322)

Compendium sensus litteralis totius sacrae scripturae [111]

This commentary was written by Peter Aureoli, a prominent Franciscan theologian and later Archbishop of Aix, in 1319 while holding the important Franciscan chair in theology at the University of Paris. It is little more than a cursory outline of the Biblical text, dividing the various books into major themes or *quaestiones* suitable for scholastic disputation. It was apparently intended as a study aid. The section covering Romans does nothing more than provide a literal paraphrasing and

[110] *ad Rom.*, fol. 25v. A final, and unusual passage concerning justification which should perhaps receive at least footnote reference occurs on fol. 35r, where, in an objection, Giles briefly analyzes justification in terms of Aristotle's four-fold scheme of causation (e.g., formal, material, efficient, and final). However, he makes no substantive theological point, since his intent is merely to resolve a hypothetical contrariety in his sources. Although interesting as a random example of Aristotelian influence upon a thirteenth century theologian, this passage is unique in the sources and mostly in the nature of an historical curiosity-piece. Neither Giles nor any other theologian attempted to formulate a concept of justification in terms of Aristotelian metaphysics.

[111] Edition : Petrus Aureoli, *Compendium sensus litteralis totius divinae scripturae*, ed. P. Seeböck (Quarrachi, 1896), pp. 244-254. Literature : Denifle, pp. 186-188; Stegmüller no. 6422 (vol. 4, pp. 233f.); Affeldt, pp. 395 f. (Spicq apparently did not consider this work of sufficient importance to list in his handbook).

summary of the Apostle's major points, and contains nothing of significance for this study.

(22) Nicholas of Lyra (*ca.* 1270-1349)

Postilla super totam Bibliam [112]

One of the greatest Biblical scholars of the Middle Ages, the Franciscan scholar Nicholas of Lyra became regent master in theology at Paris in 1308, where he taught for many years. Deploring the state of Biblical studies in his own time, he set out to reform the field by writing commentaries which would set out the literal sense of the Scriptures as opposed to the allegorizing methods which prevailed in Old Testament exegesis. Well-grounded in the history of Christian theology and exegesis, he further prepared himself by mastering Hebrew and was familiar with Jewish commentators, one of the rare medieval commentators so equipped. However, he is typical of his age in that he was strongly influenced by the great thirteenth century masters, especially St. Thomas Aquinas and St. Bonaventure, and his basic intellectual orientation is thoroughly scholastic. He is most frequently mentioned today in the Luther literature, since his commentary and the *Glossa ordinaria* were the two commentaries best known to Luther. But no specific Lutheran teaching has been found in Lyra, and the punning epigram current in the sixteenth century, "Si Lyra non lyrasset, Lutherus non saltasset", is an undoubted exaggeration; Lyra's highly esteemed commentary became the standard reference and was in common use among Biblical scholars in Luther's day. Indicative of its importance is that it was the first Bible commentary to be printed, at Rome in 1471-72; it was also translated into Flemish, German, and Italian.

Lyra's commentary on Romans (completed in 1329) is, to a much greater degree than Aquinas, independent of the earlier tradition which, as has been seen, formed a continuity from the patristic age through the twelfth century. However, it is evident that Luther could not have been decisively influenced by Lyra, for in the key sections on justification, the author gives only a brief treatment reflecting commonplace scholastic doctrine of his day. His exegesis of Romans 1:17 reflects that of St. Thomas :

---

[112] Edition : Nicolaus de Lyra, *Postilla super totam Bibliam* (Rome : Conradus Sweynheyn and Arnoldus Pannartz, 1471-72), 5 vols. Literature : Denifle, pp. 188-194; Stegmüller no. 5902 (vol. 4, pp. 76 f.); Spicq, pp. 335-342; Affeldt, pp. 389 f.

... iustitia enim dei in eo revelatur id est in Evangelio manifeste traditur *ex fide in fidem* id est ex fide informi procedendo ad fidem formatam licit enim sit idem habitus : tamen dicitur informis sine caritate existens et superveniente caritate formatus : quia per hoc actus eius efficitur meritorius vite beate et talis fides formata vivificat et iustificat perfecte ...[113]

A slightly longer gloss on 3:23-24 is purely scholastic in tone; note especially the use of the Aristotelian scheme of the four causes :

non est distinctio inter Iudeos et gentiles quantum ad iustificationem per Christi fidem. et loquitur Apostolus de fide formata caritate que iustificat. *Omnes enim* Hic consequenter ostenditur modus huiusmodi iustificationis per causam formalem efficientem et finalem et temporis congruentiam. premittitur tunc huius iustificationis necessitas : cum dicitur : *omnes enim peccaverunt* tam Iudei quam gentiles. *et egent gloria dei* id est gratia sua per quam apparet gloriosus et subditur huius iustificationis modus cum dicitur : *iustificati igitur gratis* id est sine meritis nostris per gratiam ipsius formaliter. et per redemptionem que est in Christo Iesu id est per passionem eius efficienter. meritorie tamen quam proposuit deus qui est causa efficiens nostre iustificationis principaliter. per fidem nos deo coniungentem. In sanguine ipsius ad ostensionem iusticie sue etc. scilicet finaliter ...[114]

Other *loci* add nothing of significance to these definitions.

Perhaps the only relevant comment here is that Lyra's commentary is plainly the product of a different era and departs so widely from the earlier medieval exegetical tradition as to have little evidential value for this study. It is unfair to judge the quality of Lyra's scholarship, from this commentary alone, for his Old Testament commentaries made fundamental contributions and have been much admired. It is nevertheless somewhat astonishing that the above excerpts, so weak in either historical insight or doctrinal significance, are from a work that reputedly represents the best Biblical scholarship of the fourteenth century. As in the case of Giles of Rome, Nicholas' Pauline commentaries suggest that a certain decadence had overtaken the tradition by the later medieval era. For speculative theology, the field was clearly left to the philosopher-theologians of the emerging nominalist schools.

2. CONCLUSIONS AND ANALYSIS

Overall, this survey produces a rather negative conclusion : that Paul's teaching on justification was not viewed as a topic of major importance by the medieval exegetes. There are no extended statements concerning

---

[113] *Postilla*, vol. 5, fol. 4r. Luther's reaction to this will be discussed presently.
[114] *Postilla*, vol. 5, fol. 9v.

any doctrine of justification *per se*, nor any references from which one could infer that the concept in any way formed an issue for debate among theologians. It is only in the latest commentaries (i.e., St. Thomas and Nicholas of Lyra) that there is any indication that the schoolmen had begun to find it desirable to give the term a developed and logically precise theological definition. For most of the commentators, justification was a word which happened to form part of Paul's technical vocabulary when describing the process of salvation, neither more nor less important than any one of a number of other such terms found in the Pauline epistles, and required no unusual effort of explanation different from any other aspect of Paul's teaching. In sum, justification presented no theological problem, as such, to medieval expositors.

However, there are certain firm points of doctrine that emerge from a comparative study of the texts. First, the teaching of the commentators is emphatic that faith alone pertains to justification and that it is bestowed by unmerited grace—this point is maintained in its integrity from St. Augustine on through the tradition. The basic text is Romans 3:24 ("justificati gratis per gratiam ipsius"), for which Augustine's dictum in *De spiritu et littera* became the classic statement :

Per ipsam [gratiam iniustis] justificatur gratis, id est nullis suorum operum praecendentibus meritis; alioquin gratia jam non est gratia (Rom. 11:6), quandoquidem ideo datur, non quia bona opera fecimus, sed ut ea facere voleamus.[115]

There was consequently no formal Pelagianism in the tradition, and enough commentators make explicit reference to Pelagius and Pelagianism to show that they were well aware of the heretical view that justification could result from personal merit or righteousness; for these writers also, Pelagius remained the *bête noire* of medieval theology.

The idea of faith was developed exclusively under the Augustinian rubric of *fides quae per dilectionem operatur* and integrated into the general doctrine of grace; the normative concept was of a justifying grace defined as an "efficacious" faith, that is, faith formed by love (*fides formata caritate*).[116] But, at the same time, the phrase *sola fide* was customarily given a limited and primarily negative connotation as it was construed to mean *fides sine operibus*, that is, 'faith alone' as exclud-

---

[115] *De spir. et litt.*, c. 10, n. 6. Cf. Landgraf, *Dogmengesch.* I/1, pp. 148 *et seq.*

[116] Landgraf, *Dogmengesch.* I/1 pp. 206-219, shows this concept to have been universal also in the general theological literature, and outlines the development to its first Aristotelian interpretation in Phillip the Chancellor (*ob.* 1236); see further discussion in I/2, pp. 1-17.

ing 'works of the Law', the observances and ceremonies of the old Jewish faith. Thus the term is significant for these commentators only in a narrow, literal interpretation referring back to the immediate historical occasion for Paul's epistle, the dissentions created in the infant church at Rome, as elsewhere, by the so-called "Judaizers".[117] It began to pass out of the exegetical tradition by the late twelfth century (Aquinas

[117] Here it may be appropriate to refer to the issues raised by H. Denifle in his *Die abendländischen Schriftausleger*, cited in the introductory chapter. The purpose of his study was to support a major contention in his *Luther and Luthertum* that Luther was either mendacious or ignorant in stating in his famous 1545 autobiographical statement that he had been taught only the so-called "active" or punitive justice of God; Denifle claimed to have demonstrated from sixty medieval sources that "not a single writer from the time of Ambrosiaster to the time of Luther understood this passage (Rom. 1:17) in the sense of the justice of God which punishes, of an angry God. All, on the contrary, have understood it of the God who justifies, the justice obtained by faith" (as quoted by Gordon Rupp, *The Righteousness of God* New York : Philosophical Library, 1953, p. 123). Denifle's thesis was followed by Joseph Lortz in his influential *The Reformation in Germany* (trans. by R. Walls New York : Herder and Herder, 1968, vol. I, pp. 207 ff.). On the *justitia Dei* problem, Denifle has been convincingly answered by several scholars, most directly by Karl Holl in his article, "Die *iustitia dei* in der vorlutherischen Bibelauslegung des Abendlandes" (in his *Gesammelte Aufsätze zur Kirchengeschichte* [Tübingen : J. C. B. Mohr, 1927-32], pp. 171-188), who showed that there were divergent streams of interpretation in the Pauline commentaries dating back to patristic times, with the result that there was no such clear, unambiguous doctrine of *Justitia Dei* as Denifle supposed. Holl also pointed out that most of the commentaries were unknown to Luther and that he derived his conception from other sources, especially the Nominalists (this latter topic has since been explored; see especially the important article by Heinrich Bornkamm, "Iustitia dei in der Scholastik und bei Luther", *Archiv fur Reformationsgeschichte* 39 [1942], pp. 1-46; also H. A. Oberman, " 'Iustitia Christi' and 'Iustitia Dei' : Luther and the Scholastic Doctrines of Justification", *Harvard Theological Review* 59 [1966], pp. 1-26).

As a corollary conclusion, Denifle's study also showed that the *sola fide* formula was not Luther's invention, which, for Denifle, further discredits the claims the Reformer made for the uniqueness of his "discovery" of Romans 1:17. But, as indicated above, no medieval commentator used the term in the radical sense of Luther. And, on the basis of the research presented in this study, it would not seem unfair to observe that, in general, Denifle's research was too limited and the excerpts he presents are too selective to represent the full sense and the doctrinal implications in the Pauline commentators; in particular, he concentrated on *loci* for Romans 1:17 and largely ignored the context of Romans 3:19 ff., where, traditionally, the commentators made their most significant statements concerning justification. And, as will be shown in following chapters, by ignoring the general theological literature and the systematic theologians, Denifle overlooked the sources where the essential core of the medieval concept of justification is to be found.

never uses it), having been so severely qualified by repeated emphasis upon apparently conflicting texts (i.e., James 2:26, "fides sine operibus mortua est"; also important was Romans 2:13, "Non enim auditores legis iusti sunt apud Deum, sed factores legis iustificabantur"[118]) that it virtually disappeared in the theological literature. On faith and works, the statement of Stephen Langton in his commentary on Romans can be considered as definitive :

> Dicimus, quod hec glosa respicit illum locum supra : arbitramur iustificari hominem per fidem sine operibus, ut dicit glosa, sine operibus carnalibus et [?] quibuslibet moralibus. Sed hoc intelligendum est de operibus precedentibus fidem.[119]

And the impression remains that the term 'justification' had relatively minor significance for these interpreters; it occurs in a sense which is technically little more than a synonym for remission of sins. The point is also illustrative for the relative lack of progress in medieval exegesis, for it was stated in essence at the very beginning of the history of the literature in the early eighth century by the Venerable Bede in his commentary on St. John's Gospel :

> [John 1:16] ... "Nos omnes accepimus de plenitudine ejus, et gratiam pro gratia." Aliquid primo de plenitudine ejus accepimus, et postea gratiam pro gratia, id est, de plenitudine ejus accepimus remissionem peccatorum, et postea gratiam pro gratia, id est, de plenitudine ejus accepimus gratiam, id est, vitam eternam pro gratia fide, quae per dilectionem operatur. Quae omnia ex uno fonte plenitudine Christi nobis provenire certissimum est. Quid ergo accepimus de plenitudine bonitatis illius? Ut, scilicet, remissionem peccatorum, ut justificemur in fide.[120]

---

[118] Cf. the following from Innocent III, *Sermones de diversis* 2 (MPL 217, col. 656) : Porro "fides sine operibus mortua est". Vivit autem fides illa, quae per dilectionem operatur, "quia iustus ex fide vivit". "Non enim auditores est verbi et non factor, hic comparabitur viro consideranti vultum nativitatis suae in speculo".

[119] Quoted by Landgraf, *Dogmengesch.* I, 242, n. 20. Cf. the following interpretation in a MS of Richard of St. Victor (*op. cit.* II, 13 f., n. 39) :

> Queritur ergo, utrum semper ex sola fide sit iustitia, an aliquando ex sola fide sit iustitia, an aliquando ex sola fide sine operibus, aliquando ex fide simul et operibus. Queramus super hoc ipsius apostoli testimonium. Arbitramur, inquit, hominem iustificari ex fide sine operibus legis. Sed numquid semper? Non. Nam, si tempus operandi habet, fides sine operibus mortua est. Non enim auditores legis, sed factores iustificabuntur. Absque dubio, quamdiu homini tempus operandi conceditur, ab eo nec immerito fides exigitur, que per dilectionem operatur. Ex his ergo collige, quod homo iustificatur quandoque ex sola fide, quandoque ex fide simul et legis opere, numquam vero ex sola lege.

[120] *In S. Johannis Evangelium expositio* (*MPL* 92, col. 644).

Such refinement of the concept which did take place was toward a further limitation of justification as it is conceived as a process occurring at a specific point in time, although it is not stated with unanimity exactly when it occurs, i.e., at baptism or in repentance (this, however, was to begin to receive clarification in systematic theology beginning in the early thirteenth century). And in this frame of reference, justification seems to pertain only to the removal of original and prior actual sin. After this occurrence, works are enjoined to 'fulfill' the faith which alone no longer suffices to maintain the state of grace gained in justification, but must 'work by love'. There are indications of a variant doctrine which implies a continuing justification in the practice of penance, but even here the concept still implies only a remission of sins. In general, none of these writers use their commentaries to state a complete theory of grace.

There are at least three reasons which may be suggested for this restricted interpretation. The first is a matter of linguistics : the medieval commentators were limited by their sole reliance upon the Latin language. This reason alone accounts for the superiority of the humanist and Reformers' commentaries, which expound upon the original Greek text with the resources of a vastly improved critical knowledge of classical philology. Working only in Latin, the ambiguity between 'justification' and 'righteousness' in St. Paul's Greek was not apparent. The term was understood—here St. Augustine deserves the initial credit or blame from a frequently quoted etymological aside in *De spiritu et littera* [121]—in the most literal sense as *justum facere*, 'to make just', and hence the concept had the connotation of a legal status. The concept therefore had an inherent semantic bias toward a forensic rather than an ethical interpretation, and also tended to be treated as something static, implying a status within a hierarchy of grace rather than a state of spiritual activity. And a further observation may be made concerning literary form which reinforced this propensity toward verbal literalism, noticeable especially with the rise of the gloss from the eleventh century, a tendency to fragment the text and commentary into discrete and isolated *scholia* which became increasingly pronounced in the scholasticism of the high Middle Ages. G. G. Coulton has described this characteristic with his customary acerbity, as "the fundamental weakness of medieval theology ... that false perspective by which the Bible had long been

---

[121] *De spir. et litt.*, c. 26, n. 45 : "Quid est enim aliud, justificati, quam justi facti, ad illo scilicet qui justificat impius, ut ex impio fiat justus?" (*MPL* 44, col. 228).

treated less as a whole than as a collection of separate texts, to be torn
from their context and bandied backwards and forwards as missiles
in ... verbal combats."[122]

The second point requires the discussion of Augustinianism which
was deferred in the relevant section above. As on many other points,
Augustine is not completely consistent in his concept of justification.
Loofs maintains that Augustine uses the term in two different senses,
to refer to the work of grace in : (a) remission of sins, especially original
sin in baptism, and (b) a renewal of the will, making it capable of good.[123]
The former view, of justification as removal of sins in baptism, was the
opinion common in the ancient Church. This doctrine is especially
strong in the *Enchiridion*, e.g. :

> ... the apostle goes on to speak of the great mystery of holy baptism in the
> cross of Christ, and to explain clearly to us that baptism in Christ is nothing
> else than a similitude of the death of Christ, and that the death of Christ on
> the cross is nothing but a similitude of the pardon of sin : so that just as real
> as is His death, so real is the remission of our sins; and just as real as is His
> resurrection, so real is our justification.[124]

The *Enchiridion* is often regarded as a treasury of the best of Augustinianism, but Harnack is correct, at least on this point, in his criticism
that : "Everything is combined in this book to instruct us as to the nature
of the revision ... by Augustine of the popular Catholic dogmatic doctrine that gave a new impress to the Western Church."[125] But it should
be remembered that the work is designed as what the title implies, an
enchiridion or handbook intended for the laity, and here Augustine, as
the high churchman he was, would naturally emphasize practical and
basic Church doctrine. And, while Protestant interpretation of Augustine
is often criticized for underestimating the role of his ecclesiology in
his total thought, Augustine's "high church" outlook should always
be measured against the ecclesiology of the *City of God* with its distinction between the Church visible and invisible.

---

[122] G. G. Coulton, *Medieval Panorama* (New York : Meridian paperback ed.,
1955), p. 420. On the following page, Coulton speaks with magnificent invective of
"bibliolatrous fundamentalism and text-slinging" by medieval preachers and theologians.

[123] Loofs, *Leitfaden*, pp. 309-314. For a view dissenting from Loofs and Harnack,
see Portalié, *Guide*, pp. 274 f., who argues for a necessity of works in Augustine.

[124] *Enchir.*, c. 52 (tr. J. F. Shaw; Chicago : Henry Regnery Gateway paperback
ed., 1961).

[125] Harnack, *Hist. of Dogma*, vol. 5, p. 222.

The second aspect of Augustine's doctrine, like the first, is found scattered throughout his works, especially those against Pelagius, but *De spiritu et littera* may be conveniently cited as the single work which most directly contrasts with the *Enchiridion*. The concept which is stressed here is of justification as a regeneration, in which the chief work of grace consists in infusion of charity and of a renewed, good will. The following passages are characteristic :

Our own assertion ... is this : that the human will is divinely assisted to do the right in such manner that, besides man's creation with the endowment of freedom to choose, and besides the teaching by which he is instructed how he ought to live, he receives the Holy Spirit, whereby there arises in his soul the delight in and the love of God, the supreme and changeless Good. This gift is his here and now, while he walks by faith, not yet by sight : that having this as earnest of God's free bounty, he may be fired in heart to cleave to his Creator, kindled in mind to come within the shining of the true light; and thus receive from the source of his being the only real well-being.[126]

For it is the work of the Spirit of grace to renew in us the image of God ... By grace the righteousness which guilt had effaced is written in the inward man thus renewed; and this is God's mercy upon the human race through Jesus Christ our Lord.[127]

It is this concept of justification which Augustine develops in the dialectic of this book against a justification in the law. (The language will be familiar to both the philosopher and theologian as Augustine's Christianized Neo-platonic theory of illumination). Augustine interprets 'law' in an evangelical sense, that is, broadly and unequivocally to include all natural works, whether by Mosaic law or natural law. To this he opposes a law of faith or 'law of the new covenant'; the nature of this new law Augustine defines as infused love : "... God puts his laws in their minds and writes them in their hearts with his finger, the Holy Spirit, by whom there is shed abroad in those hearts the charity which is the fulness of the law."[128]

The concept of 'faith working through love' quite naturally follows from the premises of the above doctrine as the consequence of the moral and spiritual renewal in Augustinian justification. Although the medieval commentators from Rabanus frequently appeal to this latter principle, it is always with reference to an adjustment of works to faith; they do not bridge the important gap in their Augustinianism between Augus-

---

[126] *De spir. et litt.*, c. 3, n. 5 (tr. J. Burnaby in *Augustine : Later Works. Library of Christian Classics*, VIII [Philadelphia : Westminster, 1955]).

[127] *Ibid.*, c. 27, n. 47.

[128] *De spir. et litt.*, c. 26, n. 46.

tine's concept of works and his popular doctrine of justification as forgiveness of sins, and thus overlook the more dynamic and spiritualized
ne's concept of works and his popular doctrine of justification as forgiveness of sins, and thus overlook the more dynamic and spiritualized
of Augustine's doctrines of justifying grace. It should now be apparent
as to what occurred historically : that only one aspect of the Augustinian
teaching was dominant in the exegetical tradition and developed as
dogma; this was the more traditional and popular—and cruder—
concept of 'justification from sin' as exemplified in the *Enchiridion*
with its church-sacramental emphasis upon the external sign of remission in baptism. A doctrine of "sacramental effect" for justification could
easily develop from this interpretation. Although this doctrine is implicit only in Haymo's commentary, there was much in the traditional
exegesis which contributed to a later development of the idea in support
of the sacramental-sacerdotal system of salvation in the medieval
Church.

The third limiting factor for the concept of justification is the extreme
literalism of the exegesis in the *historice* sense. As previously noted,
this is seen especially in the comments on Paul's criticism of the Jews.[129]
Here the concept of faith, and the gloss *sola fide*, is placed in apposition
to Jewish law only for purposes of antithesis. It becomes then only a
comparative concept and a logical weapon instead of a positive and
categorical article of dogma, and, in the framework of this antithesis,
can be broadened to include almost anything—sacraments, creeds.
'works of faith', 'works of justice', etc.—which does not specifically pertain to Jewish religious observances. Further, the text of the second
chapter of St. James' epistle is always at hand to support this interpretation. This is another ramification of medieval literalism : it was incon-
ceivable that James and Paul could be contradictory in doctrine, and
James consequently forces the interpretation of justification *sine operibus*
as applying only to prior works, i.e., Jewish ceremonialism.[130] The issue
involved is admirably stated from an opposing viewpoint by one of the

---

[129] Some of the commentators become most vehement on the subject; I have
noticed this esp. on Rom. 3:27-29 ("Where then is thy boasting? ..."). I have the impression that this may indicate anti-Semitic attitudes. It is known that there was
contact between Christian theologians and rabbis, and some commentators even
consulted them for linguistic assistance—e.g., Andrew of St. Victor (see Smalley,
Study of the Bible, pp. 149 *et seq.*; Spicq, pp. 90-93). But these contacts, especially
from the twelfth century, were mostly in the nature of disputation and polemics,
which these commentators seem to reflect. They may also, as I suggest, be a useful
source for medieval anti-Semitism.

[130] Here again Bede may be related to the tradition. In his interpretation of James
2:21-22, he states that James does not contradict Paul; Paul was writing against

ablest exegetes of the Reformation, John Calvin, commenting on Galatians 5:1-4 :

"Stand fast in the freedom wherewith Christ has set you free, and do not submit again to the yoke of slavery. ..." These passages surely contain something loftier than freedom of ceremonies! Of course I admit that Paul is there discussing ceremonies, for his quarrel is with false apostles who were trying to reintroduce into the Christian church the old shadows of the law that had been abolished by Christ's coming. But for the discussion of this question, the higher topics upon which the whole controversy rested had to be considered. First, because the clarity of the gospel was obscured by those Jewish shadows, Paul showed that we have in Christ a perfect disclosure of all those things which were foreshadowed in the Mosaic ceremonies. Further, because those imposters imbued the common people with the very wicked notion that this obedience obviously availed to deserve God's grace, Paul here strongly insists that believers should not suppose they can obtain righteousness before God by any works of the law, still less by those paltry rudiments! And at the same time he teaches that through the cross of Christ they are free from the condemnation of the law, which otherwise hangs over all men, so that they may rest with full assurance in Christ alone. This topic properly pertains to our argument. Finally, he claims for the conscience of believers their freedom, that they may not be obliged in things unnessary.[131]

And again, in this interpretation of Romans 1:17 :

Whereas, many think there is under these words a secret comparing of the Old with the New Testament, that is more subtle than firm. For Paul does not compare here the fathers who lived under the law with us, but notes the daily progress and proceeding in every faithful man.[132]

Calvin's *Commentary on Romans*, from which the latter quotation above is taken, is interesting in showing his familiarity with the medieval

---

Jewish claims of merit in good works (*Super epistolas catholicas expositio* [*MPL* 93, col. 22]) :

Unde apostolus Paulus dicit posse hominem sine operibus, scilicet praecedentibus, justificari per fidem. Nam justificatus per fidem, quomodo potest nisi juste operare? Cum ergo dicit Jacobus :

"Abraham pater noster nonne ex operibus justificatus est, offerens Isaac filium suum super altare?" Eleganter exemplum bonae operationis ab ipso patriarcha monuit esse discendum ...

[131] J. Calvin, *Institutes of the Christian Religion*, III, ch. 19, n. 3 (edition used here : J. T. McNeill, ed., *Calvin : Institutes of the Christian Religion*, tr. F. L. Battles, *Library of Christian Classics* XX [Philadelphia : Westminster, 1960], vol. 1, 835 f.).

[132] J. Calvin, *Commentary upon the Epistle of St. Paul to the Romans*, tr. H. Beveridge (Edinburgh : Calvin Translation Society, 1844), p. 22. I have modernized the translation in this and the following excerpt.

commentaries by treating of the traditional glosses and doctrinal position *in loco* [133]—Luther exhibits no such comparable scholarly knowledge of the details of medieval exegesis in his works. In this connection, it might be useful to digress briefly to indicate Luther's relationship to his medieval predecessors as a commentator on Romans. Here, too, the findings are largely negative—a study of the medieval commentators sheds little light on the major biographical problems of Luther's early life and development as a theologian. His sources for the *Lectures on Romans* can be easily followed in modern critical editions, which show that he directly utilized only two of the medieval commentaries on Romans, the *Glossa ordinaria* and Nicholas of Lyra; and he used the latter most often to refute him.[134] But one major example of his use of a medieval source is an important one, since it is part of his comment on Romans 1:17; here, Luther rejects Lyra's exposition of the phrase "ex fide in fide" as meaning *fides informis* to *fides formata*, which Lyra, in turn, had taken from Aquinas :

[133] It would be an interesting project to gather all of Calvin's allusions to medieval exegesis or otherwise determine just which commentaries he knew. Another example of this familiarity is the comment on Romans 3:28, where Calvin directly attacks the distinctive "faith working through Love" gloss of Rabanus and his successors taken from Augustine :

"We have determined, therefore." Now he [i.e., St. Paul] gathers the principal proposition, as though it were now out of all controversy, adding also an explication; for justification by faith is made very clear, while works are excluded by name. Therefore, our adversaries at this day labor nothing more, than that faith might be entangled with the merit of works. They confess a man is justified by faith, but not by sole faith; indeed, they place the power of justification in charity, howsoever in words they attribute it to faith. But Paul, in this place, makes justification so free that he makes it evident how in no way can it stand with any merit of works. (*ed. cit.*, p. 91).

Calvin continues in this place, as in the medieval commentaries, to cite and comment upon the relevance of James 2:26 for the interpretation of this text. Another passage may be mentioned, on Romans 3:21 f., which is especially striking in that Calvin successively refutes four major points of the customary exegesis : (1) the literal interpretation of the "law of works" as pertaining only to Jewish ceremonialism, (2) Augustine's interpretation of justification as the grace of regeneration, (3) justification as remission of sins, (4) a justification by works following justification by faith.

[134] The standard edition is by Johannes Ficker, published as vol. 56 of the *Weimar Ausgabe*, but an expanded set of notes appears in Wilhelm Pauck's English translation (*Luther : Lectures on Romans, Library of Christian Classics* XV [Philadelphia : Westminster, 1961]); Pauck's introduction has a thorough and useful discussion concerning Luther's medieval sources and his relationship to medieval theology in general at the time of his writing the Romans lectures (1515-16).

We must note further that the phrase *from faith unto faith* (Rom. 1:17) is interpreted in various ways. Lyra wants to understand it as if it meant "from unformed faith to formed faith." But this is meaningless, because no righteous man lives by an unformed faith. But Lyra says here both of these things, unless he wants to understand the unformed faith as the faith of beginners and the formed faith as that of the perfect. But unformed faith is, strictly speaking, no faith at all, but, rather, the object to which faith is directed. At any rate, I do not think that it is possible for anyone to believe by unformed faith—all that one can accomplish by it is to get an insight of what one must believe and thus to remain in suspense.[135]

This is one of the rare instances where Luther cites a medieval commentator on a substantive issue, and, even here, the significance of this reference is relatively minor; it serves in the context of his argument as little more than a further expression of his lack of sympathy with the subtleties of scholastic terminology.[136]

---

[135] Luther, *Romans, ed. cit.*, pp. 18 f. (WA 56, pp. 172 f.).

[136] It is to be noticed, however, that Luther here does not comment upon the broader doctrine implied by the definition of *fides formata* as 'faith formed by love' to which Lyra, following St. Thomas, refers in his gloss. The reason is that Luther was not familiar with the concept as it appears in the commentators, but rather associated it with the nominalist theologians (he had also earlier accepted the conventional teaching on justifying faith as 'faith working through love' in his marginal comments on the *Sentences*; see WA 9, p. 72). He explicitly rejected *fides caritate formata* elsewhere in the *Lectures on Romans*, on 7:5-6 (*ed. cit.*, pp. 196 f.) (WA 56, p. 337) :

This is what the Scholastic teachers mean when they say in their highly obscure and entirely unintelligible way that there is no valid observance of the divine commandment unless it is formed by love. This word "formed" is a cursed word, for it compels one to think of the soul as if it remained the same after and before the outpouring of love and as if the form were added to it at the moment of action, while, as a matter of fact, it must be wholly mortified and made new before it becomes capable of deeds of love.

On the concept of *fides charitate formata* in medieval theology and in Luther, see discussions in Anders Nygren, *Agape and Eros*, trans. Philip S. Watson (Philadelphia : Westminster, 1953), pp. 655-58, 716-21.

These passages are related to other *loci* where Luther emphatically rejects a corollary form of the same concept as it had been developed by the nominalists, that man is capable of loving God above all else by his natural powers without the aid of grace; see especially the comment on Rom. 4:7, one of the bitterest, as well as most difficult, passages in the *Lectures on Romans*, where he attacks the teaching propounded by Scotus, Ockham and Biel that man can possess any natural inclination or *habitus* toward the good—this, for Luther, leads only to further works-righteousness (*ibid.*, pp. 129 f. WA 56, pp. 271 *et seq.*). Luther found this an especially pernicious doctrine, and returned to an attack upon it in the *Disputation Against Scholastic Theology* of September, 1517 (see further discussion below, ch. 5).

Similarly, it is a point of minor importance that, in the text immediately following in the *Lectures*, Luther takes issue with another medieval interpretation :

Others interpret the passage as follows : "from the faith or the fathers of the old law to the faith of the new law." This interpretation is passable, though one can readily refute it by the argument that the text "The righteous man lives by faith" cannot possibly mean that the righteous man lives by the faith of his ancestors. The fathers had the same faith as we; there is only one faith, though it may have been less clear to them, just as today the scholars have the same faith as the laymen, only more clearly.[137]

These examples are not exceptional; the medieval commentaries on St. Paul played no important formative role in the development of Luther's thought or that of any other leading theologian of the sixteenth century. The medieval exegetical tradition had long since ceased to operate as a vital force in theology by the dawn of the Reformation era.

The history of this literature is perhaps more significant as it relates to the problem which was delineated in the introduction to this study : the quiescence of the Pauline doctrine of justification in the Middle Ages. The factors elucidated above can be of assistance at least in framing a partial answer. The particular reception of Augustinianism is but one facet of the extreme conservatism of the commentators with regard to all of their patristic sources, and which accounts for most of the positive doctrinal content of these works. The historical literalism of the commentators explains something of the narrowness of interpretation. Paul's letters were regarded, in the connection which has been examined here, simply as records of controversies in the apostolic Church in which the issues had long since been settled and held no contemporary urgency; if, to give an exaggerated illustration, justification was thought of only as having something to do with the fact that Christians need not be circumcised, it is unlikely that such a remote point of theological curiosity would result in polemics on "Christian freedom" or "Christian liberty".

---

[137] Luther, *Romans*, *ed. cit.*, p. 19 (WA 56, p. 173). Although the precise wording as Luther quotes it does not occur in any of the Pauline commentaries surveyed here, the concept occurs in several, as in, e.g., St. Thomas Aquinas : " 'Ex fide in fidem' : idest, ex fide veteris testamenti procedendo in fidem novi testamenti : quia ad utroque homines justificantur, et salvantur per fidem Christi ..." (*Opera omnia*, vol. 20, p. 396). Cf. Ps.-Haymo (*MPL* 117, col. 372D), Hatto of Vercelli (*MPL* 134, col. 138A), Lanfranc (*MPL* 150, col. 108), William of St. Thierry (*MPL* 180, col. 557), Hervaeus Burgidolensis (*MPL* 181, col. 608C).

This suggests what is perhaps the basic cause of the relative insignificance of justification in medieval theology, that it was not a tension-point in the accepted scheme of salvation, which, rather, centered about the sacraments and sacerdotal intercession. So long as there was no dissatisfaction with the sacramental apparatus of the Church, invested with the prestige and congeniality of centuries of cumulative tradition, it was unlikely that there would be any re-examination of the fundamental presuppositions of the system of grace. The commentaries, then, represent stages in the basic trend observable in the development of medieval dogma until the late scholastic period, an accommodation of theology to the cult-system. Justification is treated as a subsidiary and theoretical element in the general theology of grace, and in a thoroughly objective (as opposed to a subjective, mystical) frame of reference as a theological explanation of how and why the sinner is translated into a state of righteousness. The characteristics discussed above and in this conclusion, however, are only formal and immediate factors, which explain the matter positively—they do not account for the fact that other factors did not intervene to alter the basic trend. Although it is in the realm of the intangibles of history why no one—Abelard excepted—undertook the task of this re-examination, whether for personal and temperamental reasons or out of sheer intellectual curiosity, the case of Abelard is instructive here. The medieval culture-pattern curiously limited the pattern of inquiry to exclude all areas of thought which rested upon subjective assumptions—hence a total lack of a literature on aesthetics, for example, although the period was rich in the production of art and most fecund in other branches of philosophy— and also rigorously excluded any subjectivism in matters which could be given purely objective exposition. Abelard's subjectivism in his logically diffuse notion of justification by *amor Dei* was at total variance with the rationalist temperament of medieval theology and hence rejected out of hand—and with a very real sense of abhorrence, as evidenced by the treatment he received at the hands of his contemporaries. In contrast, all other commentators, formally correct as to justification *sola fide*, convey no vital sentiments as to the meaning of justification as a religious experience. This was a subjective category which medieval theologians refused to apply to systematic theology in any manner other than in terms of a formal, philosophical psychology, as applied, for example, to the concepts of attrition and contrition in penance. Religious subjectivism was rather expressed in devotional or ascetic forms.

The result, in contrast to Reformation theology, was that the evangelical dimension of justification was totally undeveloped by these exegetes, despite the intensely personal statement of religious experience in the Pauline text before them.

CHAPTER III

JUSTIFICATION IN THE EARLY SCHOLASTIC LITERATURE

Having determined the general lines of interpretation in the Biblical commentaries, it remains to determine the concept of justification as it appears in the general theological literature of the early Middle Ages. Investigation has shown that a distinct thread of tradition can be traced here also, but with its beginnings traceable only to the late eighth and ninth centuries and largely independent of patristic sources. This chapter therefore commences with an account of the historical circumstances which initiated this doctrinal tradition.

1. THE CAROLINGIAN PERIOD

In the previous chapter, reference was made to a gloss on Romans 3:24 in the mid-ninth century commentary of Pseudo-Haymo of Halberstadt in which justification was posited in baptism, but with the additional comment *postmodum per poenitentiam*. This is an isolated reference in the series of commentaries, but it is significant as reflecting a new development in the ninth-century Frankish Church, the introduction of the Anglo-Irish system of private confession and penance on the Continent. This ranks as one of the major developments in the church history of the period, along with the important doctrinal controversies and the first appearance of monographic treatises on subjects of dogma since the end of Antiquity.[1]

This private system was unknown in the ancient Church.[2] The system of penance as developed by the time of St. Augustine was a recognized

---

[1] Harnack, *Hist. of Dogma*, vol. 5, pp. 275 f.

[2] For the following remarks, I draw upon the standard work (coverage to 1215) of O. D. Watkins, *A History of Penance*, 2 vols. (London, 1920; repr. New York: Burt Franklin, 1961) and the eminently useful introduction in J. T. McNeill and H. M. Gamer, *Medieval Handbooks of Penance*, Records of Civilization XXIX (New York:

and systematized church rite, but differed in a number of important respects from the modern private system. The ceremony was public in character. It was regarded as a drastic disciplinary measure, sometimes undertaken voluntarily but more often as a means of purging a sentence of excommunication. And, in the West until the sixth century, all patristic authorities emphatically maintained that penance could be undertaken only once during one's lifetime. Because of the rigor of the penitential discipline, which involved an elaborate and lengthy regimen of ceremonial self-abasement, fasting, special garb, and other acts of self-mortification, it was often postponed until the approach of death. The rite was not obligatory and the evidence suggests that it was an extraordinary undertaking. It is important to note that this ceremony—it cannot at this period be described exactly as a sacrament although it was regarded as having a sacramental effect in remission of sin somewhat analogous to baptism—was imposed for the mortal or so-called "deadly" sins. For venial sins, the Fathers were unanimous in holding that, as in Augustine, "the daily prayer of the believer makes satisfaction for those daily sins of a momentary and trivial kind which are necessary incidents of this life."[3] The role of confession in public penance, as to whether public or private, is the source of some controversy among scholars, although the evidence seems to suggest that procedures varied in different localities. As to the practice of private confession to a clergyman of venial sins, which did not require the public or "great" penance, there was no established routine; the sources do show that confessions were occasionally received but only informally as a pastoral, rather than sacramental, function.

The ancient system of penance declined in the late Western Roman Empire both because of its inherent rigor and impracticality and due to a widespread moral relaxation attendant upon the political decadence of the Western Empire. Public penance did survive in medieval canon law, but mainly as a theological curiosity since it was seldom practiced. A newer and more workable system developed independently in Celtic

---

Columbia, 1938), pp. 1-50. Cf. Harnack, *Hist. of Dogma* V, 323-331. These works largely supersede the older classic of H. C. Lea, *A History of Auricular Confession and Indulgences in the Latin Church*, 3 vols. (Philadelphia : Lea, 1896); Lea did not sufficiently appreciate the significance of the penitentials and hence overlooks the distinct invention of a new system of private penance in Anglo-Irish Christianity. A comparatively brief historical survey is found in Bernard Poschmann, *Penance and the Anointing of the Sick*, trans. F. Courtney, S. J. (New York : Herder and Herder, 1964), pp. 5-154.

   [3] *Enchir.*, c. 71; cf. Portalié, *Guide*, pp. 260 *et seq.*

Christianity. Among the distinguishing traits of the Church in this area was its monastic, rather than episcopal, organization, which profoundly affected its institutional character; one of the most important results of this was the extension of the monastic penitential discipline to the laity. This development was accomplished in conjunction with the appearance of the penitential books. This important class of ecclesiastical literature can be traced back to Welsh sources of the sixth century and more tentatively to fifth-century Ireland, and such books came to form the exclusive basis of penitential discipline in the English church. The penitentials had important advantages : they not only prescribed the new method of private penance, but provided confessors with manuals of practical guidance in their task and also tariffs of penalties or satisfactions graded in accordance with specific offenses. For the latter reason, these documents are an especially rich source for social history. They are also an important source for legal history since the penitentials, in developed form, were in a sense codifications of church law; they also interacted with Celtic and Germanic customary law—the substitution of pecuniary satisfactions for acts of penance (a remote but apparently unconnected anticipation of the system of indulgences of the late medieval and Renaissance Church) is an example, and the similarity between the penitentials and established legal customs of northern Europe may be considered a factor in the success of the penitentials. The system was also in due course absorbed into canon law, forming substantial sections in the important medieval codifications of Burchard, Ivo, and Gratian.

The use of these manuals had declined by the twelfth century, but not without firmly fixing the novel features of the newer discipline in the practice of the Church, much as it is known today : private and repeated confessions to a priest, the seal of secrecy, and the inclusion of both venial and mortal sins within the system. The capstone of the development was the decree of the Lateran Council of 1215 making confession and penance at least once annually universally obligatory in the Latin Church.

Of immediate interest for this study is the introduction of the penitential books and the private system of penance on the Continent in the ninth century. Given the background of the general revival of church life and church reform in the Carolingian renaissance, the immediate cause of the development was the influence of the considerable number of émigré Anglo-Irish missionaries and scholars who imported and actively championed the new system in the Frankish church.

The penetration of the system can be traced in its tentative beginnings in the mid-eighth century. St. Boniface advocated confession to a priest and the prerogative of the confessor to determine appropriate penance.[4] Chrodegang of Metz (bp. 742-766) extended the monastic rule of confession to canons of his diocese, prescribing confession to a superior at least once or twice annually.[5] Moving towards the ninth century, there is an important and detailed statement of recommended practice in Paulinus of Aquileia (ca. 726-802) in which this prominent Italian prelate makes two basic points : the Christian should confess and do "true penance" before taking the Eucharist, and that even lesser sins should be confessed. This is in a *Liber exhortationis* written for Henry, duke of Friuli, about 795, and similar to other works of spiritual guidance for the laity which often provide the historian with clear statements of contemporary doctrine and practice.[6] A similar document is the capitulary written by Theodulf of Orleans (bp. 797-821) setting forth regulations for his diocese. Theodulf still recognized personal confession in daily prayer, but prescribes sacerdotal confession for the so-called eight principal sins. This was a schematization of the mortal sins received from Gregory the Great which became definitive for the penitential system;[7] it appears also in the works of Boniface and Chrodegang cited above and appears regularly in the literature thereafter.[8] From the early ninth century, references to the new system multiply greatly in all classes of literature—theological and devotional treatises, conciliar decrees, even in imperial legislation—as private penance became universal in the Frankish church.

It is not germane to the present subject to trace this development in detail.[9] Rather, it is of interest here to focus attention upon the manner in which the system of private penance was given a theological interpretation and incorporated into the general body of church doctrine. There is no attempt to argue the case theologically in the penitential books themselves, either in the Anglo-Irish literature or the later Continental specimens—these books only promulgate the positive practices

---

[4] *MPL* 89, cols. 851 and 887; cf. Watkins, *Hist. of Penance* I, 660 f.

[5] *MPL* 89, col. 1104; cf. Watkins, *Hist. of Penance* I, 662-664.

[6] *MPL* 99, cols. 230-232; Manitius I, 368 f.

[7] McNeill, *Medieval Handbooks*, pp. 19 f.

[8] Another early appearance is in Smaragdus of St. Mihiel, *Diadema monachorum*, cc. 15 f. (*MPL* 102, cols. 611-614).

[9] See Watkins, *Hist. of Penance* I, 665 *et seq.* for a comprehensive historical treatment and selection of documents.

and details of the system.[10] The system simply developed in the practice, and theological elaboration was, in the nature of the case, *ex post facto.* The beginnings of the latter process first appeared in conjunction with the introduction of private penance on the Continent. The innovation was not accepted without resistance in some quarters, notably at the Council of Chalon-sur-Sâone in 813,[11] and had to be both actively promoted and rationalized as in accordance with the ancient tradition of the Church. It is especially significant that the new system found its foremost advocate in Alcuin of York (*ca.* 735-804), the famed English scholar who held a position of unique prestige as Charlemagne's principal ecclesiastical adviser and later as abbot of St. Martin of Tours, the foremost monastic foundation in the Frankish empire. The rapid acceptance of the Anglo-Irish system is in no small measure due to his influence, backed by Charlemagne's vigorous support of this and other church reform activity.

The principal evidence for Alcuin's activity in this matter are the frequent exhortations in his extensive correspondence, but these references are negligible for doctrinal content.[12] More solid treatment is found in several of his more substantial works where sections are devoted to confession and penance. Among these is a concise statement of the *rationale* of penance as a church institution; a portion of the following context concerns justification in penance. This is from Alcuin's *Liber de divinis officiis,* one of several manuals of doctrine produced during this period of institutional, as well as intellectual, renewal :

Poenitentiae autem remedium Ecclesia catholica in spe indulgentiae fidenter alligat exercendos homines, et post unum baptismi sacramentum, quod singu-

[10] Based on a search of McNeill, *Medieval Handbooks,* and the standard source collection of F. W. H. Wasserschleben, *Die Bussordnungen der abendländischen Kirche* (Halle : Graeger, 1851).

[11] The Council of Chalon did not directly oppose private penance, but the records indicate a dispute among the participants as to the merits of personal confession in prayer as opposed to sacerdotal confession; the council concluded by recommending both courses as of benefit (Canon 33; in Mansi, *Sacrorum Conciliorum Nova et Amplissima Collectio* 14, col. 100). This and other councils of the period attempted an indirect opposition with efforts to revive the ancient public penance, but the principal objection was the indiscriminate use of penitential books of uncertain authorship which were without authority in canons or tradition. This objection was overcome by the work of Rabanus Maurus and others who, with royal and episcopal support, prepared manuals prescribing a uniform and authoritative practice for the Frankish church as a whole.

[12] Epp. 14, 44, 94, 112, 142, 152, 188, 225 (*MPL* 100, cols. 165, 210, 300, 339, 384, 402, 460, 502).

lari traditione commendatum sollicite prohibet iterandum, medicinali remedio poenitentiae subrogat adjumentum, cujus remedio egere se cuncti agnoscere debent pro quotidianis humanae fragilitatis excessibus, sine quibus in hac vita esse non possumus, honore duntaxat et dignitate servata, ita ut sacerdotibus et levitis, Deo tantum teste, fiat; a caeteris vero, attestante coram Deo solemniter sacerdote, ut hoc tegat fructuosa confessio, quod temerarius appetitus, aut ignorantiae nota contraxisse negligentius videtur : ut sicut in baptismo omnes iniquitates remitti, vel per martyrium nulli peccatum credimus imputari, ita poenitentiae compunctione fructuosa fateamur deleri peccata. Lacrymae enim poenitentium apud Deum pro baptismate reputantur. Unde et quamlibet sint magna delicta, quamvis gravia; non est tamen in illis Dei misericordia desperanda. In actione enim poenitudinis, ut supra dictum est, non tam consideranda est mensura temporis, quam doloris. Cor enim contritum et humiliatum Deus non spernit (Ps. 50:19). Verumtamen quanto in peccando fuit ad malum promptior mentis intentio, tanto devotior debet esse in poenitendo afflictio.

... Ex fine enim suo unumquemque aut justificat, aut condemnat, sicut scriptum est : "Ipse judicat extrema terrae (I Reg. 2:10). Et alibi : "Universorum finem ipse considerat (Job 28:3)". Proinde non dubitamus circa finem justificari hominem per poenitentiam et compunctionem; sed quia raro hoc fieri solet, metuendum est; ne dum ad finem differtur conversio, incerta occupet mors, antequam subveniat poenitentia. Pro qua re etsi bona est ad extremum conversio, melior tamen est, quae longe ante finem agitur, ut ab hac vita securius transeatur.[13]

Thus, the specific term *justificatio* is linked with penance. A more pointed statement occurs in Alcuin's *opusculum De virtutibus et vitiis* :

12. De Confessione.

Hortatur nos saepius Scriptura ad medicamentum fugere confessionis : non quod Deus indigeat confessione nostra, cui omnia praesto sunt quae cogitamus, loquimur, aut agimus; sed nos aliter salvi fieri non possumus, nisi confiteamur poenitentes quod inique gessimus negligentes. Qui seipsum accusat in peccatis suis, hunc diabolus non habet iterum accusare in die judicii ... Quomodo potest medicus vulnus sanare, quod aegrotus ostendere erubescit? Deus enim confessionem nostram desiderat, ut justam habeat causam ignoscendi. Qui peccata sua occultat, et erubescit salubriter confiteri, Deum testem habet nunc, et iterum habebit eum ultorem. Optime se judicat homo in hac vita, ne judicetur a Deo damnatione perpetus. ... Confessio justificat, confessio veniam peccatis donat. Omnis spes veniae in confessione consistit. Confessio

---

[13] C. 55 (*MPL* 101, cols. 1283 f.). Note that Alcuin compares penance with baptism ("Lacrymae enim poenitentium apud Deum pro baptismate reputantur"); another statement reintroduced into the literature is Jerome's statement in his famous Ep. 130 *De servanda virginitate* : "Illa [i.e., penance] quasi secunda post naufragia miseris tabula sit ..."; see Alcuin's Epp. 94 and 112 (*MPL* 100, cols. 300, 339). This continues to be a favorite patristic tag with writers on penance.

opus est misericordiae : salus aegroti unicum est viribus [*forte*, vitiis] nostris medicamentum cum poenitentia.[14]

These statements convey only portions of Alcuin's many arguments for the advantages of confession and should not be exaggerated as to their importance—there is no theology of justification in his thoughts on penance. Nevertheless, it is significant that Alcuin uses the term only in contexts where penance is discussed.[15] It is used to build up the forensic element in the doctrine, where the idea of God's judgment of the sinner is repeatedly stressed. The contrasting emphasis is penance as a manifestation of the mercy (*misericordia*) of God, and it is in this frame of reference that a theory of sacramental grace in penance is ultimately worked out. Yet the forensic element was to survive as a sanction within the system, balanced in varying degrees among individual theologians. It is perhaps the predominant theological note in Alcuin's theological treatment, for whom an accusing Devil was a veritable reality.[16]

This aspect of the theology of penance will not be explored in detail—the examples given from Alcuin are representative of the fundamentals of the concept as it continued to appear in the literature. Rather, attention will be devoted specifically to the use of the term *justificatio*. Hence, the body of conciliar legislation of this period must be passed over, as well as two important ninth-century theological works, Halitgar of

---

[14] C. 12 (*MPL* 101, cols. 621 f.).

[15] Cf. his *opusculum* to the students at St. Martin of Tours, *De confessione peccatorum* (MPL 101, cols. 649-656) in which he marshals all of his arguments in favor of sacerdotal confession and penance; the text Isaiah 43:26 is here applied to penance (col. 652B) : " 'Dic tu prior injustias tuas, ut justificeris', et non condemneris : ut maneat in te praemium poenitentiae, non vindicta peccatorum." Cf. *Expositio in psal. poenitentiales*, Ps. 141 (*MPL* 100, col. 591) where justification is referred to original sin.

[16] The following is another typical, if more striking, expression of this viewpoint (Ep. 225 [*MPL* 100, col. 502D]) :
... nullusque senior sive junior, saecularis vel monasterialis, vir aut femina sua erubescat confiteri peccata, atque per poenitentiam emendare, quidquid contra Dei voluntatem fecisset. Melius est habere unum hominem testem peccatorum suorum in salutem animae suae, quam spectare accusationem diabolicae fraudis ante Judicem omnium saeculorum, et ante angelorum choros, et totius humani generis multitudinem. Dum vero homo vivit in hoc saeculo, fructuosa est confessio et poenitentia; in futuro scilicet judicio poenitentia erit peccatorum, sed non fructuosa, quia unusquisque judicabitur secundum opera sua. Metuant criminosi et peccatis onerati aeternorum flammas tormentorum. Gaudeant justi, etiam et poenitentes de perpetuae beatitudinis gloria cum Christo, qui ait : "Ibunt impii in ignem aeternum; justi autem in vitam aeternam (Matt. 25:46)."

Cambrai's penitential and the *De institutione laicali* of Jonas of Orleans. The second author to be treated in this chapter is Rabanus Maurus who, in addition to his Pauline commentaries, produced important writings on penance and may be considered Alcuin's successor as the leading proponent of private penance in the Frankish church. He prepared a penitential designed to replace the existing unauthorized manuals which drew such strong criticism in the councils of Chalon-sur-Sâone and Paris.[17] As in other documents in this class, the doctrinal content in this work is not significant. Several other contexts are of greater interest for the present subject.

Rabanus' Homily 55 is on the subject "De confessione ac poenitentia atque compunctione cordis"; the following context closely follows Alcuin's remarks quoted above :

Quomodo potest medicus vulnus sanare quod aegrotus ostendere erubescit? Deus enim confessionem nostram desiderat, ut justam habeat causam ignoscendi. Qui peccata sua occultat et erubescit salubriter confiteri, Deum, quem testem habet, iterum habebit cum ultorem. Optime se judicat homo in hac vita, ne judicetur a Deo damnatione perpetua. Duplicem habere debet fletum in poenitentia omnis peccator, sive quia per negligentiam bonum non fecit, seu quia malum per audaciam perpetravit. Confessio justificat, confessio veniam peccatis donat. Omnis spes veniae in confessione consistit, confessio opus est misericordiae, salus aegroti, unicum est viribus nostris medicamentum poenitentiae; cujus ipse Salvator in Evangelio virtutem ostendit dicens : "Poenitentiam agite, appropinquavit enim regnum coelorum (Matt. 3:2)".[18]

In his *De ecclesiastica disciplina*, another ecclesiastical handbook, is another statement of his teaching in which Rabanus applies a number of Biblical texts, including the basic text in Matthew 3:2 and also Romans 10:10 ("Ore autem, inquit, confessio fit ad salutem").[19] Rabanus concludes this section as follows :

---

[17] *MPL* 110, cols. 467-494. Written 841. In the conclusion of his preface, Rabanus does appeal to St. Paul for the practice of penance, writing : "Unde necesse est ut in praesenti vita, juxta Apostolum, mortificemus membra nostra que sunt super terram ..." (col. 470D).

[18] *MPL* 110, col. 103. In this homily, Rabanus considers the concept of compunction, and is one of the earliest medieval theologians to give the term some technical precision. His theology of penance shows similar sophistication where he identifies and compares the *confessio* of the Latin Church with the Greek Church *exmologesis* (*De universo* VI, c. 15 [*MPL* 111, cols. 137 f.]).

[19] The Matthew text, words of St. John the Baptist repeated by Christ in Matt. 4:17, is in the Vulgate as follows : "Paenitentiam agite, adpropinquavit enim regnum caelorum." This is the main proof-text in virtually all medieval discussions of penance. But there is a hidden ambiguity in the Latin, apparently overlooked by St. Jerome,

Consideremus namque quod justus sit, peccata nostra non negligamus. Consideremus ergo quod pius sit, non desperemus. Praebet apud Deum homini fiduciam, Deus homo est nobis spes magna poenitentibus, quia advocatus noster factus est judex noster. Unde necesse est ut audiamus quia misericors est, convertamur a peccatis, recordantes quod justus est, pertimescamus recedere a justitia ... In bonis enim operibus intenti nisi contra malignos spiritus sollicite vigilemus, ipsos irrisores patimur quos ad malum habemus. Et ideo sollicite considerare debemus, ne per pusillanimitatem pereamus, ne hostes spirituales, quos innumerabiles habemus, cum vederint nos de statu justitiae corruisse, omnem laborem nostrum in novissimo in derisum sibi ducant vitam nostram, et nobis in opprobium vertant.[20]

These texts are consistent with the treatise on penance which forms a complete "book" in the three-book *De videndo Deum, de puritate cordis et modo poenitentiae.* This is the lengthiest theological treatment of penance in the Carolingian literature. The forensic emphasis is prominent throughout, of which the following excerpts are most relevant to the term *justificatio* :

... per confessionem sacerdoti patefaciat, et pro hoc ipso poenitentiam condignam gerat, sperans in misericordia opificis sui quod ipse, qui eum ex nihilo condidit, potens est post lapsum rursum recuperare, et de peccatore justum facere, atque aeterni regni simul cum sanctis angelis suis participem efficere, proh dolor!
... Et iterum dicit : Qui redit a Dei justitia ad peccatum, Dominus praecipitat eum in gladium, et sicut canis, cum revertitur ad vomitum suum, odibilis efficitur, ita et stultus cum revertitur ad peccatum suum. Non ergo hoc solum sufficit si incusans temetipsum peccata tua videaris exponere, sed eo affectu haec age, ut speres tibi in eo justificationis aliquid conferri per poenitentiam.[21]

---

as compared with the sense of the Greek. The most natural interpretation of the Vulgate *poenitentiam agite* is 'do penance' and was so understood in the Middle Ages with reference to the specific church rite, later sacrament, of penance. Modern English versions (Protestant and Roman Catholic) now render it, in accordance with the Greek, as 'repent'. This linguistic peculiarity was a major factor in the growth and propagation of the medieval doctrine, as Erasmus and the Reformers were quick to note. In Romans 10:9-10 there is a similar linguistic confusion, which also occasionally appears in medieval writers, between confession of *sins* and confession of *faith*. The Confraternity edition now has the full context (which Rabanus does not quote, but only as above) : "9. For if thou confess with thy mouth that Jesus is the Lord, and believe in thy heart that God has raised him from the dead, thou shalt be saved. 10. For with the heart a man believes unto justice, and with the mouth profession of faith is made unto salvation" (n.b. 'profession' for *confessio*). This is a particularly egregious error and example of forcing an interpretation, since the Latin of this and similar texts quoted on the point are not at all ambiguous.

[20] *MPL* 112, col. 1260.
[21] *MPL* 112, col. 1304; col. 1326. A somewhat less direct text, but which directly

2. EARLY SCHOLASTICISM : TENTH TO TWELFTH CENTURIES

The tenth and early eleventh centuries represent a *hiatus* in the history of medieval theology. In this "age of iron", the gross quantity of literary production underwent a considerable decline, with the effects especially noticeable in Biblical commentaries and speculative theology. The reasons generally advanced for this decline in letters and learning are the Viking and Magyar raids and the disintegration of the Frankish empire. But it has also been suggested that a more important reason was the retreat of learning into the monasteries correlative with the disappearance of court patronage. The tone was set by the newer institutions of the Cluniac reform, where the emphasis in Bible study was shifted from learned hermeneutic investigation to the more practical purposes of personal edification and liturgical usage.[22] Despite this proportionate de-emphasis, references to penance are numerous in the few productive theologians, as well as in sermons and in papal and conciliar legislation. Toward the end of this period, Burchard of Worms was able to draw upon an extensive literature to synthesize a well-developed body of doctrine and practice in his *Decretum* (*ca.* 1012), the first of the great canon law collections.[23] And St. Peter Damiani (1007-1072) was probably the first to include penance in an enumeration of the sacraments of the Church.[24]

---

connects penance and justification, is as follows, from the same work (col. 1315) :
... si enim Redemptor noster, qui peccatores non perdere sed justificare venit in oblivione peccantium delicata derelinquit, quis hominum condemnanda reservet? cum Apostolus dicat : "Si Deus justificat, quis est qui condemnet?" Ad fontem misericordiae recurrentes evangelicam proferamus sententiam : "Gaudebo, inquit, super uno peccatore poenitentiam agente quam super nonaginta novem justis qui non indigent poenitentia (Matt. 18:13)" ...

Note again the sense of *poenitentia* here. Another text is interesting for an adjustment of the concept of faith to penance, in Rabanus' preface to the penitential of Halitgar mentioned above (*MPL* 112, col. 1334C) :
Oportet igitur ad poenitentiam accedere cum omni fiducia, et ex fide indubitanter credere poenitentia aboleri posse peccata, etiamsi in ultimo vitae spiritu commissa poeniteat ...

[22] Smalley, *Study of the Bible*, pp. 44 f.; H. H. Glunz, *History of the Vulgate in England from Alcuin to Roger Bacon* (Cambridge, 1933), pp. 32 *et seq.*, pp. 72 f.

[23] *Decr.* XIX (*MPL* 140, cols. 949-1014): the section on penance occupies a complete book, which also was widely known by a separate informal title, the *Corrector*. Ivo of Chartres and Gratian followed Burchard in treating penance as a major subdivision of canon law.

[24] Sermo 49 (*MPL* 144, col. 901A). Cited by P. Pourrat, *Theology of the Sacraments* (St. Louis : Herder, 1910), p. 266, who also states (p. 264, n. 18) : "St. Gregory the

Sermons often provide insight into current theological opinion when more systematic sources are lacking. A tenth-century monk, Abbo of St. Germain (ob. 923) published a little collection of four sermons of rather greater doctrinal content than usual, for the benefit, he stated, of those clergy who have difficulty in understanding the Gospel "per obscura doctorum commenta et homilias". Three of the sermons are on penance. *Sermo* 2 is especially interesting for its extreme sacerdotalism, in which the author compares the role of priests with that of God *vis-à-vis* Adam : God created Adam just, but then expelled him from Paradise when Adam sinned, later redeemed him through Christ's Passion. He draws the comparison thusly :

> Igitur, fratres, nos episcopi, sumus vicarii Domini nostri Jesu Christi in hoc modo, et sumus missi, et ordinati in loco ejus, et propterea post apostolos dedit nobis Dominus potestatem ligandi animas atque solvendi, et praecepit nobis aedificare, et plantare bonos homines in domo Domini, et evellere [de ea] hoc est de Ecclesia. ...
> Fratres, istud exemplum Domini nostri Jesu Christi tenemus, nos episcopi in Ecclesia, peccatores vero tenent exemplum Adam, verbi gratia, sicut Filius Dei misit Adam sanctum et justum in paradisum, similiter nos et omnes sacerdotes mittimus in Ecclesiam homines sanctificatos, et justificatos in baptismo.[25]

This is a rare instance where baptism is said to justify, but it is consistent with the concept of justification as remission of sins in both baptism and penance as expressed in Haymo's commentary; this author implies as much in his sermon *Ad poenitentes reconciliatos* :

> Et de talibus hominibus repetentibus peccata sua quae jam fecerunt, dicit Spiritus sanctus per prophetam David, "Quia justificationes Domini non exquisierunt (Ps. 118 : 155)", id est, non permanserunt in promissionibus suis, quas promiserunt in baptismo et in confessione iniquitatum suarum.[26]

A collection of Anglo-Saxon ecclesiastical laws, attributed to the reign of Edgar, King of England (959-975), has serveral sections devoted to confession and penance, of which the first title of the section *De confessione* reads :

Great was the first to use the name *sacramentum* in connection with Penance. This usage, however, did not become general until the time of St. Peter Damian." I have been unable to verify this positively in modern authorities, although it is the earliest such reference I have noted in *MPL*. Cf. Sermo 58 (*MPL* 144, col. 834C) where penance is also referred to as a sacrament.

[25] Sermo 2 (*MPL* 123, col. 766); Abbo continues the analogy to equate the Church with Adam's paradise.

[26] Sermo 4 (*MPL* 132, col. 770D).

I. Quando aliquis voluerit confessionem facere peccatorum suorum, viriliter agat, et non erubescat confiteri scelera, et facinora se accusando; quia inde venit indulgentia, et quia sine confessione nulla est venia. Confessio enim sanat, confessio justificat.[27]

St. Peter Damiani, one of the greatest preachers of the eleventh century, has an interesting sermon on penance which, while he does not use the term *justificatio*, makes an equivalent connection of penance with *justitia*. On the text Romans 10:10, "Corde creditur ad justitiam, ore autem confessio fit ad salutem", his premise is as follows :

Haec est consummata justitia, perfecta veritas, et vera perfectio, si tamen oris confessio subsequatur. Fides enim cordis sine fide oris, aut parva, Salvatore dicente : "Qui me erubuerit et meos sermones, hunc Filius hominis erubescet coram angelis Dei (Luc. 9:26)." Et propheta : "Periit fides, ablata est de ore eorum (Jer. 7:28)." Non dixit de corde, sed de ore, quia nihil valet fides cordis, sine fide oris, nec fides oris, sine fide cordis, cum ista justitiam, illa donet salutem, quia salus a justitia, vel justitia a salute separari non possunt. Crede ergo et confitere, nihilominus confitere et crede, quia fides ad justitiam, confessio fit ad salutem.

It may seem here that Damiani means confession of faith, but from what follows it becomes clear that, as in Rabanus' *De ecclesiastica disciplina*, *confessio*, is interpreted as confession of sins. And it is this confession that he makes the vital principle of *justitia*, and not simply faith in itself :

Pro hujusmodi confessione remittes tu, Domine, impietatem cordis mei, peccati scilicet. Et, "pro hac orabit ad te omnis sanctus in tempore opportuno (Ps. 31:6)". Hoc primum in corde germinat ad justitiam, postea in ore nascitur ad salutem. ... Sic igitur in interiori homine justitia germinante, surculus erumpat in arborem, et loquatur lingua quod scientia loquebatur.[28]

The sources lead next into the period of the second revival of medieval learning, beginning with the rise of the cathedral schools from the mid-eleventh century through the twelfth-century renaissance. These writers are, properly speaking, "schoolmen", representative of the earlier period of the scholastic learning which forms the grand movement in the intellectual history of the high Middle Ages.

The earliest major figure was Lanfranc of Bec (*ca.* 1005-1089), whose Pauline commentary was previously surveyed; his other writings, however, contain nothing of interest on justification. Similarly, Anselm of Laon (*ca.* 1036-1086) and St. Anselm of Canterbury (1033-1109),

---

[27] *MPL* 138, col. 503D; Glorieux, *Pour revaloriser Migne*, p. 59, lists this as tenth century, anonymous.

[28] Sermo 58 (*MPL* 144, cols. 830, 831C, 832B).

a towering figure in the history of Western philosophy for his famous ontological argument, make little use of the term in their theology. The few occurrences of *justificatio* in their writings are as a synonym for remission of sins. Anselm of Laon uses the term to describe baptism, distinguishing between the *res* and *signum* of the sacrament (an Augustinian concept) :

Res sacramenti iustificatio est hominis, tam exterioris, que in simplici predictorum remissione, quam interioris, que in triplici constat uirtutum susceptione, scilicet, fidei, spei, caritatis, et illius quidem sacramentum uisibile est causa, istius uero signum, suscipiende quidem in paruulis, iam vero suscepte in adultis, sicut circumcisio Abrahe signaculum iustitie erat iam ex fide suscepte. ... Quoniam igitur res signum suum precedere debet, ideo et ista iustificatio causam suam habet uisibile sacramentum precedentem, que fit per penitentiam et instructionem fidei et exorcismum.[29]

In St. Anselm, the term occurs only in one passage of importance: this is in the *Cur Deus Homo* where this doctor defines the fundamental rule of God's justice :

Nullatenus ergo debet aut potest accipere homo a deo quod deus illi dare proposuit, si non reddit deo totum quod illi abstulit; ut sicut per illum deus perdidit, ita per illum recuperet. Quod non aliter fieri valet nisi ut, quemadmodum per tota humana corrupta et quasi fermentata est peccato, cum quo nullum deus assumit ad perficiendam illam civitatem caelestem, ita per vincentem iustificentur a peccato tot homines quod illum numerum completuri erant, ad quem complendum factus est homo. Sed hoc facere nullatenus potest peccator homo, quia peccator peccatorem iustificare nequit.[30]

Here, in the dogmatic framework of St. Anselm's well-known "satisfaction theory" of the Atonement, *justificatio* has no more significance than the conventional 'justification from sin'.

---

[29] *Sententie* c. 6, in *Anselms von Laon Systematische Sentenzen,* ed. F. Bliemetzrieder, *Beiträge zur Geschichte der Philosophie des Mittelalters,* Bd. XVIII, Heft 2-3 (Münster, 1919), p. 114.

[30] I, c. 23 (*MPL* 158, col. 396). According to the index of the critical edition of F. S. Schmitt, *S. Anselmi Cantuarensis Archepiscopi Opera Omnia* (Edinburgh : Nelson, 1946-61), VI, pp. 203 f., the term appears in only three places in St. Anselm's writings (one citation is apparently erroneous). This is not correct, for I have found the following additional context in one of Anselm's prayers to the Virgin, so that justification need not be unrelated to medieval Mariology (Oratio 7 [*MPL* 158, col. 875]) :

... Non est enim reconciliatio nisi quam tu casta concepisti, non est iustificatio nisi quam tu integra in utero fovisti, non est quam tu virgo peperisti. Ergo o Domine, mater es iustificationis et iustificatorum, genetrix es reconciliationis et reconciliatorum, parens es salutis et salvatorum. ...

With Rupert of Deutz (*ca.* 1070-1129?), a scholastic theologian who wrote several important Biblical commentaries, there is an approach to a more definite connotation in the term. He prefers to use *sanctificatio* for technical purposes, specifically to denote remission of sins as a gift of the Holy Spirit, although in his commentary on the first chapter of Matthew, concerning the genealogy of Christ, he frequently alludes to the 'justification' of Old Testament figures.[31] But in a similar context in his commentary on St. John's Gospel where the work of the Holy Spirit is again described as remission of sins, a synonymous use of *justificatio* occurs in a context where Rupert describes the power of baptism as given to the Church "ut baptizati a peccati [sic] omnes justificemur."[32] Rupert also has an unusual usage in one of his *opuscula* where he identifies justification with humility.[33] The idea, however, is presented in a work on the monastic life and is of no greater importance than as a hortatory conceit; this work exhibits Rupert's propensity for the traditional Benedictine mystic theology, as an "anti-dialectician" in opposition to the precise doctrinal theology of the early schoolmen of his generation.

Another example of an incidental use of the term occurs in one of several sermons on penance by an obscure *scholasticus* contemporaneous with Rupert. These sermons are likewise hortatory rather than doctrinal and of little present interest except for the following sentence : "Sed, fratres, non omnis poenitentia salvat, sed digna tantum justificat."[34]

These and other mystic theologians of the monasteries seem to use the term *justitia* in the sense of 'righteousness' rather than in the stricter forensic sense of the schoolmen.[35] The mystics, however, reflect something of the currents in contemporary theology, as evidenced by several major figures. Turning first to the Victorines, I cite the following unauthenticated passage in the *Miscellanea* of Hugh of St. Victor (*ca.* 1096-1141), a *scholia* on Psalm 84:12 :

[31] *Comment. in Matth.*, c. 1 (*MPL* 168, cols. 1307 *et seq.*, esp. cols. 1324 f.).

[32] *Comment. in Joan.* (*MPL* 169, col. 812C). Rupert does not develop a specific doctrine of penance in his writings, although he incidentally states the usual opinion that it is necessary for salvation in various places.

[33] *De vita vere apostolica* II, c. 3 (*MPL* 170, cols. 622 f.).

[34] Printed in *MPL* as Hildebert (1057-1133; archbp. of Tours), Sermo 22 (*MPL* 171, col. 442); attributed to Geoffrey Babion (*scholasticus* at Angers, 1096-1110) by Glorieux, *Pour revaloriser Migne*, p. 63.

[35] See esp. the homilies of the twelfth-century abbot Godefrid of Admont (*ob.* 1165), *passim* (*MPL* 174; see various *loci* cited under *justificatio* in the index to this vol.).

Homo confessionem ad salutem ore proprio faciebat, et misericordia precibus suis Dominum ad justificationem hominis compellebat. Veritas de terra per confessionem oriebatur, et justitia de coelo prospiciens per misericordiam Dei ad terras mittebatur. Veritas dixit prius puniendum qui prius malum fecerat. Misericordia dixit postea justificandum, et salvandum qui et malum confitendo bene fecerat. Per veritatem accusabatur, et per misericordiam propter veritatem justificabatur. Quia "veritas de terra orta est, et justitia de coelo prospexit (Ps. 84:12)".[36]

While the above passage may not be genuinely Hugh's, it is well within the spirit of his teaching. A series of passages from his *De sacramentis*, a landmark in sacramental theology, shows that *justificatio* is an important term in his theological vocabulary. A general connection is made between the sacraments and justification where Hugh explains why the sacraments were instituted—as a sign and promise of sanctification of those who receive the sacraments in faith and hope; it is by this 'remedy', he concludes, that men are saved :

Scias ergo quocunque tempore ab initio mundi usque ad finem, nullum fuisse vel esse vere bonum, nisi justificatum per gratiam, gratiam autem nunquam aliquem adipisci potuisse, nisi per Christum. Ita ut omnes sive praecedentes sive subsequentes uno sanctificationis remedio salvatos agnoscas.[37]

Hugh also has a concept of justification by faith; this also is given a sacramental interpretation. A rather lengthy excerpt must be given here to show his argument (this is a good example of Victorine mystic theology, drawing its inspiration from the Platonic-Augustinian tradition) :

Sed omnes fide una crediderunt unum, et omnes una fide justificati sunt, qui justificari meruerunt. "Sine fide enim", ut ait Apostolus, "impossibile est placere Deo (Hebr. 11:6)". Et sicut dicit beatus Augustinus : Ubi fides non erat, bonum opus non erat.
Cap. IX. De sacramento fidei et virtute.
Sacramentum fidei dupliciter potest intelligi. Sacramentum enim fidei vel ipsa intelligitur quae sacramentum est, vel sacramento fidei intelliguntur quae cum fide percipienda sunt, et ad sanctificationem fidelium praeparata sunt. Nam et quaedam sacramenta militaria dicuntur, quibus milites in sua conditione imperatori suo ad fidem conservandam obligantur; et infideles

---

[36] *Misc.* II, tit. 63 (*MPL* 177, col. 625). The *Miscellanea* is a collection of materials arranged into a theological synthesis, purportedly from Hugh's writings; but Glorieux, *Pour revaloriser Migne*, p. 70, lists the bulk of the work as not authentic.

[37] *De sacr.* I, pars 8, c. 11 (*MPL* 176, col. 313C). Cf. the preceding discussion which defines the active justice of God : I, pars 8, c. 11 (cols. 310 f.). Here Hugh seeks to show that God acts justly whether he punishes or justifies a sinner—the thought is developed, similar to the common doctrine of the commentaries, that the sinner is just not by his own justice, but "quia sine justitia sua per solam gratiam justitiam accipit." For Hugh, then, justification is by grace, and not by human merit.

quoque sacramenta quaedam habent, quae sacramenta dicuntur, quamvis nec sacra sint, nec sacrae rei signa. Sed exsecrationes potius et abominationes : quibus non sacrantur homines, sed polluuntur. Tamen ad horum differentiam sacramenta fidei dicta intelligi possunt quae a fidelibus tractantur, et cum fide ad sanctificationem suscipiuntur. Primum ergo consideramus qua ratione ipsa fides sacramentum dicatur, vel cujus rei sacramentum esse intelligatur, Apostolus dicit : "Videmus nunc per speculum in aenigmate, tunc autem facie ad faciem (I Cor. 13:12)." ... Sed quod est aenigma, et quod est speculum in quo videtur imago donecipsa res videri possit? Aenigma est Scriptura sacra. Quare? quia obscuram habet significationem. Speculum est cor tuum, si tamen mundum fuerit et extersum et clarificatum. Imago in speculo fides in corde tuo. Ipsa enim fides imago est, et sacramentum. Contemplatio autem futura, res et virtus sacramenti. Qui fidem non habent nihil vident; qui fidem habent jam aliquid videre incipiunt, sed imaginem solam. Si enim fidelis nihil videret, ex fide illuminatio non esset, nec dicerentur illuminati fideles. Si autem jam ipsam rem viderent, et non amplius videndum aliquid exspectarent, non per speculum in aenigmate, sed facie ad faciem viderent. Ergo qui per fidem vident, imaginem vident; qui per contemplationem vident, rem vident. Qui fidem habent, sacramentum habent; qui contemplationem habent, rem habent. Fides ergo sacramentum est futurae contemplationis, et ipsa contemplatio res et virtus sacramenti; et accipimus nunc interim sacramentum sanctificandi, ut perfecte sanctificati, rem ipsam capere possimus. Si ergo summum bonum hominis contemplatio creatoris sui merito creditur, non inconvenienter fides per quem absentem videre quodammodo incipit, initium boni, et principium restaurationis ejus memoratur. Quae videlicet restauratio secundum incrementa fidei crescit, dum homo per agnitionem amplius illuminatur, ut plenius agnoscat, et inflammatur per dilectionem, ut ardentius diligat. Sic ergo justus, quandiu in hoc corpore existens, peregrinatura Domino, vivere habet ex fide, quemadmodum cum eductus de hoc ergastulo fuerit, et introductus, in gaudium Domini sui vivere habebit ex contemplatione. Sed mira Dei dispensatione agitur quod nunc malitia interim hostis antiqui ad persequendos et impugnandos fideles relaxatur, quatenus videlicet hoc homini reputetur pro merito; si nunc per fidem ambulans, viam veritatis etiam impugnatus non deserat, qui prius visione praesentis Dei roboratus, sola persuatione prostratus erat. Ut autem in hoc praelio invictus stare possit, et bonum suum illaesum custodire, dantur ei at dictum est in sacramentis arma, quibus se muniat; in operibus bonis tela quibus hostem prosternat, ut scilicet fidei charitate et spe adjuncta, interius pariter roboretur et vivat.[38]

Hugh, then, approaches a concept of *sola fides* in his notion of faith as justifying and sanctifying, but in effect rejects it as insufficient—the sacraments are necessary as 'weapons' against the 'ancient enemy', i.e., the Devil. In later contexts, the paramount emphasis is the usual sacramental interpretation of justification. For example, in the section *Quando institutum sit sacramentum baptismi*, Hugh compares a justifi-

---

[38] *De sacr.* I, pars 8, c. 8-9 (cols. 341-344); cf. II, pars 9, c. 1 (col. 473A.)

cation in the Old Testament sacrament of circumcision with justification in baptism; the burden of the argument is indicated in the conclusion :

Propterea autem quia obscurum signum fuit emundationis in decimatione, data est circumcisio ut virtutem justificationis evidentius demonstraret, quando dictum est homini, ut portionem carnis suae, non quidem superfluam, sed illius quod superfluum erat in homine, signum auferret, ut per hoc agnosceret quod culpam quam natura per illam partem corporis traheret, gratia per sacramentum circumcisionis emundaret. Sed quia circumcisio eas tantum quae foris sunt enormitates amputare potest, eas vero quae intrinsecus sunt pollutionum sordes mundare non potest, venit post circumcisionem lavacrum aquae totum purgans, ut perfecta justitia signaretur. Rursus quia prioris populi qui sub timore serviebat mundatio laboriosa fuit, propterea sacramentum circumcisionis in carne quae dolorem habet illi datum est. Novo autem populo qui voluntate et dilectione servit, sacramentum justificationis in lavacro aquae, quae suavem habet purificationem propositum est; et sic quidem rationem reddendam existimamus pro eo quod sacramentum circumcisionis mutatum est, et sacramentum baptismi institutum.[39]

Similarly, the purpose of confession in justification :

Antiqua lex peccata confiteri jubet, et homines ad sacerdotes mittit ut confiteantur peccata sua, ut indulgentiam accipiant. Illic ergo praevaricatio legis confessione et oblatione aboletur, quando adhuc umbra fuit, et adhuc confessio criminis poenam potius timere debuit, quam misericordiam exspectare. Si haec auctoritas non sufficit, audite Scripturam alibi manifeste dicentem : "Qui abscondit scelera sua non justificabitur (Prov. 28:13)." Quid enim est abscondere nisi tacere, et confiteri nolle? Nam qui scelera sua per impudentiam prave agendi manifestant, non justificationem merentur sed damnationem. Igitur tegenda sunt mala quantum pertinet ad impudentiam pravi operis, et revelanda sunt per humilitatem confessionis. ...
... Confitemini alterutrum peccata vestra, et orate pro invicem. Ad quid? Ut salvemini. Confitemini ut salvemini. Quid est confitemini ut salvemini? Hoc est non salvamini, nisi confiteamini. Hoc fortassis tu audire noluisti, quia latebras quaeris et abscondis scelera tua ut non justificeris. Non tibi placet quod dicitur, quod ii qui confiteri nolunt peccata sua salvari non possunt; propterea fortassis conaris ad aliud dictum Apostoli intorquere, ut intelligatur confitentibus non negasse justificationem. Audi ergo. Augustinus dicit : Non potest quis justificari a peccato, nisi confessus fuerit ante peccatum. Item Beda in eamdem epistolam Jacobi de qua superius testimonium sumpsimus. Sine confessione, inquit, nequeunt dimitti peccata. Sed in hoc illa discretio esse debet, ut quotidiana leviaque peccata alterutrum coaequalibus confiteamur, ut orationibus invicem salvemur. Porro gravioris leprae immunditiam sacerdoti pandamus, et ad ejus arbitrium justificari curemus.[40]

---

[39] De sacr. II, pars 6, c. 3 (col. 449).
[40] De sacr. II, pars 14, c. 1 (cols. 550-553); cf. II, pars 14, c. 4 (col. 559A).

The quotation above attributed to Augustine ("Non potest quis justificari a peccato, nisi confessus fuerit ante peccatum") requires a digression since it assumed some importance through further authoritative quotation. It appears, with the same attribution, along with the following quotation from Bede, in a sermon of Richard of St. Victor (*ob.* 1173).[41] Abelard has it in his *Sic et non*, prefaced with the citation "Augustinus lib. I De poenitentia". He is doubly wrong, having both the wrong author, who was Ambrose (the *De poenitentia* was at that time known to be Ambrosian) and the wrong title, since it is in another of Ambrose's works. But Abelard at least correctly followed the text in question by placing after it Ambrose's proof-text of Isaiah 43:26 ("Dic iniquitates tuas, ut justificeris").[43] Gratian commences the sections of the *Decretum* on penance with this quotation and the Isaiah proof-text, but here gives the correct and precise citation to Ambrose's *Liber de paradiso*, c. 29.[43] Peter Lombard also has it in the *Sentences* with correct attribution.[44] St. Bernard paraphrases the quotation in one of his writings without indication of source.[45] This *obiter dicta* of Ambrose thus acquired an immense authority, especially from its use in the *Decretum* and *Sentences*, and is the most important single piece of evidence to be presented in this study for the medieval understanding of justification as especially inhering in the sacrament of penance. It is also an example of the numerous patristic authorities which are cited by all medieval writers on penance—it is ironic that the patristic arguments, which were formulated in support of the ancient public penance, could now be vigorously applied with perfect consistency to the newer system of sacerdotal confession and private penance. A conspicuous example is the *Liber de misericordia et justitia* of Alger of Liège

---

[41] It appears as Sermo 54 among dubious works of Hugh of St. Victor (*MPL* 177, col. 1051A); Glorieux, *Pour revaloriser Migne*, p. 70, now attributes it to Richard.

[42] *Sic et non*, c. 51 (*MPL* 178, col. 1599A). É. Amann in his *DTC* art. (vol. 12, col. 734) was unfortunately misled by Abelard and states that Abelard quotes the "classic phrase" from the pseudo-Augustinian *De vera et falsa poenitentia* (MPL 40, cols. 1113 *et seq.*), emending Abelard's citation as a reference to that work. The phrase appears nowhere in this work, which was, however, taken as Augustinian and quoted by all important writers on penance, despite the fact that in one place the anonymous author quotes Augustine and cites it as such. It is now generally dated as eleventh century (Glorieux, *Pour revaloriser Migne*, p. 29).

[43] *De poenitentia*, Dist. I, c. 38 (*Decret.* pars II, causa 33, quaest. 3 [*MPL* 187, col. 1532A]). In Ambrose, *loc. cit.* above (*MPL* 14, col. 328).

[44] *Sent.* IV, Dist. 17, c. 1 (*MPL* 192, col. 880).

[45] *Tractatus de interiori domo seu de conscientia aedificanda*, c. 1 (*MPL* 184, col. 509B).

(*ca.* 1070-*ca.* 1131), a *catena* of patristic authorities arranged under the heading of *quaestiones*, many of which are on penance. An interesting example quotes Augustine on justification :

Ipse autem Dominus cum in templo orarent Publicanus et Pharisaeus, peccatorem confitentem peccata sua magis justificatum dicit, quam Pharisaeum jactantem merita sua. Quanquam enim justificatus destiterit esse peccator, tamen ut justificaretur orabat, et peccata confitebatur. Exauditur, justificatus est. Non desineret esse peccator nisi prius exaudiretur peccator.[46]

Two further passages from Richard of St. Victor may be added to the quotation of Ambrose cited above. In the same sermon, Richard continues to say :

In facienda autem confessione talis discretio esse debet, ut quotidiana leviaque peccata alterutrum coaequalibus confiteamur, ut orationibus pro invicem factis salvemur. Porro gravioris leprae immunditiam sacerdoti, id est nostro summo praelato, scilicet abbati, pandere debemus, ut ad ejus arbitrium justificari curemus.[47]

He is here, of course, elaborating on the passage of Hugh's *De sacramentis* quoted above. Another sermon of interest does not directly concern penance, but rather discusses justifying faith in terms of the Augustinian 'faith working through love'; note the definition of *sola fides* :

Fides origo est in nobis ac fundamentum virtutum et bonorum operum. Unde ut ait Apostolus : "Sine fide impossibile est placere Deo (Hebr. 11:6)." Fides ei in sola cognitione sit non sufficit, nisi per dilectionem vivificetur et ex dilectione, si possit, operetur. Si non potest operari, si habeat dilectionem, ipsa dilectio ei est operatio. ... Sola ergo fides, illa fides dicendo est cui comas est dilectio, et quae per dilectionem, si tamen potest, operatur. ... Haec est enim quae justificat, "quae", secundum Apostolum, "per dilectionem operatur (Gal. 5:6)".[48]

In St. Bernard of Clairvaux (1090-1153) one encounters, as in Abelard, one of the truly original theologians of the Middle Ages. He is impossible to categorically classify in any general scheme of the history of dogma. There are indubitable traces of evangelical doctrine in his theology which have attracted the attention of Protestant historians, notably Ritschl, yet in relationship to progressive tendencies in the theology of his day he was implacably conservative and anti-intellectualist.

---

[46] *MPL* 180, col. 888D, quoting Aug., *Contra epistolam Parmeniani* II, c. 8, n. 17 (*MPL* 43, col. 61), interpreting Luke 18:10-14.

[47] Sermo 53 (*MPL* 177, col. 1051C).

[48] Sermo 35 (*MPL* 177, col. 984).

He was, it will be remembered, the most relentless opponent of Abelard, to the point of unscrupulous violation of canon law in securing the condemnation of Abelard at the Council of Sens (1141). The same paradoxical character of Bernard as mystic theologian and as ultraconservative churchman is also manifested in his ideas on justification. Ritschl has demonstrated this in his classic *Christian Doctrine of Justification and Reconciliation*.[49] Ritschl cites *De gratia et libero arbitrio* to show how Bernard stressed grace as the immanent principle of the Christian life in his discussion of the concept of merit. On the orthodox side, Bernard states that it is the free will that is saved and that the bestowal of grace is brought about by the active consent of the will—merits deserve to be rewarded on account of this cooperation of the free will with grace. But Bernard refers this concurrence of man's will and grace to a prior perfecting of the will which is also a work of grace. Hence, at the conclusion, Bernard can say on the subject of justification :

Quis est qui ignorat Dei justitiam? Qui se ipsum justificat. Quis est qui se ipsum justificat? Qui merita sibi aliunde, quam a gratia praesumit. Caeterum, qui fecit quod salvaret, etiam dat unde salvet. ...
... Deus igitur auctor est meriti, qui et voluntatem applicat operi, et opus explicat voluntatis. Alioquin, si proprie appellentur ea, quae dicimus nostra merita; spei quaedam sunt seminaria, charitatis incentiva, occultae praedestinationis indicia, futurae felicitatis praesagia, via regni, non causa regnandi. Denique, quos justificavit, non quos justos invenit, hos et magnificavit (Rom. 8:30).[50]

Yet in other places St. Bernard enjoins works for salvation. One example given by Ritschl which expresses this in relation to justification, *Sermones de diversis* 105, distinguishes between justification and glorification, and holds that the former demands our effort :

Duo sunt in quibus consistit nostra salus, justificatio et glorificatio. Altera initium, altera perfectio est. In illa labor, in hac autem fructus laboris est. Et nunc quidem justificatio fit per fidem; nam glorificatio erit per speciem. ... Ipsa est enim via, per quam fit transitus ad glorificationem, dicente Apostolo : "Quos praedestinavit, hos et vocavit; et quos vocavit, hos es justificavit; quos autem justificavit, hos et magnificavit (Rom. 8:30)." Neque enim poterit obtineri magnificatio, nisi justificatio praecesserit; cum ista meritum, illa praemium sit. ...
Notandum autem, quod sicut in illo beatitudinis regno praesentem se electis suis exhibebit Dominus ad glorificationem, ita etiam se eisdem ipsis exhibet in via peregrinationis ad justificationem; ut a quo scilicet glorificandi sunt

[49] Vol. 1, *A Critical History*, pp. 90 f., 95-101.
[50] *De grat. et lib. arbit.*, c. 14, nos. 48, 51 (*MPL* 182, cols. 1027C, 1030A).

per speciem, ab ipso prius justificentur per fidem. Et quidem tria sunt, a quibus abstinere debent quicunque justificari desiderant. Primo utique, ab operibus pravis; secundo, a carnalibus desideriis; tertio, a curis saeculi. Item tria sunt, quibus debent insistere, quae etiam continet sermo Domini in monte (Matt. 5-7) : eleemosyna, jejunium, oratio. Sic enim adimpletur justificatio, dum ab interdictis vitiis abstinent, et bona quae praecepta sunt fideliter exercent.[51]

Ritschl cites other passages where justification is regarded in the traditional medieval sense as remission of sins; e.g., in his polemic against Abelard :

Itaque ubi reconciliatio, ibi remissio peccatorum. Et quid ipsa, nisi justificatio? Sive igitur reconciliatio, sive remissio peccatorum, sive justificatio sit; sive etiam redemptio, vel liberatio de vinculis diaboli a quo captivi tenebamur ad ipsius voluntatem : intercedente morte Unigeniti obtinemus, justificati gratis in sanguine ipsius ...[52]

Another sermon can be cited to show that this is how St. Bernard basically understood Paul, yet again referring all merit to grace :

Hoc est testimonium quod perhibet in corde tuo Spiritus sanctus, dicens : Dimissa sunt tibi peccata tua. Sic enim arbitratur Apostolus, gratis justificari hominem per fidem (Rom. 3:28). Ita de meritis quoque si credis non posse haberi nisi per ipsum, non sufficit, donec tibi perhibeat testimonium Spiritus veritatis, quia habes ea per illum. Sic et de vita aeterna habeas necesse est testimonium Spiritus, quod ad eam divino sis munere perventurus. Ipse enim peccata condonat, ipse donat merita, et praemia nihilominus ipse redonat.[53]

A parallel example is interesting in that Ritschl cites the following for Bernard's traditionalism :

Sic ergo omne quod erat angelis, factus est nobis. Quid? Sapientia, justitia, sanctificatio, redemptio. Sapientia in praedicatione, justitia in absolutione peccatorum, sanctificatio in conversatione, quam habuit cum peccatoribus; redemptio in passione, quam sustinuit pro peccatoribus. Ubi ergo haec a Deo factus est; tunc Ecclesia odorem sensit, tunc cucurrit.[54]

But Loofs points out that this sermon continues with an amplification which this latter historian considers a correct expression of the Pauline concept :

---

[51] *MPL* 183, cols. 731 f. The same concept is in *Tractatus de conscientia*, c. 1 (*MPL* 184, col. 554B).

[52] *Tractatus de erroribus Abaelardi*, c. 8, no. 29 (*MPL* 182, col. 1069C).

[53] *In festo annuntiationis B. Mariae* Sermo I, n. 3 (*MPL* 183, col. 384A).

[54] *Sermones in Cantica Canticorum* 22, n. 6 (*MPL* 183, col. 880D). According to Melanchthon, this passage deeply influenced Luther (see E. G. Schwiebert, *Luther and His Times* [St. Louis : Concordia, 1950], p. 171).

Et primo quidem veritatis doctor depulit umbram ignorantiae tuae luce sapientiae suae. Per justitiam deinde, quae ex fide est, solvit funes peccatorum, gratis justificans peccatorem. ... Addidit quoque sancte inter peccatores vivere, et sic tradere formam vitae, tanquam viae, qua redires ad patriam. Ad cumulum postremo pietatis tradidit in mortem animam suam, et de proprio latere protulit pretium satisfactionis, quo placaret Patrem ... Quamobrem quisquis pro peccatis compunctus esurit et sitit justitiam, credat in te qui justificas impium, et solam justificatus per fidem, pacem habebit ad Deum.[55]

These apparent contradictions in doctrine may be variously explained. Loofs considers this a result of the mystic orientation of Bernard's theology, in which contrarieties in systematics are of little consequence. Ritschl gives a more analytical interpretation, stating that Bernard's idea of grace is two-fold : in a moral sense, merit and forgiveness can be earned by virtue of man's free exercise of the will, but in a religious sense (and this, presumably, would be St. Bernard's ultimate thought), all of man's activity for good originates in grace. And, Ritschl maintains, it is in this religious aspect that Bernard occasionally rises to the level of Reformation thought.[56] It is probably impossible to make a definitive judgement between the views of these two eminent historians of dogma, by the nature of the case—the saintly temperament is not amenable to objective explanation and any scholarly comment can only illuminate one or another of the shifting modes of St. Bernard's mystic theology. One can, however, add to the stock of paradoxes. In a letter written to a certain young man named Thomas, St. Bernard urged him to fulfill his vow to enter Clairvaux; in a style of great fervor, the saint counsels the prospective monk to seek after his justification :

Prodit in lucem ad miseri consolationem magnum consilium, quod ad aeterno latuerat in sinu aeternitatis : quod nolit videlicet Deus mortem peccatoris, sed magis ut convertatur et vivat. Habes, homo, hujus arcani indicem spiritum justificantem, eoque ipso testificantem spiritui tuo, quod filius Dei et ipse sis. Agnosce consilium Dei in justificatione tui; confitere et dic, "Consilium meum justificationes tuae (Ps. 118:24)." Praesens namque justificatio tui, et divini est consilii revelatio, et quaedam ad futuram gloriam praeparatio. Aut certe praedestinatio ipsa potius praeparatio est, justificatio autem magis jam appropinquatio. Denique ait : "Agite poenitentiam, quia appropinquavit regnum coelorum (Matt. 3:2)." ...

Cum ergo geminum teneamus nostrae salutis indicium, geminam sanguinis et Spiritus effusionem, neutra sine altera prodest. Nam nec Spiritus datur

---

[55] Ibid., nos. 7-8 (col. 881); Loofs, Leitfaden, p. 427.

[56] Both Loofs and Ritschl give much more documentation than I have included here; I have selected only those passages where Bernard makes specific use of the term justificatio.

nisi credentibus in Crucifixum, nec fides valet, si non operatur ex dilectione. Dialectio autem donum Spiritus est. Quod si secundus homo (Christum loquor) factus est non solum in animam viventem, sed etiam in spiritum vivificantem, ex uno videlicet moriens, ex altero mortuos suscitans; quid mihi prodesse potest quod in ipso moritur, absque eo quod vivificat? Denique ipse ait : "Caro non prodest quidquam, Spiritus est qui vivificat (Joan. 6:64)." Quid est autem, "vivificat", nisi, justificat? Cum enim mors animae peccatum sit, (anima quippe quae peccaverit ipsa morietur [Ezech. 18:4]); vita ejus sine dubio justitia est, quoniam justus ex fide vivit. Justus autem quis est, nisi qui amanti se Deo vicem rependit amoris? quod non fit nisi revelante Spiritu per fidem homini aeternum Dei propositum super sua salute futura. Quae sane revelatio non est aliud quam infusio gratiae spiritualis, per quam, dum facta carnis mortificantur, homo ad regnum praeparatur, quid caro et sanguis non possident; simul accipiens in uno Spiritu, et unde se praesumat amatum, et unde redamet, ne gratis amatus sit.

Hoc itaque est illud sacrum secretumque consilium, quod a Patre Filius in Spiritu sancto accipiens, suis, quos novit, per eundem Spiritum, justificando eos, communicat, et communicando justificat : quando id quisque accipit in sui justificatione, ut incipiat et ipse cognoscere, sicut et cognitus est; cum videlicet datur et ipsi praesentire aliquid de sua ipsius futura beatitudine, quemadmodum ab aeterno latuit in praedestinante, plenius appariturum in beatificante.[57]

The following, which places St. Bernard within the tradition traced here of associating justification with penance, has a less evangelical ring than the context of the exhortation *agite poenitentiam* in the letter above :

Homo igitur per veritatem stimulatus, peccata sua confitetur : Deus autem per misericordiam flexus, confitenti miseretur. Omnis namque spes veniae et misericordiae in confessione est, nec potest quis justificari a peccato, nisi prius fuerit confessus peccatum. Ex eo enim unusquisque justus esse incipit, ex quo sui accusator exstiterit.[58]

It is perhaps not inappropriate to note the opinion of Bernard's equally original contemporary against whom Bernard carried through a successful prosecution for heresy. Although Abelard approved of sacerdotal confession, he was highly critical of current practices with regard to the confessional. Further, he denied the sacerdotal power of binding and loosing, limiting the confessor to aiding and advising concerning the nature of satisfaction for offenses committed. Abelard's rejection of the Power of the Keys is consistent with the doctrine of the Atonement in his Romans commentary. He declares that repentance

---

[57] Ep. 109 (*MPL* 182, cols. 246 f.); Eng. tr. in *The Letters of St. Bernard of Clairvaux*, tr. B. S. James (Chicago : Regnery, 1953), pp. 162 f.

[58] *Tractatus de interiori domo* ..., c. 1 (*MPL* 184, col. 509B).

must spring from love of God alone; the subjective act which results from this pure motive, contrition, is sufficient to remove guilt and further absolution from a priest is not necessary.[59] (Abelard's other writings add nothing to the concept of justification in the commentary discussed in the previous chapter, hence he will not be further discussed here.)

The sublime tone, if somewhat ambiguous doctrine, of St. Bernard's mystic theology could not be sustained within the general dogmatic synthesis of medieval theology. The rare and extremely personal spirituality of this saint could not be readily imitated, nor could his thought be reduced to the systematic exposition essential for the foundation of a distinct school of theology. Nor were the patently suspect views of Abelard widely received. For the most authoritative statements of the positive theology of the period it is necessary to turn to two key works which, together with Irenaeus' gloss on the Roman law, mark the summit of the intellectual renaissance of the twelfth century. These are Gratian's *Decretum* and the *Sentences* of Peter Lombard. The former work was accepted as the standard codification of canon law which, with subsequent additions by later popes, was the official church law of the Roman Church until 1917; the latter work was the basic text-book of theology until the Reformation. Both works are also a culmination of the development of the dialectic method in early scholasticism and the method of reconciling conflicting authorities pioneered in Abelard's *Sic et non*; the method of the two works is well described by the formal title of Gratian's collection : *Concordia discordantium canonum*. Both are massive compilations of legal and theological materials ranging in authority from Scripture to decrees of local synods, all systematically arranged and duly considered in accordance with their relative weight of authority.

Each has an extensive section on penance. There are numerous points of correspondence between the two, in materials as well as method, and it has been established that Lombard was working after and often following Gratian on this topic.[60] An example has already been cited,

---

[59] *Scito teipsum*, c. 25 (*MPL* 178, col. 669D). See, for a full discussion of the point, Sikes, *Peter Abailard*, pp. 193-200; Sikes states (p. 193) that Abelard, by expressing these views, was "the first theologian to make penance a part of theology"; he was certainly the first since ancient times to explore its *rationale* in detail, and his conclusions exhibit his usual originality and iconoclasm. Cf. Harnack, *Hist. of Dogma* VI, 243, n. 3; 244, n. 2,

[60] J. de Ghellinck, *Le mouvement théologique du XIIe siècle*, 2d ed. (Bruges : Éditions "De Tempel", 1948), pp. 470 f.

the common quotation in Gratian, Lombard, and others of the dictum : "Non potest justificari a peccato, nisi confessus fuerit ante peccatum."

It is necessary to observe, however, that Gratian himself leaves open the question of the necessity of confession for remission of sin.[61] He was too acute and honest a scholar to overlook those passages in Augustine and other patristic authorities which tend to deny this necessity. The problem seems to arise because Gratian did not appreciate the difference between the ancient public penance and the broader medieval system which included both mortal and venial sins—this considerably affected his interpretation of patristic authorities who were writing of two different things, public penance for mortal sin and personal prayers of confession for trivial sins, which Gratian took as one. However, in accordance with his method he makes a case for both sides. It is a portion of the affirmative argument which is of concern in the following excerpt. The passages relevant to justification commence with the Ambrosian quotation noted above. Gratian then places next a second excerpt from Ambrose :

C. XXXIX. Idem *in serm. I. Quadragesimae.*

Ecce nunc tempus acceptabile adest, in quo confessio a morte animam liberat, confessio aperit paradisum, confessio spem salvandi tribuit. Unde scriptura dicit : "Dic tu iniquitates tuas ut justificeris." His verbis ostenditur, quia non meretur justificari qui in vita sua peccata non vult confiteri. Illa ergo confessio nos liberat, quae fit cum poenitentia. ...[62]

Gratian later sums up the affirmative case, beginning as follows :

IV. Pars. Gratian. Ex his apparet, quod sine confessione oris et satisfactione operis peccatum non remittitur. Nam si necesse est, ut iniquitates nostras dicamus, ut postea justificemur; si nemo potest justificari a peccato, nisi antea confessus fueris peccatum; si confessio paradisum aperit, veniam acquirit; si illa solum confessio utilis est, quae fit cum poenitentia, in quo notatur aliud esse confessio, aliud poenitentia, sive interior sive exterior accipiatur; si ille, qui promittit veniam occulte apud Deum non apud ecclesiam poenitentiam

---

[61] *De poenit.* Dist. I, c. 89 (*MPL* 187, col. 1562; Friedberg, *Corpus iuris*, t. 1, col. 1189). (I give references here to that part of the *Decretum* [pars 1, causa 33, quaestiones 3-4] which is subtitled *Tractatus de poenitentia*; it is thought that this may have been a separate, earlier work which Gratian incorporated bodily into the *Decretum*. I also give parallel references to the standard critical edition of A. Friedberg, *Corpus iuris canonici* [Leipzig, 1879 : repr. Graz : Akademische Druck- u. Verlagsanstalt, 1955]). Cf. Watkins, *Hist. of Penance*, vol. 2, p. 774 f.

[62] *De poenit.* Dist. I, c. 39 (*MPL* 187, col. 1532A; Friedberg, *Corpus iuris*, t. 1, col. 1167). The quotation is Ambrose, Sermo 25 (*MPL* 17, col. 676); there is some doubt as to its authenticity since the main evidence is citation here and in Peter Lombard.

agenti, frustratur evangelium et claves dates ecclesiae, promittit etiam quod Deus negat delinquenti; si nemo potest consequi veniam, nisi quantulam cunque, etsi minorem quam debeat, peccati solverit poenam; si solis sacerdotibus ligandi solvendique potestas a Deo tradita est; si nullus veniam accipit, nisi ecclesiae supplicationibus ipsam impetrare contendat : concluditur ergo, quod nullus ante confessionem oris et satisfactionem operis peccati abolet culpam.[63]

There is another important context which further evidences Gratian's definition of justification as remission of sins (Gratian here is specifically adjusting the concepts of God's justice and foreknowledge, following the solution of St. Bernard by distinguishing between justification—which can occur in this life—and glorification in eternal life) :

Gratian. Secundum justitiam deletur qui gratia subtracta ea operari permittitur, quibus aeternam damnationem meretur. Hinc Propheta loquens ex persona Christi ait : "Deleantur de libro viventium," hoc est : subtrahatur eis gratia, qua subtracta ii in profundum vitiorum, deinde in aeternam damnationem praecipitentur, "et cum justis non scribantur", id est non apponatur eis gratia, qua fiant digni aeterna salute. Sic itaque peccata secundum praescientiam remittuntur, quum ab aeterna gratia preparentur, qua vocatus justificatur, justificatus tandem aeternaliter glorifietur. Secundum justitiam vero peccata remittuntur, quum vel baptisma plana fide accipitur, vel poenitentia toto corde celebratur, quae remissio et ipsa secundum praescientiam non inconvenienter fieri dicitur. Ut enim ex praemissa auctoritate Apostoli datur intelligi, duae sunt praeordinationes : una, qua quisque praeordinatur hic ad justitiam et remissionem peccatorum percipiendam; altera, qua aliquiis praedestinatur ad vitam aeternam in futuro obtinendam. Harum effectus sunt praesens justificatio, et futura glorificatio, quae omnia in praemissa auctoritate convenienter distinguuntur.[64]

Peter Lombard, in contrast to Gratian, definitely commits himself to the necessity of confession, or at least the intention of oral confession (to accommodate death-bed situations where time may be insufficient to summon a confessor). Also significant is the fact that he discusses penance as a sacrament—part of the historic importance of the *Sentences* is that it contains the first categorical enumeration of the seven sacraments of the Roman Catholic Church. There is also a definitive statement of the doctrine of the Power of the Keys which earlier theologians had been developing as the foundation of the sacerdotal power of remission in the confessional. His important *distinctio* defining penance begins as follows, with the tag from Jerome common in the literature since Alcuin :

[63] *Ibid.*, c. 60 (*MPL* 189, cols. 1541 f.; Friedberg, *Corpus iuris*, t. 1, cols. 1233 f.).
[64] *De poenit.* Dist. IV, c. 10 (*MPL* 187, cols. 1624 f.; Friedberg, *Corpus iuris*, t. 1, cols. 1233 f.).

Distinctio XIV. De Poenitentia.

1. Post haec, de Poenitentia agendum est. Poenitentia longe positis a Deo necessaria est, ut propinquent. Est enim, ut ait Hieron., secunda tabula post naufragium, quia si quis vestem innocentiae in Baptismo perceptam peccando corruperit, Peonitentiae remedio reparate potest. Prima tabula est Baptismus, ubi deponitur vetus homo, et induitur novus; secunda, Poenitentia, qua post lapsum resurgimus, dum vetustas reversa repellitur, et novitas perdita resumitur. Post Baptismum prolapsi per Poenitentiam renovari valent, sed non per Baptismum. Licet homini saepius poenitere, sed non baptizari. Baptismus tantum est sacramentum; sed Poenitentia dicitur et sacramentum, et virtus mentis. Est enim Poenitentia interior, et est exterior. Exterior, sacramentum; interior, virtus mentis est; et utraque causa salutis est et justificationis.[65]

The other important statement on justification in penance follows in a later *distinctio* where Lombard considers the question of the necessity of penance. Here he reproduces many of Gratian's authorities, along with material of his own, to support an affirmative conclusion; in this place he has both the Ambrosian quotations cited above in Gratian.[66] It deserves mention, however, that much the same dualism exists in the Lombard's theology as noted in St. Bernard. Several other *distinctiones* contain a purely theological interpretation of justification, heavily documented with quotations from Augustine familiar from the Pauline commentaries. His argument here completely subsumes justification by faith into the doctrine of merit. He commences by identifying justifying faith with prevenient grace or Augustinian *gratia operans* which 'prepares the human will to do good' :

Fides enim qua justificatus es, gratis tibi data est. Hic aperte ostenditur quod fides est causa justificationis, et ipsa est gratia et beneficium quo hominis praevenitur voluntas et praeparatur.[67]

He then proceeds to identify this *gratia voluntatem proveniens* with the Augustinian *fides cum dilectione.*[68] This done, in the next *distinctio* he continues the argument to a 'merited' justification :

Sicut, verbi gratia, ex fidei virtute et hominis arbitrio generatur in mente motus quidam bonus et remunerabilis, scilicet, ipsum credere; ita ex charitate et

---

[65] *Sent.* IV, Dist. 14, c. 1 (*MPL* 192, cols. 868 f.).

[66] *Ibid.* IV, Dist. 17, c. 1 (*MPL* 192, col. 880).

[67] *Sent.* II, Dist. 26, c. 4 (*MPL* 192, col. 711).

[68] This theme is elsewhere in pure Augustinian form, quoting the often cited distinction of degrees of belief (*credere in Deum, credere Deo, credere Deum*); e.g., *ibid.* III, Dist. 23, n. 4 (*MPL* 192, col. 805) :

Credere in Deum, est credendo amare, credendo in eum ire, credendo ei adhaerere et ejus membris incorporari. Per hanc idem justificatur impius, ut deinde ipsa fides incipiat per dilectionem operari.

libero arbitrio alius quidam motus bonus provenit, scilicet, diligere, bonus valde; sic de caeteris virtutibus intelligendum est. Et isti boni motus vel affectus merita sunt, et dona Dei, quibus meremur et ipsorum augmentationem, et alia quae consequenter hic et in futuro nobis apponuntur.

Ex qua ratione dicitur fides mereri justificationem et alia.

6. Cum ergo dicitur fides mereri justificationem et vitam aeternam, ex ea ratione dictum accipitur, quia per actum fidei meretur illa. ...[69]

Yet a third strain can be deduced from the Lombard's treatment of the Atonement, combining the primitive medieval concept of justification as remission of sins with the basic feature of Abelard's theory of the Atonement (an example of Abelard's limited but unmistakable influence in some areas of dogma) :

A diabolo ergo et a peccato per Christi mortem liberati sumus, quia ut ait Apostolus, Rom. 5, "in sanguine ipsius justificati sumus"; et in eo quod sumus justificati, id est, a peccato soluti, a diabolo sumus liberati, qui nos vinculis peccatorum tenebat. Sed quomodo a peccatis per ejus mortem soluti sumus? Quia "per ejus mortem", ut ait Apostolus, Rom. 8, "commendatur nobis charitas Dei", id est, apparet eximia et commendabilis charitas Dei erga nos in hoc quod Filium suum tradidit in mortem pro nobis peccatoribus. Exhibita autem tantae erga nos dilectionis arrha, et nos movemur accendimurque ad diligendum Deum, qui pro nobis tanta fecit; et per hoc justificamur, id est, soluti a peccatis justi efficimur. Mors ergo Christi nos justificat, dum per eam charitas excitatur in cordibus nostris. Dicimur quoque et aliter per mortem Christi justificari, quia per fidem mortis ejus a peccatis mundamur.[70]

Peter Lombard thus provided three possible lines of development. In the next century an integration of these disparate conceptions would be effected by St. Bonaventure and St. Thomas. But for the remainder of the twelfth century, the evidence suggests that the traditional idea of a penitential justification continued to dominate the thought of those few ecclesiastical writers who had occasion to make reference to the topic. Two such *loci* may be briefly cited, both from treatises on the sacraments.

Peter of Blois (*ob. post* 1204), a prominent English churchman and a prodigious, if not profound, writer, wrote a *Liber de confessione sacramentali*, a tract which sums up much of the Church's popular teaching on the subject. The following are significant excerpts :

Omnia sane in confessione lavantur; et sicut "corde creditur ad justitiam", ita oris "confessio fit ad salutem (Rom. 10:10)". Magna est confessionis virtus : quia, sicut beatus Ambrosius in libro De paradiso scribit : Confessio lavat animam, confessio aperit paradisum : haec est secunda post naufragium tabula, baptimus que poenitentiae.

[69] *Sent.* II, Dist. 27, cc. 5-6 (*MPL* 192, col. 715).

[70] *Ibid.* III, Dist. 19, c. 1 (*MPL* 192, col. 795).

Sciebat quod sicut Deus judex et ultor est culpas suas abscondentium, sic advocatus est confitentium. Nec melius causam nostram justificare possumus, quam si accusando et puniendo nos partes judicis exsequamur. Dic ergo iniquitates tuas, ut justificeris. Sicut enim testatur beatus Ambrosius : Confessio justificat, omnesque sordes, quas negligenter vita congessit, evacuat.[71]

Finally, a *quaestio* from the *Sententiae de sacramentis* of Petrus Manducator, written probably between 1165 and 1170, summarizes the basic opinion on the necessity of confession among the generation of churchmen after Lombard :

Queritur, utrum remittatur peccatum sine oris confessione et exterioris operis satisfactione.

Audi Ysaiam : "Dic tu iniquitates tuas, ut iustificeris" : quasi diceret, nisi dixeris non iustificaberis.

Item Ambrosius in libro *De paradiso* : "Non potest quisquam iustificari a peccato, nisi peccatum fuerit ante confessus."

Idem : "Confessio liberat animam a morte. Confessio aperit paradisum. Confessio tribuit spem salutis, quia non meretur iustificari qui in vita sua peccatum non vult confiteri."

Item Augustinus, super illum locum : "Non absorbeat me profundum," etc. : "Puteus," inquit, "est profundum iniquitatis, in quem si cecideris, non claudet super te puteus os suum, nisi clauseris os tuum. Confitere ergo et dic : De profundis clamavi," etc., "et evades." Claudit autem super illum qui existens in profundo peccatorum negligit ea et contempnit.

Item, quod sine exteriori satisfactione nemo liberatur a peccato, testatur Augustinus : "Nemo," inquit, "debite pene accipit veniam, nisi qualemcumque, etsi longe minorem quam debeat, solverit penam."

Hiis auctoritatibus probatur, quod nullus sine oris confessione et exteriori satisfactione solvitur a peccato. Si vera sit contricio et votum habeat in mente confitendi, fit peccati remissio; oportet tamen confiteri si tempus habuerit. Nam qui negligit vel erubescit confiteri, non meretur iustificari.[72]

[71] *MPL* 207, cols. 1078C, 1079D, 1081D. A similar, less direct statement is in his Sermo 15 on penance and justice (cols. 603 f.).

[72] *Sententiae de sacramentis*, ed. R. M. Martin, O.P., in H. Weisweiler, S.J., *Maître Simon et son groupe De sacramentis : Textes inédits* (Louvain : *Spicilegium sacrum Lovaniense*, fasc. 17 [1937]), pp. 97 f. Another *locus* found in *MPL* is the following excerpt from a commentary on the Song of Songs by a Premonstratensian, Philip of Harvengt (*ca.* 1100-1182) :

Et quis audebit David beatum virum dicere, qui adulterium tam leviter commisit, et eidem adulterio, quod pejus est, homicidium copulavit? Sed secundum apostoli Pauli (I Cor. 6) vocem ablutus est, justificatus est, sanctificatus est in nomine Domini nostri et in Spiritu Dei nostri. Justificatus est, inquam, per confessionem quando ait ad Nathan prophetam: "Peccavi Domino, ora pro me"; et Nathan prophetam ad eum: "Noli, inquit, timere, nequaquam morte morieris, qui Dominus transtulit peccatum tuum a te (II Reg. 12)." Ecce quam velociter iste homo per confessionem ablutus est, justificatus est, sanctificatus est.

(*In Cantica Canticorum moralitates* V [*MPL* 203, col. 552B]).

CHAPTER IV

THE COMPLETION OF THE MEDIEVAL DOCTRINE :
THE *PROCESSUS JUSTIFICATIONIS*

Thus far, the concept of justification has been traced as it was transmitted through early medieval theology in a traditional association
with those sacraments pertaining to justification, baptism and penance.
The concept received little elaboration among theologians of this period,
with but rare exceptions such as St. Bernard and Peter Lombard. And
the imprecision with which the latter used the term shows that there
was no doctrine, properly speaking, of justification; it was never treated
as a special problem or as a discrete category in theological discussion,
nor did it give rise to any controversy.[1] Toward the end of the twelfth
century, however, there are indications of a re-examination of the tradition and an attempt to achieve an integrated doctrine in the matter.
This development is an important example signalling the beginnings
of that fundamental review and revision in all areas of theology which
formed the major task of the theologians of the high scholastic age and
ultimately issued in the great systems of the summists.

1. FIRST STATEMENTS

The appearance of a new doctrinal framework in which, at last,
a precise concept of justification was developed and applied as a major
component in systematic theology is associated with several doctors
of the emergent University of Paris, and approximately concurrent with
the rise of its theological faculty to the pre-eminent position it was to
enjoy until the close of the Middle Ages. This was the so-called *processus
justificationis*, for which priority apparently rests with Peter of Poitiers,
one of the prominent late twelfth-century theologians responsible for
the rise of Paris in theology; Peter was chancellor of the cathedral
school from 1193 until his death in 1205, occupying a key position of

[1] Cf. Rivière, art. "Justification", DTC 8, cols. 2106 f.

leadership during the transition period when the several Paris schools were formed into the University. In his commentary on Lombard's *Sentences*, Peter commences his discussion with a schematization of the component parts of the *processus* :

Sciendum est autem quod ad justificationem impii quatuor occurrunt : Infusio gratiae, motus surgens ex gratia et libero arbitrio, contritio, peccatorum remissio. Nullum istorum prius est aliquo eorumdem tempore, sed tamen naturaliter praecedit gratiae infusio et per ordinam sequuntur alia tria, non tempore, sed natura. Sciendum est autem quod quodlibet istorum quatuor dicitur justificatio, nec unum potest esse in homine sine aliis tribus.[2]

He then proceeds to a discussion of this scheme in relationship to grace and merit :

Cum autem Deus non det primam gratiam, ut dictum est, meritis, sed tantum gratis, inter praedictas quatuor justificationes, facienda est quaedam distinctio, non negligenter sed corde tenus retinenda. Primam igitur justificationem nec meremur nec ea meremur, secundam non meremur sed ea meremur, tertiam meremur et ea meremur; quartam meremur sed ea non meremur. Primam non meremur quia gratis datur, nec ea meremur, quia non meremur virtute, sed virtutis opere interiori vel exteriori; secundum, id est motum non meremur, nulla enim praecedunt merita, sed ea mere mur contritionem et peccatorum remissionem; tertiam, id est contritionem, meremur per motum, naturaliter non tempore praecedentem, et ea meremur quartam, id est peccatorum remissionem; quartam meremur per motum, per contritionem, sed ea non meremur.[3]

The next several pages of Peter's discussion are devoted to an explanation and demonstration of this position.

Landgraf's research has shown that there were a number of anticipations of Peter's theory,[4] including a threefold scheme proposed earlier, about mid-twelfth century, by the important Biblical scholar Peter Comestor (*ob. ca.* 1180) :

Tria enim sunt, in quibus iustificatio consistit, scilicet primarie gratie infusio, cordis contritio, peccati remissio. Prima iustificatio est, cum iustificatur impius, id est fit de impio pius. Iustificari non potest sine fundamento. Primo ergo infunditur ei fundamentum, id est fides. Sed, quia sine caritate non iustificatur, infunditur ei fides caritates [sic]. Et quam cito gratia infunditur, tam cito conteritur, tam cito ei peccatum remittitur. Vide ergo, quia hec tria non se precedunt tempore, sed causa; nam infusio gratie causa est contritionis; contritio causa est remissionis.[5]

---

[2] *Sententiarum libri quinque* III, c. 2 (*MPL* 211, col. 1044A).

[3] *Sent., loc. cit.* (col. 1045).

[4] Landgraf, *Dogmengesch.* I/1, pp. 287-302.

[5] In his commentary on Luke (Paris, Nat. Lat. 15269, fol. 44); quoted by Landgraf, *Dogmengesch.* I/1, p. 291, n. 11.

Iustificatio etiam in tribus consistit vel notatur: in gratia infusione, in liberi arbitrii cooperatione, tondem in consummatione : primum est incipientiem, secundum proficienteium, tertium pervenientium.[6]

But the four-fold schematization gained the field; Landgraf cites a number of theologians who took it up in the years around the turn of the thirteenth century, including Stephen Langton, Peter Cantor, Odo of Ourscamp, Roland of Cremona, and others, as well as in several anonymous collections of *Quaestiones*, indicating the popularity of the topic in the schools. It was then fully received into the tradition toward mid-century with its acceptance by the forerunners of St. Thomas Aquinas, such as the first of the summists, William of Auvergne in his *Summa aurea*,[7] and the first of the great Franciscan doctors, Alexander of Hales.[8]

---

[6] Sermo 17 (*MPL* 198, col. 1769); cited by Landgraf, *loc. cit.* Landgraf derives these passages from anticipations of a *processus justificationis* in at least two of the Biblical commentaries. He cites the following excerpt from Bruno the Cathusian's commentary on the Psalms (*MPL* 152, col. 1087A) :

Notandum, quod haec beneficia non narrat ordine : prius enim fuit a captivitate per fidem averti, postea vero peccata opereri et sic post iniquitatem remitti; et ad ultimum in bonis operibus et virtutibus benedici.

Also, a passage in the Romans commentary of Hervaeus Burgidolensis, on 3:20 (*MPL* 181, col. 642D) :

Per legem enim cognitio peccati, per fidem impetratio gratiae contra peccatum; per gratiam sanatio animae a vitio peccati; per animae sanitatem libertas arbitrii; per liberum arbitrium iustitiae dilectio; per iustitiae dilectionem legis operatio. Ac per hoc lex non destruitur, sed statuitur per fidem, quia fides impetrat gratiam, qua lex impleatur, gratia sanat voluntatem, qua iustitia libere diligatur.

[7] William discusses justification in connection with contrition and the role of free will in commentary on Books III and IV of the *Sentences* (*Summa aurea in quattuor libros sententiarum* [Paris, 1500], fols. 122r., 247v.).

[8] One *locus* in Alexander is especially illustrative of the kind of doctrinal questions discussed by these pre-Thomist writers. Here Alexander is discussing the differing operation of grace in the justification of a child (i.e., in baptism), of an adult convert, and the penitent believer. A portion of his argument follows :

De quatuor quae exiguntur ad iustificationem habetur etiam in illo Psalmo [59:4] : "Deus repulisti," versus : "Commovisti terram et conturbasti eam" etc. Unum est infusio gratiae, alterum motus liberi arbitrii in Deum, tertium motus contritionis sive detestationis in peccatum, quartum remissio peccati. Duo istorum sunt, Dei et duo hominis. Per hoc quod dicitur : "Commovisti terram", notatur motus liberi arbitrii a gratia. Per "conturbasti eam" notatur motus liberi arbitrii in peccatum. Per hoc : "quia commota est", motus liberi arbitrii in Deum. Per hoc : "sanat contritiones", notatur remissio peccati.

Quaeritur ergo quare haec quatuor exigantur, et quo ordine, et utrum sint simul tempore; et principaliter quaeritur utrum infusio gratiae sit prior quam remissio peccati vel e converso.—Praeterea, in quo differat iustificatio prout est in parvulo

By the time of St. Albert the Great, it was *opinio communis*; St. Albert could open one of his lengthy treatments with the words, "Dicitur ab omnibus, quod quatuor exigantur ad justificationem impii, scilicet infusio gratiae, motus liberi arbitrii in peccatum sive contritio, quod idem est, motus liberi arbitrii in Deum, et remissio peccati. ..."[9] It became a standard feature of commentaries on the *Sentences*, which were written by nearly every professor of theology in connection with his teaching duties; traditionally, the topic was discussed in comment at one of two places in the *Sentences*, either at *distinctio* 28 of Book II, or at Lombard's treatment of penance in Book IV, *dist.* 17. The further history of the fourfold scheme includes nearly every theologian of rank

---

et prout est in adulto; [item, prout est in adulto] converso ad fidem, prout est in poenitente fideli, prout est in exercitante se in operibus bonis ...

Per dicta etiam patet quod plura exiguntur ad iustificationem poenitentis fidelis quam parvuli vel conversi adulti. Exigitur enim infusio gratiae, quae communis est; et remissio peccati, quae similiter communis est, sed hic originalis peccati, ibi vero actualis. Exigitur motus liberi arbitrii, qui non est communis parvulo, sed adulto. Liberum autem arbitrium est "facultas rationis et voluntatis". Motus autem rationis principaliter exigitur in converso ad fidem; cui superadditur in poenitente motus voluntatis, ut satisfaciat secundum quod debet; ex quo, ex consequenti, requiritur motus in peccatum vel contra. Sic ergo remissio peccati fit per tria, in quibus figuratur opus Trinitatis; per gratiam, a qua potestas est vivificandi animam; et per motum rationis illuminatae per gratiam fidei; et per motum voluntatis detestantis peccatum : accensae per caritatem, paratae per iustitiam ad satisfaciendum. Primus actus est Patri appropriatus, secundus Filio, tertius Spiritui Sancto; remissio vero est actus communis.

The *quaestio* concludes with one of the earliest statements distinguishing *gratia gratis data* or prevenient grace and *gratia gratum faciens*, sanctifying grace :

Ad aliud dicimus quod gratiam est dupliciter considerare, et uno modo simul est cum remissione peccati, alio modo praecedit. Si enim accipiatur gratia gratum faciens, simul infunditur gratia et remittitur peccatum; et haec proprie dicitur gratia 'infusa'—Si vero sumatur gratia gratis data, quae superfunditur animae, illa potest esse prior tempore quam remissio peccati, et secundum hoc ista iam ordinata incipiunt a gratia gratis data et procedunt usque ad gratiam gratum facientem, et tunc oportet loqui de fide informi et iustitia informi.—Si vero omnia ista dicantur esse in gratia gratum faciente, aut sumetur remissio peccati quoad culpam, auto quoad poenam. Si primo modo, tunc simul tempore; secundum prius tamen et posterius natura sunt haec quatuor. Si vero de remissione quoad poenam, possunt esse secundum prius et posterius tempore sicut natura. Simul autem in instanti oportet esse infusionem gratiae gratum facientis et remissionem culpae quoad culpam.

(*Glossa in quatuor libros Sententiarum Petri Lombardi* IV, dist. 17, no. 7 [Bibliotheca Franciscana, tom. 15 (Quarrachi, 1957), pp. 275-278]).

[9] IV *Sent.*, dist. 17A, art. 10.

to the end of the fifteenth century, including St. Thomas, St. Bonaventure, Peter of Tarantasia, Richard of Middleton, and Duns Scotus; the basic scheme makes its last appearance in Gabriel Biel.[10] The *processus justificationis* formed the basic conceptual framework for the theology of penance as it was formulated and taught throughout the high and late scholastic periods.

What could explain the attraction, and durability, of this concept? Limiting our attention for the moment to the earlier sources in this tradition, the reasons are fairly obvious. An examination of these writers reveals that, while individual theologians developed variations of the system in detail, the range of problems discussed is essentially identical because of the solutions which this schematization could so usefully provide in bringing together disconnected strands in the theology of their common master, Peter Lombard, especially concerning fundamental problems concerning the operation of grace and free will, as well as special problems connected with the sacrament of penance, such as the nature of contrition.[11]

This is well illustrated in Peter of Poitiers himself; his first two "justifications" neatly integrate the concepts of prevenient and cooperating grace in relationship to free will, and at the same time retains a functional concept of faith in the *processus* (in other sources, faith is usually more directly equated with infused or "first" grace which initiates the process). Peter accomplishes this in the following passage (note that this author builds upon mere fragments of the Pauline text to make his case) :

Ad primam ergo justificationem refertur quod legitur : "Justificati estis gratis (Rom. 3)". Prima ergo gratia gratis datur non meritis; aliter enim non esset gratia. Ad eamdem refertur quod legitur : "Justificationem operatur Deus in homine sine homine", quod videtur esse falsum. Quam cito enim gratia infunditur, liberum arbitrium cooperatur eodem momento, et ita non est illa gratiae infusio sine homine. Ad quod dicendum quod haec praepositio, "in", duo potest notare, et comitantiam temporis et causam. Si "in" notet tempus, falsum est quod infusio gratiae sit sine homine, imo quando infunditur, cooperatur homo libero arbitrio; si vero notet causam, verum est causa quare ei infundatur gratia. Ad secundam justificationem, id est ad motum proce-

[10] Johann Auer, *Die Entwicklung der Gnadenlehre in der Hochscholastik* : 2. Teil, *Das Wirken der Gnade* (Freiburg : Herder, 1951), pp. 50 *et seq.*

[11] A comprehensive examination of these sources is impractical here; it would require a lengthy excursus into the vast topic of scholastic theories of grace, as well as the large controversial literature on contrition among modern Roman Catholic theologians. Probably the best synthetic treatment is, in addition to Landgraf, for the early scholastic period, Johann Auer, *Die Entwicklung der Gnadenlehre in der Hochscholastik*, 2 vols. (Freiburg : Herder, 1942 and 1951).

dentem ex libero arbitrio, et gratiam praecedentem, non tempore, sed natura, refertur quod dicitur : "Justificati estis ex fide (Rom. 5)", id est quia creditistis. Credere enim motus est proveniens ex fide et libero arbitrio.[12]

In the context following, the argument continues to state that the "third justification", contrition, proceeds from free will, resulting in remission of sins. Thus, all the desired phenomena are saved : justification by faith, by both species of Augustinian grace, and by human effort, all in an integrated, 'natural' process. Another important problem given a solution concerns the idea of merit : whether or not man can be said to merit remission of sins—and hence justification—or whether this is also given *gratis* (Landgraf finds this to be the issue of greatest concern in the literature he has surveyed). The answer in all of these writers, as illustrated in the previous quotation from Peter of Poitiers, is an ingenious combination of both a negative and positive answer.

This schematization was capable of adjustment in a variety of combinations to attain similar conclusions, reconciling both the evangelical and sacerdotal-ecclesiastical elements in the received doctrine on justification. The obvious objection to a modern reader is that these conclusions seem highly artificial, produced *ex machina*, as it were, by a sort of dialectical manipulation or sleight-of-hand, and the resulting doctrine seems highly remote from authentically spiritual sources of inspiration. But to a mind trained in the scholastic tradition, in which a highly exacting system of logic functioned as the core of all science, the cogency and, above all, the unity of this theory would have been overwhelming in its persuasiveness. The *processus justificationis* is noteworthy as the first attempt to deal with the concept of justification wholly within the framework of a systematic theology. And it also fulfilled the leading tendency of the tradition which has been traced in the previous chapter, the close identification of justification with the sacraments of baptism and, more especially, penance. The final two elements of the *processus*, contrition and remission of sins, refer directly to this latter sacrament, and indicate the genesis of the problem to which the *processus* was addressed—a clarification of the relationship of justifying grace to penance.[13] The summit of the pre-Thomist speculation on justification is therefore also a systematic theology of penance.

[12] *Sent.* III, c. 2 (*MPL* 211, col. 1044BC).
[13] This is also the opinion of Landgraf, *Dogmengesch.* I/1, 289 f.

2. THE COMPLETED DOCTRINE

The doctrine of the *processus justificationis* continued to be further developed during the course of the thirteenth century, receiving its most elaborate exposition in St. Albert the Great, who treats the subject in his usual encyclopedic fashion.[14] The doctrine also received a wide popular dissemination in such works as the *Speculum* of Vincent of Beauvais (ca. 1190-1264), a kind of dictionary of universal knowledge which replaced Isidore of Seville's *Etymologies* as the standard encyclopedia of the Middle Ages. Vincent gives a concise outline in his section on grace, under a *distinctio* entitled "De effectu gratiae".[15] Here he systematically treats what had become a standard series of questions as developed by Alexander of Hales and St. Albert : what is justification? whether remission of sins requires infusion of grace? whether justification requires a movement of the free will? and if this is a movement of faith? and the nature of the faith required for justification. In fact, examination of the text reveals that Vincent's discussion consists almost exclusively of selections from the *Summa theologica* of St. Thomas Aquinas. On a yet more popular, rather than academic, level, the doctrine appears in Caesarius of Heisterbach's *Dialogue on Miracles*, a book designed to instruct novice monks on major points of Church doctrine and practice by means of a series of illustrative anecdotes. In a chapter on contrition, Caesarius states that the *processus* is called the "four justifications".[16] In another place, he gives this maxim for the novice monk in a chapter "On temptation" :

Cum peccator ad Dominum corpore, deserendo saeculum, fuerit conversus, corde pro peccatis suis contritus, et oris confessione iustificatus atque confirmatus, tunc ad pugnam tentationis procedet securius, et cum hoste dimicabit efficacius.[17]

The definitive development of the doctrine, as with most other theological matters in this era, occurs in the two greatest theologians of the thirteenth century, St. Bonaventure and St. Thomas Aquinas. In general,

---

[14] Some *loci* are *Comment. in IV Sent.*, IV, dist. 17A, arts. 8-16 (*Opera omnia*, ed. S. C. A. Borgret [Paris : Vivès, 1894], vol. 29, pp. 669-686); *De sacramentis*, VI, *De paenitentia*, pars 1, q. 7, arts. 1, 7; pars 2, arts. 4-6 (*ed. cit.*, vol. 26, pp. 73 *et seq.*).

[15] *Speculum quadruplex sive Speculum maius* (Paris : Baltazaris Belleri, 1624; repr. Graz : Akademische Druck- u. Verlagsanstalt, 1964), vol. 3, cols. 167 f.

[16] *Dialogus miraculorum*, dist. 2, c. 1 (ed. J. Strange [Cologne : J. M. Heberle, 1851], p. 57). This work has appeared in an English translation by H. von E. Scott and C. C. S. Bland (London : George Routledge, 1929).

[17] *Dialogus*, dist. 4, c. 1 (*ed. cit.*, p. 171).

the most important observation to be made is that these doctors add relatively little of substance to the ideas of Peter of Poitiers and his successors. There occur differences of nuance and emphasis, but the overall development is one of continuity. The more traditional of the two, St. Bonaventure, is treated here first. His doctrine of justification appears in several contexts of his major theological work, a commentary on the *Sentences*. It appears first in a *distinctio* concerning grace and free will, where Bonaventure has the conventional *processus justificationis* exactly :

Dicendum quod justificatio dupliciter potest dici : uno modo justificatio. dicitur justitiae infusio; alio modo justificatio dicitur in justitiae exercitatio. Secundum autem quod justificatio dicitur in justitia exercitatio, sic verbum Magistri verum est, et planum : nemo enim in justitia exercitatur, nisi mediante fide operante per dilectionem : et hic dicitur impetrare justificationem, id est profectum justitiae, quae consequitur ex bonorum operum et meritorum multiplicatione, quod non contingit esse sine fide et charitate : "Sine fide" enim, sicut dicitur et epistola ad Hebraeos, "Impossibile est placere Deo." Sine charitate etiam impossibile est, sicut dicitur, ad Corinthios. Si autem dicatur justificatio justitiae infusio, sic adhuc habet veritatem, licet non ita plene : aut enim est infusio justitiae in parvulo, aut in adulto : si in parvulo, sic dicitur esse justificatio per fidem, non propriam, sed parentum, vel totius Ecclesiae, sicut dicit Augustinus *ad Bonifacium*. Si autem sit justificatio in adulto, sic cum quatuor concurrant ad justificationem, scilicet gratiae infusio, contritio, motus liberi arbitrii, et peccati remissio, sicut dicunt magistri, et motus liberi arbitrii sit motus qui pertinet ad virtutem fidei; non inconvenienter dicitur adultus per fidem justificari. Nec huic obstat quod justificatur per gratiam; illa enim quatuor necessario requiruntur ad justificationem impii; et ideo aliquando homo dicitur justificari per gratiam, aliquando per fidem, aliquando per poenitentiam, quia peccati remissio praesupposit illa tria. ...[18]

In another context, a typically scholastic exercise resolving an apparent contradiction between Paul's *dictum*, "The letter kills, but the spirit gives life (II Cor. 3:6)" with Paul's words in Romans 7:12 : "the Law indeed is holy" (the burden of the argument is that Paul means in the latter passage the Law of the New Testament), Bonaventure explains how justification is to be regarded in terms of works and sacraments, with a decided emphasis upon the importance of the latter :

... Et sic legi evangelicae justificare secundum triplicem modum, videlicet formaliter ratione gratiae sacramentalis, et in effectu ratione amoris spiritualis, et in exercitio ratione multiplicis boni operis ad quod dirigitur homo per consilia et praecepta. ...

[18] *II Sent.*, dist. 26, art. 1, dub. 3 (*Opera omnia*, ed. A. C. Peltier [Paris : Vivès, 1864-71], vol. 3, pp. 238 f.). Bonaventure here as elsewhere most closely follows the earlier Franciscan doctor, Alexander of Hales.

Ad illud quod objicitur, quod cum lex Evangelii spectet ad doctrinam, quod ideo non justificet, etc., dicentum, quod lex Evangelii non dicitur justificare prout legitur et cognoscitur, sed prout in opere servatur, et secundum eam vivitur : hoc autem fit per sacramentorum susceptionem, aeternorum expectationem, et mandatorum impletionem : et secundum hoc assequitur plenam justificationem ...

Ad illud quod objicitur, quod lex evangelica attenditur in praeceptis quae respiciunt opera, dicendum, quod non tantummodo lex Evangelii claudit in se praecepta; imo claudit in se promissa et sacramenta, et magis dicitur justificare ratione sacramentorum quam ratione praeceptorum.[19]

While these *loci* contain the essentials of Bonaventure's doctrine, his major statement is included in commentary on Lombard's treatment of penance in the Fourth Book of the Sentences, where this sacrament is characterized as 'man's part' in justification [20] and the commentary on Lombard's key *Distinctio* 17 is devoted to a detailed development of the *processus justificationis*. It consists of a discussion of each of the four elements of the *processus* in the standard order, and is quite conventional in doctrinal content. Bonaventure first establishes the necessity of infusion of grace.[21] But a movement of the free will is necessary, a movement of faith, which he identifies with a Pauline reference in Romans 5:1 :

Et quia primus motus, per quam consentit gratiae, est motus fidei; ideo motus iste est motus fidei. Unde : "Justificati per fidem"; Glossa prima : "Ex motus liberi arbitrii, qui est ex fide." Ideo dicitur : "Fide purificans corda [Acts 15:9]."; quia motus fidei primo requiritur ad purificationem.[22]

On contrition, the third element in the *processus*, there is the usual anti-Pelagian *caveat*, in which the priority of grace is carefully preserved :

[19] *III Sent.*, dist. 40, art. 1, q. 2 (*ed. cit.*, vol. 5, pp. 236 f.). Cf. *IV Sent.*, dist. 1, pars 1, art. 1, q. 5 (*ibid.*, p. 263), where justification and sacramental theory are treated *re* sacraments of the Old Law and the New Law; discussing Hugh of St. Victor's *De sacramentis*, Bonaventure holds that : "Et novae legis sacramenta non solum ex prima cause et institutione ordinata sunt, ad significandum, set etiam ad gratiam obtinendam : ideo per se ordinata sunt ad justificationem. ...", and that the NT sacraments justify by conferring grace *ex opere operato*.

[20] *IV Sent.*, dist. 14, pars 1, art. 2, q. 3 (*ibid.*, vol. 5, p. 566) :
Nam etsi simul stet motus liberi arbitrii cum contritione, qui quidem motus a pluribus dicitur motus fidei; tamen gratia adveniens per modum reparantis, et expellentis culpam, immediate respicit motum vel actum poenitentiae. Sicut enim gratia prius culpam expellit per naturam, quam habilitet ad bonum; sic necesse est quod homo ex parte sua in justificatione primo aspernetur culpam, quam dirigatur in bonum opus.

[21] *IV Sent.*, dist. 14, pars 1, art. 1, q. 1 (*ed. cit.*, vol. 5, pp. 659 f.).

[22] *Ibid.*, q. 2 (pp. 661 f.).

Sed certe, si ad hoc quod gratia infundatur, necesse est quod homo se praeparet consentiendo gratiae, et detestando peccatum, necesse est in ipsa gratiae infusione ista quatuor esse, scilicet gratiae infusionem, et liberi arbitrii motum, et contritionem, et peccati expulsionem : Deus enim expellit culpam infundendo gratiam; sed non infundit, nisi ei qui concordat; et necesse est concordare gratiae advenienti, et peccatum expellenti. Gratiae sic advenienti concordat per motum liberi arbitrii; gratiae ut peccatum expellenti, per motum contritionis. Unde duo sunt ibi a Deo, scilicet gratiae infusio, et peccati expulsio; et duo a nobis his duobus modis consonant. Et haec quatuor tanguntur in illo versiculo Psalmi [84:14] : "Commovisti terram, et conturbasti eam : sana contritiones ejus, quia commota est. Gratia enim adveniens in animam commovet rationem secundum quod est pars liberi arbitrii, et conturbat voluntatem per contritionem; et postmodum sanat per peccati expulsionem : et ratio hujus redditur, quia praecessit duplex commotio, per quam anima ipsa se gratiae justificanti conformavit; et ideo subjungit : "Quia commota est."[23]

Lastly, Bonaventure treats the fourth element, confession.[24] The only unusual feature here is that he holds that sacerdotal oral confession is not absolutely essential to justification (contrition, as the *res* or essence of the sacrament is always necessary), a point which had been left unclear in earlier writers on the *processus*. The problem itself, however, was not new. The necessity of confession and the positive effect of the priest's absolution *ex opere operato* had been left open by Gratian (he referred to it as a "quaestio multiplex") while Lombard sought to preserve the integrity of the sinner's inner disposition in contrition as the sole precondition of God's forgiveness by making the priestly absolution a merely declarative act, proclaiming the sinner's justification to the Church at large. Alexander of Hales offered a solution which preserved the sacerdotal role by redefining contrition to include the intention to confess as a necessary element in the sinner's disposition to receive forgiving grace. This is a position followed by both Bonaventure and St. Thomas.[25] This slight relaxation of the requirement for confession does not modify the conception of justification as, above all, a penitential theory.

Bonaventure thus shares a general tendency among theologians of this period, to reduce the problem of justification to one major preoccu-

[23] *Ibid.*, q. 3 (pp. 662 f.).

[24] *Ibid.*, q. 4 and art. 2, *passim* (pp. 663 *et seq.*).

[25] *IV Sent.*, dist. 17, art. 2, q. 4. In St. Thomas, *Summa theol.* III, q. 86, art. 2 and q. 87, art. 2 ad 2. The problem of the *propositum confitendi* was not merely theoretical; one reason for this teaching was to make provision for the case of a person on the point of death but without access to a priest to whom to make confession; Church doctrine came to hold that, in such cases, confession to a layman or, at a minimum, a genuine desire to confess (other than prompted by immediate fear of death) was sufficient to receive remission of sins.

pation : the sinner's disposition for grace. The role of faith and the phrase
justificati per fidem is characteristically de-emphasized as merely the
primus motus of the free will in contrition, a preparatory stage for reception of the sacrament of penance. In this regard, one other passage should
be cited here for later discussion; this is in commentary on Lombard's
Distinctio 14 ("De poenitentia in generali") where the author posits
and responds to the question, "An poenitentia concipitur per timorem".
It is important as one of the earlier appearances of the phrase *facere
quod in se est*. Although not a major emphasis in Bonaventure's theology,
this *dictum* became fundamental in nominalist doctrine and notorious
among the Reformers (and has been frequently discussed by modern
students of pre-Reformation theology) :

> Resp. ad arg. Dicendum quod origo poenitentiae virtutis effectiva Deus
> est, sed dispositiva a nobis, quia qui creavit nos sine nobis, non justificat nos
> sine nobis [Augustine]. Dispositio autem hoc ordine procedit. Primo necesse
> est Dei bonitatem et justitiam cognoscere, cui displicet omne malum, et inor-
> dinatio, et ab illa offenditur, et nullo modo malum relinquit impunitum :
> et se debet cognoscere aliquid fecisse, quod suae displicere debeat bonitati :
> et haec est cognitio culpae : et ex hoc cognoscit se homo ex divina sententia
> obligatum ad poenam. Necesse est etiam secundo cognoscere Dei misericor-
> diam, qua paratus est omni revertenti, et dolenti de culpa commissa sibi,
> remittere et indulgere. Ex prima cognitione generatur timor; ex secunda gene-
> ratur spes remissionis : et ex his voluntas revertendi, confoederandi Deo, et
> satisfaciendi per gemitum et alias poenas : et si incipiat facere quod in se est,
> dispositus est ad justificationem.[26]

Unlike St. Bonaventure, St. Thomas Aquinas does not place his doctrine of justification in his treatment of penance in the *Summa theologica*,
but refers his readers back to his famous discussion in Question 113 of
the *Summa* (I-II).[27] It is this section which has claimed the attention of
historians of dogma. But there is virtually nothing original in the doctrine of the ten articles which comprise this question; the chief difference
between Thomas' treatment and those of his predecessors is his usual
superiority in precision and elegance of presentation (for which his
summae are justly regarded as exemplifying the perfected form of the
scholastic *quaestio* method). An analysis of Question 113 shows that
the logical framework is based on the conventional scheme of the *processus justificationis*.[28] The first article defines justification as remission

[26] *IV Sent.*, pars 1, art. 2, q. 2 .(*ed. cit.*, p. 565).

[27] *Summa theol.* III, q. 85, art. 6; q. 86, art. 6, ad 1.

[28] His construction of this series of articles follows most closely the set of questions
propounded by his teacher, St. Albert, in his *Sentences* commentary, although St.
Thomas' logical sequence is much more closely-knit and logically compact.

of sins : "Ergo, remissio peccatorum est justificatio."[29] Article 2 corresponds to the first stage of the *processus*, as Thomas affirmatively answers the question, "utrum ad remissionem culpae, quae est justificatio impii, requiratur gratiae infusio". Articles 3 and 4 correspond to the second requirement of the *processus*, a movement of free will on the part of the penitent sinner. Here, the argument is carefully balanced to avoid Pelagian implications :

Et ideo in eo qui habet usum liberi arbitrii, non fit motio a Deo a justitiam absque motu liberi arbitrii; sed ita infudit donum gratiae justificantis, quod etiam simul cum hoc movet liberum arbitrium ad donum gratiae acceptandum in his qui sunt hujus motionis capaces.[30]

This movement of the free will is also a movement of faith, but must be 'faith formed by love : "... motus fidei non est perfectus, nisi sit caritate informatus : unde simul in justificatione impii cum motu fidei est etiam motus caritatis."[31] A few lines later, Thomas shifts the emphasis slightly, and the role of faith is given a more evangelical interpretation :

... sicut Apostolus dicit ad *Rom.*, "Credenti in eum qui justificat impium, reputabitur fides ejus ad justitiam, secundum propositum gratiae Dei." Ex quo patet quod in justificatione impii requiritur actus fidei quantum ad hoc, quod homo credat Deum esse justificatorem hominum per mysterium Christi.[32]

But this statement must be read in the light of Thomas' definition of faith as a *habitus* and one of the three infused theological virtues, as was pointed out in discussing his Romans commentary; this is the technical means by which Thomas fits the *fides per dilectionem operatur* into his moral theology. The practical result is as has been previously noticed in other writers : justification by grace, but not necessarily by faith alone.[33]

---

[29] Elsewhere (*Summa theol.* III, q. 56, art. 2, ad 4), Thomas gives a more extended definition : "... quod in justificatione animarum duo concurrunt : scilicet remissio culpae, et novitas per gratiam." He does not elucidate the second part of this definition in any other place (it does occur in his doctrine of the Atonement, but only incidentally in an obscure *responsio*); this 'renewal by grace' was, however the definition taken up at the Council of Trent and given currency as the classic Thomist definition of justification.

[30] *Summa theol.* I-II, q. 113, art. 3.

[31] *Ibid.*, art. 4, ad. 1.

[32] *Summa theol.* I-II, q. 113, art. 4, ad. 3.

[33] Cf. Loofs, *Dogmengesch.*, p. 463 and the following comment by Nygren, *Agape and Eros*, p. 656 :

With respect to the justification of the sinner and his entry into fellowship with

The fifth article, entitled "utrum ad justificationem impii requiratur motus liberi arbitrii in peccatum", corresponds to the third stage of the *processus*, contrition. Thomas concludes as follows :

... in tempore praecedente justificationem oportet quod homo singula peccata quae commisit detestetur, quorum memoriam habet; et ex tali consideratione praecedenti subsequitur in anima quidam motus detestantis universaliter omnia peccata commissa; inter quae etiam includuntur peccata oblivioni tradita, quia homo in statu illo est sic dispositus, ut etiam de his quae non meminit contereretur, si memoriae adessent; et iste motus concurrit ad justificationem.[34]

Article 6 treats the fourth and final stage of the *processus*, remission of sin; in the body of this article, Thomas sums up with the usual statement of 'the four things that are required for justification' :

Dicendum quod quatuor enumerantur quae requiruntur ad justificationem impii, scilicet, gratiae infusio, motus liberi arbitrii in Deum per fidem, et motus liberi arbitrii in peccatum, et remissio culpae. Cujus ratio est quia, sicut dictum est, justificatio est quidam motus pro anima movetur a Deo a statu culpae in statum justitiae. In quolibet autem motu, quo aliquid ab altero movetur, tria requiruntur : primo quidem, motio ipsius moventis; secundo, motus mobilis; tertio, consummatio motus, sive perventio ad finem. Ex parte igitur motionis divinae accipitur gratiae infusio; ex parte vero liberi arbitrii moti accipiuntur duo motus ipsius, secundum recessum a termino a quo, et accessum ad terminum ad quem. Consummatio autem, sive perventio ad terminum hujus motus importatur per remissionem culpae : in hoc enim justificatio consummatur.[35]

The seventh and eighth articles concern the question of the temporal sequence of the *processus*; as in prior theologians, Thomas answers

---

God, it is true that the Pauline language about "justification by faith" can be used. But it is never a question of faith pure and simple, but of faith in so far as it is perfected by love. The decisive thing for man's justification is not faith, but love, Caritas. That is what is meant when, on the basis of the Aristotelian distinction between "form" and "matter", use is made of the formula "fides caritate formata", faith "formed" by Caritas. The form—in Aristotelian thought—is the thing of value which, by imprinting its stamp upon the matter, imparts value which, by imprinting its stamp upon the matter, imparts value to this too. This idea is now applied to the relation between faith and love, fides and Caritas. Faith is the matter, and as such it is insubstantial and powerless. Love is the form, the formative principle, which by setting its stamp or "forma" upon faith, gives to faith, too, worth and real being. So it is ultimately not by faith, but by love, that man is justified and comes into fellowship with God.

[34] *Summa theol.* I-II, q. 113, art. 5, ad. 3.
[35] *Summa theol.* I-II, q. 113, art. 6.

that the stages occur simultaneously. It is in these two questions that Thomas is especially careful to safeguard his doctrine against any semi-Pelagian taint beyond any possible misunderstanding. He categorically states : "... tota justificatio impii originaliter consistit in gratiae infusione. Per eam enim et liberum arbitrium movetur, et culpa remittitur."[36] In terms of the *processus*, the infusion of grace precedes any movement of the free will toward God and hence precludes any possibility of an acquired merit. For Thomas, as for previous theologians, a problem arises in that the four stages of the *processus* are said to occur simultaneously in time—how, then, can grace precede the movement of faith? The resolution of this problem is accomplished by distinguishing between a temporal order, in which all parts of justification occur in an instant, and a natural order in which, in terms of a cause-and-effect relationship, infusion of can be said to be prior to the movement of the will in the second and third stages of the *processus*. Thomas is able to explain this thesis only by a complex excursus into Aristotelian metaphysics, an explanation that would be shown to be highly vulnerable by the nominalists in the century following St. Thomas. As in many other points in his teaching, the subtle balance between potentially opposing concepts was a very fragile one.

It is also to be noticed that, while Thomas does not directly treat the subject of merit in justification (as does Peter of Poitiers), he follows logically in the next question (q. 114) with his doctrine of merit, considered as an increase of the grace received gratuitously in justification. The connection between the two is man's cooperation in justification and merit as the effect of cooperating grace. The separation between justification and merit is formally present but similarly fragile.

These considerations suggest that a proper interpretation of St. Thomas' question on justification must take into account the continuity of tradition which it represents. Thomas' doctrine is designed to accomplish exactly the same purpose as that of Peter of Poitiers, to "save the phenomena" in a synthesis that is at once quasi-evangelical and ecclesiastical-sacramental. An understanding of the peculiar mechanism of the four-fold *processus* is essential to avoid the error of such critics as Ritschl, who fails to appreciate the subtlety of its logical structure when he states that Thomas failed to prove the proposition that *transmutatio a statu injustitiae* results *per remissionem peccatorum*.[37] Rather,

---

[36] *Ibid.*, art. 7.
[37] Ritschl. *Critical History*, pp. 78 f.

one can well agree with B. Poschmann, who states : "The great and epoch-making achievement of Aquinas' teaching on penance was the integration of the sacrament in the process of justification, and consequently the proof that it was an indispensable cause of the forgiveness of sins."[38]

3. THE LATER SCHOLASTICS

It is beyond the scope of this volume to follow out the history of the doctrine of the *processus* in the numerous *Sentences* commentaries of the later thirteenth and early fourteenth centuries which mark the transition to nominalism in theology, nor beyond through the nominalist period proper. Although a definitive history of nominalist theology is yet to be written, the main outlines of this history are known and will be familiar to anyone acquainted with the relevant Luther literature. But a brief sketch will perhaps be useful in relating the substance of this chapter to key developments in later medieval theology.

In general, the importance of the *processus justificationis* itself receded in the writings of the nominalists. The classic thirteenth-century *schema* might be quoted by a very conservative theologian outside the nominalist tradition such as St. Antoninus as late as the early fifteenth century,[39] but appears in the major nominalist theologians, if at all, only in a very attenuated form.[40] Nevertheless, the *processus* had a definite influence in conditioning the nominalist debate both as it had established the basic concepts and suggested problems that had not been fully resolved by the thirteenth century doctors. No less for the nominalists

---

[38] Poschmann, *Penance and Anointing of the Sick*, p. 178.

[39] *Summa theologica* (Verona, 1740), pars 4, tit. 9, c. 6 (vol. 4, pp. 486-90).

[40] As, for example, in Gabriel Biel, in his *Commentarius in quartum librum Sententiarum* (Brixiae : Thomas Bozolam, 1573), dist. 14, q. 2 (pp. 248-50). This occurs in a section where Biel is disputing Scotus' opinion that penance does not require perfect contrition. He begins by stating the following propositions : "... ad iustificationem impii requiritur motus liberi arbitrii, ut dispositio praevia : sed per sacramentum poenitentie iustificatur impius : ergo." Citing Thomas, Bonaventure, the *Glossa*, and other authorities, he continues : "Iustificati per fidem, id est ex motul iberi arb. qui est ex fide ..." Analyzing the question, he asserts, citing Bonaventure, that justification is only by the will of God, but with man's consent through an act of free will: also, that infusion of grace is necessary for justification, but a disposition for this grace is also required, consisting of a movement of the free will in detestation of sin and a turning ('conversion') to God. He concludes as follows : "Et his duobus motibus voluntatis, odii in peccatum : voluntatis in deum, respondet duo, quae a deo sunt justificante, secundum sanctum Bonav. scilicet gratiae infusio, et peccati expulsio."

than for the scholastics, the grand issue remained the sinner's disposition for grace—that is, what are the requisite conditions which make
it possible for man to receive sanctifying or justifying grace by which
alone God fully forgives sins. Specifically, the *processus* shaped two
major issues which predominate in nominalist theology: First, the requirement of a movement of the free will toward God (the second element in
the classic *processus*) presented the whole problem of the role of free will
and the precise nature of man's participation in justification. Secondly,
the requirement of contrition (the third element in the *processus*)
raised a similar problem with regard to the movement of the free will
in detestation of sin, and more specifically the range of questions concerning the nature of contrition and attrition. (A third major issue
among the nominalists, the doctrine of merit, is of separate origin in
the tradition and will be discussed only peripherally here; as has been
noted earlier, the thirteenth century theologians did not develop their
teaching on merit directly in the context of discussions of the *processus*,
although they recognized the connection.)

How these issues developed can best be explained by a brief discussion
of the major trends in late medieval penitential theology.[41] Although
the debate involved the entire area of the theology of grace, the sacrament of penance continued to be a major point of focus. One of the major
crises in later medieval theology was precipitated, in part, over a controversy concerned with a major feature of penitential theology, the
concept of contrition. In keeping with the voluntaristic bias of his
general philosophy, Duns Scotus taught that attrition, defined as a
purely human act of sorrow unassisted or "unformed" by grace, can
be a sufficient disposition for justification; this imperfect form of contrition is made perfect in an instant with the infusion of grace.[42] Hence,
"Even in a state of sin a man is able by his natural powers to make in
attrition an act of moral perfection in which all the circumstances
required for moral goodness are verified, including in particular the circumstance of finality—*circumstantia finis*—which directs the act to
man's last end, so that it is elicited out of the love of God."[43] By this

---

[41] For the following, see especially Poschmann, *Penance and Anointing of the
Sick*, pp. 184 *et seq.* and H. A. Oberman, *The Harvest of Medieval Theology* (Cam-
bridge, Mass. : Harvard University Press), pp. 146 *et seq.* See also J. Alton Templin,
"Justification in Late Medieval Theology and Luther's Thought," *The Iliff Review*
XXV, no. 2 (1968), pp. 29-38.

[42] *Quaest. in IV Lib. Sent. (Oxon.)*, dist. 14, q. 2, nn. 14-15 (*Opera omnia* [Paris :
Vivès, 1894], pp. 74-76).

[43] Poschmann, *Penance and Anointing of the Sick*, p. 185.

definition, attrition for Scotus is nearly identical with contrition as it was defined by the earlier scholastics, save only that it is not informed by grace (Scotus held with the normal definition of contrition as requiring "information" by grace). Scotus recognized that this form of attrition, in which a true sorrow is achieved—not merely a "fear sorrow" from fear of punishment for sin—occurs in relatively few cases. He accordingly taught that, is His mercy, God has provided two different ways to salvation. In contrast to St. Thomas, who integrated contrition into the sacrament of penance and hence made it indispensable for justification, Scotus held that there is a form of justification which can be extra-sacramental, in which the penitent sinner's attrition is of a sufficiently intense quality as to merit justification. This was against all thirteenth century opinion that a perfect contrition is necessary in the *processus* and that the movement of the free will in contrition is only made possible by a prior or prevenient grace.

Scotus' doctrine is not overtly Pelagian, however—it is saved from this by his particular development of the doctrine of merit. Man cannot wholly earn his justification, or, in scholastic terminology, achieve it by condign merit (*meritum de condigno*), that form of merit which can be said to be "owed" to man by God in return for morally good acts. The issue was never in doubt that this ultimate form of merit can only be achieved in a state of grace. But he maintained that an intense attrition was sufficient for justification by the so-called "congruent" merit (*meritum de congruo*). Since, Scotus argued, the effects of the Fall of Man were not total, a sufficient portion of man's powers of reason and will remained for him to recognize the good and act toward it, albeit with limited capabilities. Therefore man could perform some good deeds, including the essential first step of a morally genuine detestation of and sorrow for his sins. Although by no means a total recompense for man's offenses against God, such acts were said to be "fitting" and rewardable by God and that, in His mercy, God would accept them as sufficiently meritorious to dispose the sinner to receive grace which would elevate his attrition to contrition and complete the process of justification. If, however, these conditions cannot be met, there remains the second way to justification through the sacrament of penance, an easier way because it does not require the high degree of attrition necessary to produce congruent merit. Here it is only required that the sinner be "barely attrite" (*parum attritus*), i.e., desirous of receiving the sacrament and avoiding mortal sins. In this case the sacrament produces justification *ex opere operato*, the power of the sacrament itself taking the place of merit.

For the standpoint of historical theology, it is not difficult to elucidate the objectionable features of Scotus' two-fold doctrine of justification. It cannot be charged that Scotus taught that man could earn his salvation; nevertheless, he held that, in a sense, man could assist in his own justification, and hence fell into a form of semi-Pelagianism. His rather complicated and tenuous theory of merit does not sufficiently insulate his teaching from Pelagian implications. It is difficult to see, for example, why man's will cannot be regarded as at least a proximate cause of his own justification, for man has it within his power to initiate the process in either of the two ways to justification. Secondly, Scotus has been frequently assailed by critics, both contemporary and modern, for his doctrine of *parum attritus*. It had the effect of considerably lowering the spiritual requirements demanded of the sinner coming to the sacrament of penance and, more generally, of promoting a superstitious conception of the sacrament itself, in which its operation is regarded as mechanistic and virtually automatic. To what extent the Scotist doctrine influenced penitential practice in the later medieval Church is a matter of debate among historians; but it is conceded on all sides that such a conception was prevalent in the Church's popular teaching at the outbreak of the Reformation.

In essentials, the nominalist school of Ockham and his disciples further developed these concepts in the same direction as Scotus out of a philosophy which, although different in certain of its metaphysical principles, similarly stressed a voluntaristic concept of man's freedom and his ability to perform morally worthy acts by his own natural powers. There were certain important differences in specific doctrine, but none of which worked to alter this basic orientation. Gabriel Biel rejected Scotus' notion of an extra-sacramental justification; to receive the first grace of justification, man must at least have the intention to confess at the first convenient occasion (historically, this means that Biel's teaching further reinforced the traditional identification of justification with the sacrament of penance). The nominalists also rejected Scotus' attritionism and taught the necessity of contrition in justification, although again in a formulation that academic, made the difference almost since they also taught that man could raise attrition to a kind of imperfect contrition through an act of unassisted free will, love of God. The moment that an act of love is present, God rewards it with an infusion of justifying grace which perfects the movement of contrition.

This latter teaching is intimately connected with what can be regarded as the most significant addition of the nominalists to the theological vocabulary and as the consummation of the voluntaristic tendencies which characterize this entire line of development in the later medieval theological tradition. This was the frequent appearance of the formula *facere quod in se est* ("from those who do their very best, God will not withhold His grace"). The phrase is of thirteenth century provenance, apparently first used by Alexander of Hales and followed by St. Bonaventure (as previously cited). It was elevated to the status of a doctrine by the nominalists and formed a fundamental concept in their theology of grace to the very end of the period, familiar to nearly every churchman.[44] For the nominalists, this conception provided the definitive solution to the major problem of the disposition for grace.

Here, also, one can discern a logical and developmental connection with the earlier theology of justification. In its broadest application, the *facere quod in se est* was used to emphasize the possibility of man performing morally worthy acts, but it was also given a specific theological content by the nominalists as they assert that, by "doing his very best", man can by his natural powers fulfill two standards : love of God "above all else" (or *propter Deum*, "for His own sake"), and that hatred of sin which, in the nominalist formulation, removes any interior "obstacle" (*obex*) to the infusion of grace. This, it was held, constituted a sufficient preparation for grace, and by means of which a man could achieve *meritum de congruo*. The *facere quod in se est* forms the nominalist equivalent of the second and third steps in the older formulation of the *processus justificationis*. And the teaching that man can love God above all else can be similarly regarded as a logical extension of the concept of justifying faith as *fides caritate formata*. With the advantage of historical hindsight, it can be seen that the possibility of an exaggeration of the role of free will was inherent in the very dialectical structure of the *processus justificationis*; the *facere quod in se est* represents precisely such a development.

As expounded by the nominalists, the *facere quod in se est* was at the same time a doctrine of salvation; beyond positing a means by which man could achieve a degree of merit, it also implied an automatic obliga-

---

[44] It appears in the writings of Luther's superior and spiritual mentor, Staupitz; see David Curtis Steinmetz, *Misericordia Dei : The Theology of Johannes von Staupitz in its Late Medieval Setting* (Leiden : E. J. Brill, 1968), pp. 93 *et seq.* See also, for the case of the prominent preacher John Geiler (*ob.* 1510), E. J. Dempsey Douglass, *Justification in Late Medieval Preaching* (Leiden : E. J. Brill, 1966), pp. 141 *et seq.*

tion on the part of God to respond and hence reward the sinner with a saving grace. Thus, the doctrine left an opening for a kind of earned salvation which no amount of theological subtlety could completely erase.[45] But it is possibly a mistake, in any critique, to emphasize exclusively its semi-Pelagian character, for it was not simply a crude doctrine of works-righteousness (no medieval theologian, scholastic or nominalist, ever held that purely exterior acts could merit justification). It was perhaps meant with the best of intentions as a doctrine of assurance, and the dictum does make some sense considered as a bit of practical, pastoral advice. But the doctrine was also interpreted to lay a positive obligation upon man to "do his very best" in preparation for grace. This in itself would impose a heavy burden upon anyone of acute religious sensibilities, but this was compounded by the further problem that the nominalists were never able to explain any means by which a sinner could be absolutely sure that he had done his best. The standards required—abhorrence of sin and wholehearted love of God—are essentially subjective, and no one can be objectively sure that he has totally met these standards. The practical effects of the *facere quod in se est* were, on the one hand, to further heighten the doctrinal uncertainties concerning the nature of attrition and contrition (a matter made all the more acute in the absence of a definitive pronouncement in the official dogma of the Church at this time), and, on the other hand, to create possible difficulties of a pastoral nature as it held the potential to engender a certain anxious scrupulosity on the part of the penitent.[46] This latter seems to have occurred at least in the case of Martin Luther.

The intimate connection between justification and the sacrament of penance thus continued to the very end of the Middle Ages. The development of these concepts in later scholasticism has been traced here primarily in terms of the theology of the period and its inner logical necessities. But this is perhaps to ignore a broader historical perspective. Johan Huizinga, in his classic *Waning of the Middle Ages*, portrayed the late medieval period as, above all, one of profound pessimism and

---

[45] Cf. Oberman, *Harvest of Medieval Theology*, esp. pp. 132-39 and 169-78.

[46] Cf. *ibid.*, p. 160; Rupp, *Righteousness of God*, remarks (p. 104) : "The Nominalist theology, with its dialectic of possibilities and its recurring 'perhaps', was ill calculated to support trembling spirits. Despite its apparent optimism, the common-sense stress on 'doing what in one lies' and the careful balance of grace and merit, it remained a system which threw a practical emphasis on the human will."

insecurity.[17] The preoccupation with sin and forgiveness and the search for an assurance of salvation was also a reflection of the age; it is possibly the underlying historical reason for the persistence of this peculiarly narrow concept of justification and the strained efforts on the part of theologians to make penitential justification a secure road to salvation.

[47] (Garden City, N. Y. : Doubleday Anchor Books, 1954); cf. Robert E. Lerner, *The Age of Adversity* : *The Fourteenth Century* (Ithaca, N. Y. ; Cornell University Press, 1968).

CHAPTER V

CONCLUSIONS

The purpose of this study has been to demonstrate that the close identification between justification and the sacrament of penance characteristic of the Church's teaching on the eve of the Reformation was no aberration of the nominalist theologians, but had undergone a long preparation in the entire medieval theological tradition. On this point, at least, it is impossible to agree with the thesis of Joseph Lortz that the "Occamist system" by which Luther was allegedly victimized was "radically uncatholic".[1] Certainly the nominalists developed the doctrine in directions that were divergent from the thirteenth century scholastics. But the fact remains that they were working within an established and accepted doctrinal structure, one in which certain key conceptions and underlying assumptions were already present which predetermined the issues and categories of the nominalist doctrine. This was not only restricted to the explicit doctrine of penance, but to more fundamental conceptions in the theology of grace. Remarking on the history of this theology in the high Middle Ages, the contemporary Roman Catholic theologian Hans Küng observes :

... It was then that the categories of habitus and qualitas were taken over from Aristotle and the notion of infused virtues took shape. Thus the accent, in the matter of actual grace, was shifted from what is now called "actual" grace (the liberating delectatio) to "habitual" grace (grace as form), from preparation for justification to co-operation with it, from justification as a gradual process of conversion to justification as instantaneous happening and as metaphysical reality seen from the viewpoint of the matter-form schema.[2]

It was in this philosophical atmosphere that justification could be conceived as a process and this concept subsequently manipulated and rationalized to a point where it became, to many men living in the immediate post-Renaissance world, literally incredible.

---

[1] Lortz, *Reformation in Germany*, vol. 1, p. 196.
[2] Hans Küng, *Justification : The Doctrine of Karl Barth and a Catholic Reflection*, trans. T. Collins *et al.* (New York : Thomas Nelson & Dons, 1964), p. 216.

With this observation, it may be relevant to make two historical digressions before proceeding to a final statement of conclusions. The first concerns Luther; the second is a brief consideration of the *Nachleben* of medieval conceptions of penance at the Council of Trent.

What role or influence, it may be fairly asked, did the earlier medieval doctrines of justification have upon Luther himself? In the light of all that is known about his education and early theological development, it seems conclusive that there was no direct influence. For various circumstantial reasons, he was simply not in touch with the sources for the high scholastic tradition and knew relatively little about the theology of the thirteenth century masters. It is well known that, for systematic theology, the author whom he knew best was Gabriel Biel, followed by d'Ailly and Ockham; throughout his earlier writings, his detailed refutations of medieval doctrine are most often directed against distinctive points in the teaching of these nominalist authorities. However, an indirect influence seems indubitable. Although one cannot establish any direct connection with his celebrated "discovery" of Romans 1:17, it is apparent that his well-known spiritual crises and specifically his compulsive scrupulosity and his failure to find comfort in the remedy of confession and penance led him into an inquiry in the area of penitential theology. This can be inferred with certainty from numerous references in his earlier writings from at least as early as the *Lectures on Romans* of 1515-16.[3] Whenever Luther discusses the key topics of justification and the righteousness of God, his argument usually includes either a reference to confession and penance or an attack on one or more points related to the nominalist theology of penance. When he speaks of "works righteousness", he most often has in mind some spiritual abuse connected with contemporary penitential practise. Obviously, what had initially led him to the notion of justification was the medieval theology of penance as justification—he could not have failed to encounter it in his sources.

Beyond this rather elementary fact, one enters into a realm of more or less uncertain speculation. But there is one passage in the *Lectures on Romans* which impressed the present author as more than a little revealing of Luther's interior thought-process as he arrived at his evangelical conception of justification. This occurs in a lengthy corollary to his comment on Romans 4:7 where, in a discussion of the nature of sin

---

[3] See Rupp, *Righteousness of God*, pp. 102-120, for citations to many of these passages and a good discussion of this matter.

and forgiveness, his attack upon the nominalists reaches a point of crescendo. It is also a passage laden with autobiographical reference, as the following context shows :

... I must say either that I have never understood the matter or that the Scholastic theologians did not deal adequately with sin and grace. For they imagine that original sin, just like actual sin, is entirely taken away, as if sins were something that could be moved in the flick of an eyelash, as darkness is by light. ...
Fool that I was, I could not understand, in the light of this, in what way I should regard myself as a sinner like others and in what way I should not put myself ahead of anyone, inasmuch as I had contritely made confession of my sins, for I thought that thereby they had been taken away and made of no effect, also inwardly. But if I should regard myself as a sinner like them on account of my past sins which, they say, must always be remembered (and here they speak the truth but not emphatically enough), then, I thought, they are really not forgiven, though God has promised to forgive them to such as confess them. Thus I fought with myself, because I did not know that though forgiveness is indeed real, sin is not taken away by the gift of grace which starts this removal, so that it is only not reckoned as sin.

What is so striking here is that Luther immediately continues in this passage with what appears to be an abrupt change of subject, one which has no apparent logical connection with his foregoing remarks, but which to him is obviously most closely related :

For this reason it is sheer madness to say that man can love God above everything by his own powers and live up to the commandment in terms of the substance of the deed but not in terms of the intention of Him who gave it, because he does not do so in the state of grace. O you fools, you pig-theologians! So, then, grace was not necessary except in connection with a new exaction over and above the law! For if we can fulfill the law by our own powers, as they say, grace is not necessary for the fulfillment of the law but only for the fulfillment of a divinely imposed exaction that goes beyond the law. Who can tolerate such sacrilegious opinons! Does not the apostle say that "the law works wrath" (Rom. 4:15) and "that it was weak through the flesh" (Rom. 8:3) and that it can absolutely not be fulfilled without grace?
Even their own experience could have made them aware of the utter stupidity of this opinion and caused them to be ashamed of themselves and to repent. For willy-nilly they must sense the wrong desires in their own selves. Therefore, I say now : Hui! Go to work, please! Be men! Try with all your powers to eliminate these coverings that are in you! Give proof of what you say, namely that it is possible to love God "with all one's strength" (Luke 10:27) naturally, in short, without grace!

He then again returns to his original theme, an attack upon the nominalists' doctrine of sin :

... These monstrous views were made possible by the fact that the Scholastic theologians did not know the nature of sin and forgiveness. For they reduced sin as well as righteousness to some very minute motion of the soul. They said, namely, that when the will is subject to synteresis, it is, only slightly to be sure, "inclined toward the good." And this tiny motion toward God (of which man is naturally capable) they imagine to be an act of loving God above everything!

... Our theologians, however, have neglected to consider the nature of sin and have concentrated their attention upon good works; they have been concerned to teach only how good works might be made secure, but not how with fervent prayers one must humbly seek the grace that heals and how one must acknowledge himself a sinner. And so they inevitably bring it about that people become proud, thinking that they are already righteous by having done good works outwardly, unconcerned as they are to make war on their evil desires by unceasing prayer and devotion to the Lord. This is also the reason why there is, in the church today, such frequent relapse after confessions. The people do not know that they must still be justified, but they are confident that they are already justified; thus they come to ruin by their own sense of security, and the devil does not need to raise a finger. This certainly is nothing else than to establish righteousness by means of works. ...[4]

Here, the bitterness of his remarks bespeaks more than a doctrinal disagreement; Luther is touching upon very painful personal experience. What is noteworthy is that he is referring to the two aspects of the *facere quod in se est*, detestation of sin and love of God "above everything" and the opinion that man has it within his natural powers to achieve these requirements. The vehemence of his remarks regarding the latter teaching, man's ability to love God, is particularly suggestive of earlier struggles of mind and spirit (taken together with the fact that, approximately two years later, Luther returned to the attack on this point in his *Disputation Against Scholastic Theology*).[5] Perhaps we have a clue here to Luther's inability to achieve a satisfactory penance—why, as he wrote in his 1545 autobiographical statement : "For, however irreproachably I lived as a monk, I felt myself in the presence of God to be a sinner with a most unquiet conscience nor could I trust that I had pleased him with my satisfaction." He writes in the next sentence : "I did not love, nay, rather I hated this just God who punished sinners ..."[6] This should be read with the implication of a causal relationship :

---

[4] *Lectures on Romans* (Pauck translation), pp. 128-30 (WA 56, pp. 273-76). A similar reference is in his *Lectures on Galatians*, on 5:4 (trans. Jaroslav Pelikan, in *Luther's Works* 27 [St. Louis : Concordia, 1964], p. 13) (WA 60, Abt. 2, pp. 14 f.).

[5] E.g., article 13 : "Therefore it is quite absurd to argue that because sinful man is able to love creation more than anything else he can on that account also love God", and articles following (in James Atkinson, *Luther : Early Theological Works, Library of Christian Classics* XVI [Philadelphia : Westminster, 1962], p. 267) (WA 1, p. 224).

[6] As quoted by Rupp, *Righteousness of God*, pp. 121 f.

Luther felt himself to be a sinner because he could not achieve a love of God through his penitential exercises.[7] What is being suggested here is that among the complex of factors involved in his spiritual crises was the *facere quod in se est*. He associated penance with the obligation to love God, and knew that the former could not be successful without the latter—but his dilemma was that he could not love God, and hence could find no relief in the remedy of the sacrament.[8] One of the major results of the "discovery" of Romans 1:17 was that it removed this tension; since he broke through to his radical principle of the priority of faith and the conception of a passive justice, the requirement to love God by a voluntary act is obviated—as, indeed, is the possibility

[7] Cf. Nygren, *Agape and Eros*, pp. 693-95.

[8] Further evidence is Luther's letter to Staupitz of 1518, especially the following excerpts, "Therefore I accepted you as a messenger from heaven when you said that *poenitentia* is genuine only if it begins with love for justice and for God and that what they consider to be the final stage and completion is in reality rather the very beginning of *poenitentia*." And especially the following : "... formerly almost no word in the whole Scripture was more bitter to me than *poenitentia* (although I zealously made a pretense before God and tried to express a feigned and constrained love for Him) ..." (*Letters*, vol. 1, trans. Gottfried S. Krodel, in *Luther's Works* 48 [Philadelphia : Fortress Press, 1963], pp. 64-70) (WA 1, p. 515). I would therefore agree with Krodel's note to the first of the above excerpts :
So taught, e.g., Gabriel Biel ... one of the Nominalist theologians whose works Luther had studied. According to Biel, man constantly fears to transgress God's holy will and to become guilty and the object of God's wrath. This servile fear has to be transformed into love for God, if the sinner is to be absolved. Man should be able to attain such love by an intense training of his mind and will and by keeping God's commandments. Ostensibly this would create a truly contrite heart, thus completing *poenitentia* ... Under the influence of von Staupitz, Luther learned that *poenitentia* begins with love for God, that is, with a heart turned to God. He also learned that a heart may be brought to this love (that is, to repent) only by the God of grace and love who reveals himself in Jesus Christ (therefore Luther's reference to Christ's wounds at the end of the following paragraph), and not by servile fear of breaking the commandments and thus becoming guilty and deserving God's wrath. When this change in the understanding of *poenitentia* took place in Luther's life is highly controversial and is assumed by various scholars to have been sometime between 1508 and 1517. ...
Also included in this development was Luther's rejection of the *facere quod in se est*; this is definitive by 1518 in the *Disputation Against Scholastic Theology* (art. 26; see *ed. cit.*, p. 268) (WA 1, p. 225) and the *Heidelberg Disputation* (art. 16; trans. Harold J. Grimm, in *Luther's Works* 31 [Philadelphia : Muhlenberg Press, 1957], pp. 50 f.) (WA 7, pp. 360 f.). For this subject, see the important article by H. A. Oberman, "*Facientibus Quod in se est Deus non Denegat Gratiam* : Robert Holcot O.P. and the Beginnings of Luther's Theology", *Harvard Theological Review* 55 (1962), pp. 312-342.

CONCLUSIONS

of any preparation for the reception of grace. With this insight, Luther would proceed over the next several years to dismantle the entire edifice of scholastic theories of grace.

These remarks are not intended to propose still another solution to the "discovery" or *Turmerlebnis* problem; what has been discussed is rather a probable effect of the *Turmerlebnis*. The interior process by which Luther achieved his redefinition of justification will probably never be completely explained with the existing evidence, although it is asserted here that the problem of forgiveness and the scholastic doctrines of penance were what initially directed his attention to the concept itself. It is due to this same circumstance that, once he had made the necessary objective adjustments in his anthropology and theology of grace—rejecting the nominalist doctrine and returning to the Augustinian conception of man's inability to achieve merit unassisted by grace—much of his career unfolded as the logical outcome of an attack upon the nominalist theology of penance. As a theologian, this occurred as his theology developed in dialectical opposition to the nominalists on many points; as a churchman and reformer, in his attacks on the penitential system of the Church culminating in the *95 Theses*.

Somewhat more positive conclusions can be stated concerning the influence of the earlier medieval doctrines of justification upon sixteenth century Catholicism; here the evidence is sufficient to demonstrate the continuity of the medieval tradition in relevant pronouncements of the Council of Trent. Here we shall be concerned specifically with the decree of justification of the Sixth Session (promulgated January 13, 1547). Two passages will suffice to illustrate :

CAPUT VII. *Quid sit justificatio impii, et quae ejus causae*
 Hanc dispositionem seu praeparationem justificatio ipsa consequitur, quae non est sola peccatorum remissio, sed et sanctificatio et renovatio interioris hominis per voluntariam susceptionem gratiae et donorum, unde homo ex injusto fit justus et ex inimico amicus, ut sit "haeres secundum spem vitae aeternae (Tit. 3:7)". Hujus justificationis causae sunt : ... instrumentalis item, sacramentum baptismi, quod est sacramentum fidei, sine qua nulli unquam contigit justificatio. Demum unica formalis causa est justitia Dei, non qua ipse justus est, sed qua nos justos facit, qua videlicet ab eo donati renovamur spiritu mentis nostrae, et non modo reputamur, sed vere justi nominamur et sumus, justiam in nobis recipientes unusquisque suam secundum mensuram, quam Spiritus Sanctus partitur singulis prout vult, et secundum propriam cujusque dispositionem et cooperationem. Quamquam enim nemo possit esse justus nisi cui merita passionis Domini nostri Jesu Christi communicantur, id tamen in hac impii justificatione fit, dum ejusdem sanctissimae passionis merito "per Spiritum Sanctum caritas Dei diffunditur in cordibus

eorum (Rom. 5:5)" qui justificantur atque ipsis inhaeret. Unde in ipsa justificatione cum remissione peccatorum haec omnia simul infusa accipit homo per Jesum Christum, cui inseritur : fidem, spem et caritatem. Nam fides, nisi ad eam spes accedat et caritas, neque unit perfecte cum Christo neque corporis ejus vivum membrum efficit. Qua rationae verissime dicitur, fidem sine operibus mortuam et otiosam esse, et "in Christo Jesu neque circumcisionem aliquid valere, neque praeputium, sed fidem, quae per caritatem operatur Gal. 5:6)." ...
CAPUT VIII. *Quomodo intelligatur, impium per fidem et gratis justificari*

Cum vero Apostolus dicit, justificari hominem per fidem et gratis, ea verba in eo sensu intelligenda sunt, quem perpetuus ecclesiae catholicae consensus tenuit et expressit, ut scilicet per fidem ideo justificari dicamur, quia fides est humanae salutis initium, fundamentum et radix omnis justificationis, sine qua "impossibile est placere Deo (Heb. 11:6)" et ad filiorum ejus consortium pervenire; gratis autem justificari ideo dicamur, quia nihil eorum quae justificationem praecedunt, sive fides sive opera, ipsam justificationis gratiam promeretur; "Si enim gratia est, jam non ex operibus; alioquin" (ut idem Apostolus inquit) "gratia jam non est gratia (Rom. 11:6)."h

There are several points of interest in these chapters : e.g., it commences with the Thomist two-fold definition of justification; baptism, as the 'sacrament of faith', is the justifying sacrament; God's justice is received according to 'disposition and cooperation'. But most interesting is the treatment of faith. It manifests two major influences : the 'faith working through love' concept, and, most prominently, the traditional texts and interpretations from the medieval Pauline commentaries which deny a merit for justification but also enjoin faith with works.

The latter point is of particular interest in view of the history of the composition of these chapters.[10] There was a prolonged debate among the council fathers as to whether or not to make some insertion of the *sola fides* in the text, but the idea was discarded as coming too close to the Lutherans. Then it was proposed to deal with the Pauline *sine operibus legis* (Romans 3:28 was at one point in the proposed draft) or simply *sine operibus*; this was rejected because it would conflict with the James text and require explanation too lengthy to be appropriate in such a document. In effect, the council was unable to come to grips with any of the crucial Pauline texts. Yet, in view of the religious and political situation, it was felt to be essential that some pronouncement should be made on faith as a cause of justification. The result was a definition of faith which is almost meaningless in a theological sense,

[9] H. J. Schroeder, *Canons and Decrees of the Council of Trent* (St. Louis : Herder, 1941), pp. 312 f.

[10] I follow here H. Jedin, *A History of the Council of Trent*, tr. E. Graf (London : Nelson, 1961), II, 294-296; cf. Rivière in *DTC* 8, col. 2186. Also see the critical analysis of the justification decree in Harnack, *Hist. of Dogma* VII, 60-72.

but a ringing reaffirmation of justification by *gratia gratis datur*—here the council fathers took no chances, eliminating mention of both faith and works, completing the argument with another familiar medieval text applied to justification : "alioquin gratia jam non est gratia."

Finally, to document the continued emphasis upon penance for justification, this chapter should be cited :

CAPUT XIV. *De lapsis et eorum reparatione*

Qui vero ab accepta justificationis gratia per peccatum exciderunt, rursus justificari poterunt, cum excitante Deo per poenitentiae sacramentum merito Christi amissam gratiam recuperare procuraverint. Hic enim justificationis modus est lapsi reparatio, quam secundam post naufragium deperditae gratiae tabulam sancti patres apte nuncuparunt.[11]

Thus was consummated a development with its genesis among Anglo-Irish scholars of the ninth-century Carolingian court.

In conclusion, certain remarks should be made directed toward an analysis of the historical factors which influenced the development of the medieval doctrine of justification.

A general observation which should first be made is that this development appears to have occurred entirely within the dogmatic and institutional structure of the late ancient and medieval Latin Church. There is nothing in the documents to indicate that any external factors, such as heretical movements, motivated or accentuated the development until the Reformation when, as has been demonstrated, the major elements of the Roman Catholic doctrine had long since been formulated (for the possible exception of Pelagianism, it has been seen that Pelagius himself was not at variance, at least verbally, with the thought of the early church on this point). Nor was this development subject to any manifest dissenting influence internally in the form of doctrinal controversy. Rather, the appearance here is of an orderly process which can be most nearly described as evolutionary in character, and one which proceeded by stages largely conceptual in nature. As such, the topic is not only included in the history of Christian dogma but may also be properly treated under the rubric of history of ideas. However, it is not a pure

---

[11] Schroeder, *Canons and Decrees*, p. 317. Cf. the decree on penance (Sess. 14., Nov. 25, 1551), esp. pp. 364, 367, which refers back to the justification decree. The final chapter of this decree preserves the order of presentation of St. Thomas and treats of merit under the rubric "fruits of justification". Also, see the prologue of the decree of Session 7 on the sacraments (March 3, 1547), p. 329, in which : "... consentaneum visum est, de sanctissimis ecclesiae sacramentis agere, per quae omnis vera justitia vel incipit vel coepta augetur vel amissa reparatur."

example of the history of a theoretical idea developing in an ideological vacuum, but rather of a religious idea as it was given a theoretical dogmatic expression yet subtly but decisively shaped by factors arising out of the character of the Church as an institution and its special institutional requirements for a supporting structure of dogma. It is this aspect which enhances the subject with its distinctive scholarly fascination for the student of intellectual history as a case-history highly illustrative of the relationship of ideas and institutions. The following analytical summary of the history of the medieval idea of justification is intended to describe both sets of historical factors—its theoretical, conceptual evolution and the institutional influences—which were operative in its development.

It seems a matter of certainty that the earliest theologians of the Church never completely understood or else never trusted the Pauline principle of the primacy of faith. This circumstance is partly explained by the difficulty of reconciling Paul's teaching with that of James; the compromising interpretation in the earliest commentaries on Romans passed into the medieval tradition unaltered as part of the patristic legacy. But this interpretation sufficed only to explain a technical point raised by several difficult passages in Romans. Other tendencies were, conceptually, more important in diluting the principle. It has been shown that various modifications where made through the centuries to enlarge the concept of faith. The most important of these was the Augustinian interpretation of *fides quae per dilectionem operatur*, which provided a useful concept for expositing the relationship between faith and works, but which also considerably adulterated the notion of *sola fides*. This concept was worked out in the commentaries as the definitive resolution of the faith-works problem. In another direction, the principle of faith was further diminished as it was subsumed under the category of grace, a development which occurred primarily in theological treatises of the Middle Ages. The need seems to have been felt to give a more efficacious principle to justification and also to avoid any appearance of Pelagianism. The solution was to refer all aspects of the Christian life to grace, and hence occurred that proliferation of various species of grace in the theologians of the high Middle Ages. In this development the concept of faith, to a great extent, lost its distinctive attributes as it was categorized as but another form of grace.

At this point it is well to note that there is no suspicion of any gross justification by works in this development, despite the frequent citation of James' *fides sine operibus mortua est*. The intensive cultivation of the concept of grace worked in total opposition almost to the point of anxiety in avoiding this danger by referring the totality of man's goodness and fate to a divine source through the idea of grace. Where the question of medieval semi-Pelagianism is concerned, its genesis was not in any "works righteousness" but, rather, wholly conceptual. The key to this development and its relationship to justification is found in the prevailing theory of salvation, and it is here that the semi-Pelagian tendency was manifested by engendering a view of righteousness which, as Seeberg states, "makes its aim not a personal intercourse with God, but the making of man capable of performing good works."[12] The first object of man, according to the medieval tradition, was always forgiveness, and justification came to be defined as the means to this end—hence the very literal medieval concept of justification as a 'making just' and the pre-scholastic and early scholastic definition of the term as consisting essentially in remission of sins. The manner in which the salvation "problem", as it might appear to a medieval theologian, was framed around remission of sins largely determined the solution; in the general theological literature, the definition of justification was amplified into a doctrine of penance and thus came to be identified with the sacrament of penance, then further broadened and developed into a comprehensive general theory of salvation. Assuredly, a distinct rule had to be preserved for free grace because of the teaching of the Pauline and Augustinian tradition. But it must be remembered that the medieval doctrine of justification was never characterized by the slightest hint of Luther's essential principle of imputation of righteousness (not even in Augustine, by Luther's account), but rather views justification exclusively as a matter of divine acceptation. Therefore the hybrid nature of the finished doctrine of the *processus justificationis*, initiated by grace but requiring an efficacious faith in love and good works on the part of the sinner. Inherent in this view was an irresistible potential toward an emphasis upon the latter to effect this acceptation. Hence, that development continued to a terminal point where, for the late medieval theologian, "The sinner is justified by meeting the requirements of God, a part of which is the habit of grace, another part of his own righteousness, the legal righteousness of observing the commandments."[13]

The above explanation, however, accounts for the evolution of this body of doctrine only upon the somewhat superficial level of its concep-

[12] R. Seeberg, *Text-book of the History of Doctrines*, 2 vols., tr. C. E. Hay (Philadelphia : Lutheran Publication Society, 1905), vol. 2, p. 121.

[13] Obermann, *Harvest of Medieval Theology*, p. 183.

tual development, without touching upon the historically operative factors which determined its basic direction. It would seem that the general semi-Pelagian character of the concept was not due to any single defect of logic or of doctrine, such as, the lack of Luther's notion of imputation of righteousness. The absence of this or any other specific Lutheran teaching need not have been fatal to the preservation of evangelical elements in the medieval theory of salvation. The fundamental criterion in any evangelical conception of Christianity is the priority given to maintaining a vital sense of a direct and personal relationship between man and God within an overall structure of doctrine. The resources for an adequate theology in this direction were not lacking in, for example, the Augustinian concept of *charitas*, as Abelard abundantly demonstrated. Instead, the prevailing trend in the medieval church was an opposing tendency of externalizing the channels of grace through institutional forms, resulting in a sacramental approach to the problem of salvation to the near-exclusion of an evangelical one, and the manifestation of, in Harnack's apt phrase, an increasing "sacramental mechanicalism" in the life and practice of the Church. This present study suggests that the latter development was the vital, or more exactly, the stabilizing principle in the medieval doctrine of justification; further, that this was essentially historically conditioned, and irreversibly so with the introduction of the private system of penance on the European continent in the ninth century when the Carolingian theologians forthwith committed the Latin Church to a view connecting justification with this ubiquitous sacramental instrument for the remission of sins; and, for all practical purposes, the concept of justification by faith was subsumed and absorbed into those categories of theology which formed the principal buttress of the sacramental and sacerdotal system of the medieval church.

BIBLIOGRAPHY

A. PRIMARY SOURCES

1. General Collections

Migne, J. P. *Patrologiae cursus completus. Series latina.* 221 vols. Paris, 1844-64.
—, Supplementum, accurante Adelberto Hamman. Vol. 1. Paris : Éditions Garnier Frères, 1958.
Wassenschleben, F. W. H. *Die Bussordnungen der abendländischen Kirche.* Halle : Graeger, 1951.

2. Miscellaneous Editions

Albertus Magnus, St. *Opera omnia.* Edited by S. C. A. Borgret. 38 vols. Paris : Vivès, 1890-99.
Alexander of Hales. *Glossa in quatuor libros Sententiarum Petri Lombardi, IV In librum Quartum.* Bibliotheca Franciscana scholastica, tom. XV. Quaracchi, 1957.
Ambrosiaster. *Das Corpus Paulinum des Ambrosiaster.* Edited by Heinrich Josef Vogels. *Bonner Biblische Beiträge* XIII (1957).
Anselm, St. *S. Anselmi Cantuarensis Archepiscopi Opera Omnia.* Edited by F. S. Schmitt. 6 vols. Edinburgh : Thomas Nelson, 1946-61.
Anselm of Laon. *Anselms von Laon Systematische Sentenzen.* Edited by Franz P. Bliemetzrieder. *Beiträge zur Geschichte der Philosophie des Mittelalters,* Band XVIII, heft 2-3. Münster, 1919.
Antoninus, St. (of Florence). *Summa theologica.* 4 vols. Verona, 1740.
Biel, Gabriel. *Commentarius in quartum librum Sententiarum.* Brixiae : Thomas Bozolam, 1573.
Bonaventure, St. *Opera omnia.* Edited by A. C. Peltier. Paris : Vivès, 1864-71.
Caesarius of Heisterbach. *Dialogus miraculorum.* Edited by J. Strange. Cologne: J. M. Heberle, 1851.
Corpus iuris canonici. Edited by Emil Albert Friedberg. 2 vols. Leipzig, 1879. Reprinted Graz : Akademische Druck- und Verlagsanstalt, 1955.
Duns Scotus, John. *Quaestiones in IV Librum Sententiarum (Oxoniensis). Opera omnia,* vol. 18. Paris : Vivès, 1894.
Luther, Martin. *D. Martin Luther's Werke : kritische Gesammtausgabe.* Vols. 1- . Weimar : H. Bohlau, 1883- .
Nicolaus de Lyra. *Postilla super totam Bibliam.* 5 vols. Rome : Conradus Sweynheym and Arnoldus Pannartz, 1471-72.

Pelagius. Souter, Alexander (ed.). *Pelagius' Expositions of Thirteen Epistles of St. Paul.* Cambridge Texts and Studies, IX, no. 1, *Introduction*; No. 2, *Text*; No. 3, *Pseudo-Jerome Interpolations.* 1922-31.

Petrus Aureoli. *Compendium sensus litteralis totius divinae scripturae.* Edited by P. Seebock. Quaracchi, 1896.

Petrus Manducator. *Sententiae de sacramentis.* Edited by R. M. Martin, in H. Weisweiler, *Maître Simon et son groupe De sacramentis* : *Textes inédits.* Louvain : *Spicilegium sacrum Lovaniense,* XVII (1937).

Robert of Melun. *Oeuvres de Robert de Melun.* Edited by R. M. Martin. Tome II, *Questiones [theologice] de epistolis Pauli.* Louvain : *Spicilegium sacrum Lovaniense* XVIII (1938).

Thomas Aquinas, St. *Opera omnia.* 34 vols. Paris : Vivès, 1871-90.

—, *Summa theologiae.* 60 vols. Blackfriars (New York : McGraw-Hill and London : Eyre and Spottiswoode), 1964.

Vincent of Beauvais. *Speculum quadruplex sive Speculum maius.* 4 vols. Paris : Baltazaris Belleri, 1624. Reprinted Graz : Akademische Druck- und Verlagsanstalt, 1964.

William of Auvergne (Guilelmus Autissiodorensis), *Summa aurea in quattuor libros sententiarum.* Paris, 1500.

3. English Translations

Augustine, St. *Augustine* : *Later Works.* Translated by John Burnaby. *Library of Christian Classics,* VIII. Philadelphia : Westminster Press, 1955.

—, *The Enchiridion on Faith, Hope and Love.* Translated by J. F. Shaw, edited by Henry Paolucci. Chicago : Henry Regnery, 1961.

Bernard of Clairvaux, St. *The Letters of St. Bernard of Clairvaux.* Translated by Bruno Scott James. Chicago : Henry Regnery, 1953.

Caesarius of Heisterbach. *Dialogue on Miracles.* Translated by H. von E. Scott and C. C. S. Bland. London : George Routledge, 1929.

Calvin, John. *Commentary upon the Epistle of St. Paul to the Romans.* Translated by H. Beveridge. Edinburgh : Calvin Translation Society, 1844.

—, *Institutes of the Christian Religion.* Translated by F. L. Battles, edited by John T. McNeill. *Library of Christian Classics,* XX. 2 vols. Philadelphia : Westminster Press, 1960.

Fairweather, Eugene R. *A Scholastic Miscellany* : *Anselm to Ockham. Library of Christian Classics,* X. Philadelphia : Westminster Press, 1965.

Hugh of St. Victor. *Hugh of St. Victor on the Sacraments of the Christian Faith.* Translated by Roy J. Deferrari. Cambridge, Mass. : Mediaeval Academy of America, 1951.

Luther, Martin. *Luther* : *Early Theological Works.* Translated by James Atkinson. *Library of Christian Classics,* XVI. Philadelphia : Westminster Press, 1962.

—, *Luther* : *Lectures on Romans.* Translated by Wilhelm Pauck. *Library of Christian Classics,* XV. Philadelphia : Westminster Press, 1961.

—. *Luther's Works.* 55 vols. Edited by Jaroslav Pelikan (vols. 1-30) and Helmut T. Lehman (vols. 31-55). St. Louis : Concordia Publishing House, 1955- , and Philadelphia : Muhlenberg Press, 1957- .

McCracken, George E., in collaboration with Allen Cabaniss. *Early Medieval*

142 BIBLIOGRAPHY

Theology. *Library of Christian Classics,* IX. Philadelphia : Westminster Press, 1957.

McNeill, John T., and Helena M. Gamer. *Medieval Handbooks of Penance. Records of Civilization* XXIX. New York : Columbia University Press, 1938.

Oberman, Heiko A. *Forerunners of the Reformation.* New York : Holt. Rinehart and Winston, 1966.

Palmer, Paul F. *Sacraments and Forgiveness. Sources of Christian Theology,* Vol. 2. Westminster, Md. : Newman Press, 1959.

B. SECONDARY SOURCES

1. Articles and Essays

Affeldt, Werner. "Verzeichnis der Römerbriefkommentare der lateinischen Kirche bis zu Nikolaus von Lyra," *Traditio* XIII (1957), 396-406.

Amann, Émile. "Pénitence," article in *Dictionnaire de Théologie Catholique.* 15 vols. Paris : Leouzy et Ané, 1903-50. Vol. XII, cols. 734-948.

Bischoff, Bernhard. "Wendepunkte in der Geschichte der lateinischen Exegese im Frühmittelalter," *Sacris Erudiri* VI (1954), 189-95.

Bornkamm, Heinrich. "Iustitia dei in der Scholastik und bei Luther," *Archiv für Reformationsgeschichte* XXXIX (1942), 1-46.

Cabaniss, Allen. "Florus of Lyons," *Classica et Medievalia* XIX (1958), 212-232.

Caplan, Harry. "The Four Senses of Scriptural Interpretation and the Medieval Theory of Preaching," *Speculum* IV (1929), 282-290

Charlier, Célestin. "La compilation augustinienne de Florus sur l'Apôtre," *Revue Bénédictine* LXII (1947), 132-186.

Dümmler, E. "Über Leben und Lehre des Bischofs Claudius von Turin," Akademie der Wissenschaften, Berlin. *Sitzungsberichte,* 1895. Pp. 427-443.

Grant, Robert M. "History of Interpretation of the Bible : I. Ancient Period," article in *The Interpreter's Bible,* vol. I, 106-114. New York : Abingdon Press, 1952.

Hägglund, Bengt. "The Background of Luther's Doctrine of Justification in Late Medieval Theology," *Lutheran World* VIII (1961), 24-46.

Halblitzel, J. B. "Hrabanus Maurus und Claudius von Turin," *Historisches Jahrbuch* XXVII (1906), 74-85.

Holl, Karl. "Die *iustitia dei* in der vorlutherischen Bibelauslegung des Abendlandes," *Gesammelte Aufsätze zur Kirchengeschichte,* vol. 3. Tübingen : J. C. B. Mohr, 1932. Pp. 171-188.

Jenkins, Claude. "Bede as Exegete and Theologian," in *Bede, His Life, Times and Writings : Essays in Commemoration of the Twelfth Centenary of His Death.* Edited by Alexander H. Thompson. Oxford : Oxford University Press, 1935. Pp. 152-200.

Laistner, M. L. W. "Antiochene Exegesis in Western Europe during the Middle Ages," *Harvard Theological Review* XL (1947), 19 ff.

—, "Bede as a Classical and Patristic Scholar," *Transactions of the Royal Historical Society,* 1933. Pp. 69-94.

—, "The Library of the Venerable Bede," in *Bede, His Life, Times and Writings : Essays in Commemoration of the Twelfth Centenary of His Death.*

Edited by Alexander H. Thompson. Oxford : Oxford University Press, 1935. Pp. 237-266.

Landgraf, Artur Michael. "Untersuchungen zu den Paulinenkommentaren des 12. Jahrhunderts," *Recherches de théologie ancienne et médiévale* VIII (1936), 253-281, 345-368.

McNeill, John T. "History of Interpretation of the Bible : II. Medieval and Reformation Period," article in *The Interpreter's Bible*, vol. I, 115-126. New York : Abingdon Press, 1952.

Oberman, Heiko A. *"Facientibus Quod in se est Deus non Denegat Gratiam* : Robert Holcot O. P. and the Beginnings of Luther's Theology," *Harvard Theological Review* LV (1962), 312-342.

—, " 'Iustitia Christi' and 'Iustitia Dei' : Luther and the Scholastic Doctrines of Justification," *Harvard Theological Review* LIX (1966), 1-26.

Rivière, J. "Justification," article in *Dictionnaire de Théologie Catholique*. 15 vols. Paris : Letouzy et Ané, 1903-50. Vol. VIII, cols. 2042-2227.

Smalley, Beryl. "La Glossa ordinaria," *Recherches de théologie ancienne et médiévale* IX (1937), 365-400.

Souter, Alexander. "The Character and History of Pelagius' Commentary on the Epistles of St. Paul," *Proceedings of the British Academy, 1915-16.* Pp. 261-296.

—, "The Commentary of Pelagius on the Epistles of Paul : The Problem of its Restoration," *Proceedings of the British Academy*, 1905-06. Pp. 409-439.

—, "The Sources of Sedulius Scottus' *Collectaneum* on the Epistles of St. Paul," *Journal of Theological Studies* XVIII (1917), 184-228.

Southern, Richard W. "Lanfranc of Bec and Berengar of Tours," *Studies in Medieval History Presented to Frederick Maurice Powicke.* Edited by Richard W. Hunt *et al.* Oxford, 1948. Pp. 27-48.

Templin, J. Alton. "Justification in Late medieval Theology and Luther's Thought," *The Iliff Review* XXV, No. 2 (1968), 29-38.

Wilmart, André. "La collection de Bède le Vénérable sur l'Apôtre," *Revue Bénédictine* XXXVIII (1926), 16-52.

Willmes, Ansgar. "Bedas Bibelauslegung," *Archiv für Kulturgeschichte* no. 3 (1962), 281-314.

2. Books and Monographs

Auer, Johann. *Die Entwicklung der Gnadenlehre in der Hochscholastik.* 2 vols. Freiburg : Herder, 1942-51.

Bardenhewer, Otto. *Geschichte der altkirchlichen Literatur.* Second edition. 5 vols. Reprinted Darmstadt : Wissenschaftliche Buchgesellschaft, 1962.

Bouillard, Henri. *Conversion et grâce chez St. Thomas d'Aquin.* Paris : Aubier, 1944.

Cabaniss, Allen. *Agobard of Lyons : Churchman and Critic.* Syracuse : Syracuse University Press, 1953.

—, *Amalarius of Metz.* Amsterdam : North Holland Publishing Co., 1954.

Chenu, M.-D. *La théologie au XIIe siècle. Études de philosophie médiévale* XLV. Paris : J. Vrin, 1957.

—, *Toward Understanding Sr. Thomas.* Translated by A.-M. Landry and D. Hughes. Chicago : Henry Regnery, 1964.

Coulton, G. G. *Medieval Panorama*. New York : Meridian Books, 1955.

Dekkers, Eligius, and Aemilius Gaar. *Clavis patrum latinorum*. Revised edition. *Sacris Eriduri* III (1961).

Denifle, Heinricj. *Die abendländischen Schriftausleger bis Luther über Justitia Dei (Rom. 1,17) und Justificatio*. Ergänzungen zu Denifle's *Luther und Luthertum*, I. Band. Quellenbelege. Mainz : Kirchheim, 1905.

Douglas, E. J. Dempsey. *Justification in Late Medieval Preaching*. Leiden : E. J. Brill, 1966.

Duckett, Eleanor Shipley. *Carolingian Portraits*. Ann Arbor : University of Michigan Press, 1962.

Dudden, F. Holmes. *Gregory the Great : His Place in History and Thought*. 2 vols. London : Longmans, Green, 1905.

Feckes, Carl. *Die Rechtfertigungslehre des Gabriel Biel*. *Münstersche Beiträge zur Theologie* VII. Münster i.W. : Aschendorf, 1925.

Ferguson, John. *Pelagius*. Cambridge : Heffer, 1956.

Franks, Robert S. *The Work of Christ : A Historical Study of Christian Doctrine*. Reprinted London : Thomas Nelson, 1962.

Frede, Hermann Josef. *Pelagius, der irische Paulustext. Sedulius Scottus*. Freiburg : Herder, 1961.

Ghellinck, Joseph de. *Le mouvement théologique du XII*e *siècle*. Second edition. Bruges : Éditions "De Tempel", 1948.

Gilson, Etienne. *History of Christian Philosophy in the Middle Ages*. London : Sheed and Ward, 1955.

Glorieux, P. *Pour revaloriser Migne : Tables rectificatives*. *Mélanges de science religieuse* IX (1952), cahier supplémentaire.

Glunz, H. H. *History of the Vulgate in England from Alcuin to Roger Bacon*. Cambridge : Cambridge University Press, 1933.

Grabmann, Martin. *Die Geschichte der scholastischen Methode*. 2 vols. Freiburg : Herder, 1909. Reprinted Graz : Akademische Druck- und Verlagsanstalt, 1957.

Grant, Robert M. *The Bible in the Church : A Short History of Interpretation*. New York : Macmillan, 1948.

Halblitzel, J. B. *Hrabanus Maurus, Ein Beitrag zur Geschichte der Mittelalterlichen Exegese*. *Biblische Studien*, Band XI, Heft 3. Freiburg : Herder, 1906.

Harnack, Adolf. *History of Dogma*. Translated by Neil Buchanan. 7 vols. in 4. Reprinted New York : Dover Publications, 1961.

Jaeger, Werner. *Early Christianity and Greek Paideia*. Cambridge, Mass. : Harvard University Press, 1961.

Jedin, Hubert. *A History of the Council of Trent*. Translated by E. Graf. Vol. 1. London : Thomas Nelson, 1957.

Küng, Hans. *Justification : The Doctrine of Karl Barth and a Catholic reflection*. Translated by T. Collins *et al.* New York : Thomas Nelson & Sons, 1964.

Landgraf, Artur Michael. *Dogmengeschichte der Frühscholastik*. 4 vols. Regensburg : Gregorius-Verlag, 1952-56.

— *Einführung in die theologische Literatur der Frühscholastik unter dem Gesichtspunkt der Schulenbildung*. Regensburg : Gregorius-Verlag, 1948.

Lea, Henry C. *A History of Auricular Confession and Indulgences in the Latin Church*. 3 vols. Philadelphia : H. C. Lea, 1896.

Leff, Gordon. *Bradwardine and the Pelagians*. Cambridge : Cambridge University Press, 1957.

Lietzmann, Hans. *A History of the Early Church*. Translated by B. L. Woolf. 4 vols. in 2. New York : Meridian Books, 1961.

Loofs, Friedrich. *Leitfaden zum Studium der Dogmengeschichte*. Sixth edition revised by Kurt Aland. Tübingen : Niemeyer Verlag, 1959.

Lortz, Joseph. *The Reformation in Germany*. Translated by R. Walls. 2 vols. New York : Herder and Herder, 1968.

Lubac, H. de. *Exégèse médiévale : les quatre sense de l'écriture*. 4 vols. Paris : Aubier, 1959-64.

McCallum, J. Ramsey. *Abelard's Ethics*. Oxford : Oxford University Press, 1935.

MacDonald, Alan John. *Berengar and the Reform of Sacramental Doctrine*. Oxford : Oxford University Press, 1930.

—, *Lanfranc : A Study of his Life, Work, and Writing*. Oxford : Oxford University Press, 1926.

Mackinnon, James. *Luther and the Reformation*. 3 vols. London : Longmans, Green, 1925.

McNally, Robert E. *The Bible in the Early Middle Ages*. Woodstock Papers No. 4. Westminster, Md. : Newman Press, 1959.

Maître, Léon. *Les écoles episcopales et monastiques en Occident avant les universités (786-1180)*. Paris : A. Picard et fils, 1924.

Manitius, Max. *Geschichte der lateinischen Literatur des Mittelalters*. 3 vols. Munich : C. H. Beck, 1911-31.

Mayer, Charles B. *The Thomistic Concept of Justifying Contrition*. Mundelein, Ill. : Seminarii Sanctae Mariae ad Lacum, 1949.

Nygren, Anders. *Agape and Eros*. Translated by Philip S. Watson. Philadelphia : Westminster Press, 1953.

Oberman, Heiko A. *Archbishop Thomas Bradwardine : A Fourteenth Century Augustinian*. Utrecht : Kemink, 1957.

—, *The Harvest of Medieval Theology*. Cambridge, Mass. : Harvard University Press, 1963.

Ozment, Steven E. (ed.). *The Reformation in Medieval Perspective*. Chicago : Quadrangle Books, 1971.

Paré, Gérard, and A. Brunet, P. Tremblay. *La renaissance du XIIe siècle. Les écoles et l'enseignement*. Publications de l'Institut d'Études Médiévales d'Ottawa, III (1933).

Pfleiderer, Otto. *The Influence of the Apostle Paul on Christianity*. Hibbert Lectures, 1885. New York : Scribner's, 1885.

Pieper, Josef. *Guide to Thomas Aquinas*. New York : Pantheon Books, 1962.

Plinval, Georges de. *Pélage, ses écrits, sa vie et sa réforme*. Lausanne : Librairie Payot, 1943.

Poole, Reginald Lane. *Illustrations of the History of Medieval Thought and Learning*. Second edition. Reprinted New York : Dover Publications, 1960.

146 BIBLIOGRAPHY

BIBLIOGRAPHY

Portalié, Eugéne. *A Guide to the Thought of St. Augustine.* Translated by Ralph J. Bastien. Chicago : Henry Regnery, 1960.

Poschmann, Bernard. *Penance and the Anointing of the Sick.* Translated by F. Courtney, S. J. New York : Herder and Herder, 1964.

Pourrat, Pierre. *Theology of the Sacraments.* Authorized translation from the third French edition. St. Louis : Herder, 1910.

Rashdall, Hastings. *The Idea of Atonement in Christian Theology.* Bampton Lectures, 1915. London : Macmillan, 1920.

Ritschl, Albrecht. *The Christian Doctrine of Reconciliation and Justification.* Vol. I : *A Critical History.* Translated by J. S. Black. Edinburgh : Edmunston and Douglas, 1872.

Rost, Hans. *Die Bibel im Mittelalter. Beiträge zur Geschichte und Bibliographie der Bibel.* Augsburg : Kommissions-Verlag M. Seitz, 1939.

Rupp, Gordon. *The Righteousness of God.* New York : Philosophical Library, 1953.

Saarnivara, Uuras. *Luther Discovers the Gospel.* St. Louis : Concordia Publishing House, 1951.

Scheper, John B. *Justitia Dei und Justificatio (Romans I, 17) in Early Latin Literature.* Wahsington : Catholic University of America, 1932.

Schwiebert, E. G. *Luther and His Times.* St. Louis : Concordia Publishing House, 1950.

Seeberg, Reinhold. *Text-book of the History of Doctrines.* Translated by Charles E. Hay. Philadelphia : Lutheran Publication Society, 1905.

Sikes, Jeffrey Garrett. *Peter Abailard.* Cambridge : Cambridge University Press, 1932.

Smalley, Beryl. *The Study of the Bible in the Middle Ages.* Second edition. Oxford : Blackwell, 1952. (also University of Notre Dame Press, 1964).

Souter, Alexander. *The Earliest Latin Commentaries on the Epistles of St. Paul.* Oxford : Oxford University Press, 1927.

—, *A Study of Ambrosiaster. Cambridge Texts and Studies* VII, no. 4 (1905).

Spicq, C. *Esquisse d'une histoire de l'exégèse latine au moyen âge.* Paris : J. Vrin, 1944.

Spitzig, Joseph A. *Sacramental Penance in the Twelfth and Thirteenth Centuries.* Washington : Catholic University of America, 1947.

Stegmüller, F. *Repertorium biblicum medii aevi.* 7 vols. Barcelona, 1950-61.

Steinmetz, David Curtis. *Misericordia Dei : The Theology of Johannes von Staupitz in its Late Medieval Setting.* Leiden : E. J. Brill, 1968.

Vogels, H. J. *Das Corpus Paulinum des Ambrosiaster. Bonner Biblische Beiträge* XIII. Bonn : Peter Hanstein Verlag, 1957.

Watkins, Oscar D. *A History of Penance.* 2 vols. London, 1920. Reprinted New York : Burt Franklin, 1961.

Whale, J. S. *The Protestant Tradition.* Cambridge : Cambridge University Press, 1955.

Wood, James D. *The Interpretation of the Bible : A Historical Introduction.* London : Gerald Duckworth, 1958.

INDEX

Abbo of St. Germain, 89
Abelard, Peter, 3-4, 13, 47-48, 77, 96-98,
  101-102, 106, 139
Aegidius Romanus. *See* Giles of Rome
Albert the Great, Saint, 111, 114
Alcuin of York, 28, 83-85, 104
Alexander of Hales, 110-111*n*, 114, 117,
  126
Alger of Liège, 96-97
Ambrose, Saint, 96, 103, 107
Ambrosiaster, 15, 17-20, 24, 29, 33, 38,
  42
Anselm of Canterbury, Saint, 90-91
Anselm of Laon, 13, 44, 90-91
Aquinas, Thomas. *See* Thomas Aqui-
  nas, Saint
Atto of Vercelli. *See* Hatto of Vercelli
Attrition, 123-125, 127
Augustine, Saint, 2, 4, 13, 20-21, 27, 29,
  33, 34, 41, 42, 44, 62, 66, 69, 70-72,
  79, 80, 105, 107, 138

Baptism: and justification, 25, 27, 33, 37-
  38, 50, 60, 69, 70, 95, 105, 134-135
Bede, The Venerable, 13, 28, 68, 72*n*, 96
Bernard of Clairvaux, Saint, 48, 96, 97-
  102, 104, 105, 108
Biel, Gabriel, 112, 122*n*, 125, 130
Bonaventure, Saint, 61, 64, 106, 112, 114,
  115-118, 126
Bruno of Cologne, Saint, 13, 45

Caesarius of Heisterbach, 114
Calvin, John: discusses medieval *Romans*
  commentaries, 72-74

Cassiodorus, 13, 25-27, 33
Confession. *See* Penance and confession
Contrition: in Scholastic theologians,
  113, 115, 117; importance in Nominalists, 123-125, 127; and Luther, 131

Denifle, Heinrich: study of Luther's doctrine of justification, 10-11, 67*n*
Duns Scotus, John, 112, 123-125

Edgar, King of England, 89-90
Erasmus, 4, 6, 17, 22, 87*n*

"*facere quod in se est*": in St. Bonaventure, 118; in Nominalists, 126-127;
  Luther's reaction, 131-133
Faith and works: mentioned, 54, 59, 115;
  citations of *James* 2:26 ("faith without
  works is dead"), 24, 26-27, 33, 39-40,
  44, 49, 50, 56, 60, 67-69, 72, 74*n*, 137;
  cited by Luther, 132; in Trent decrees,
  135-136; discussed, 137-138
Faith, formed and unformed (*fides formata* and *informata*), 59, 65, 66, 74-75,
  119
"faith working through love" (*fides per
  dilectionem operatur*): in medieval
  Romans commentaries, 29, 33, 35, 44,
  47, 53, 57, 59, 63, 66, 69, 71, 74*n*; in
  medieval theologians, 97, 101, 105,
  119; and Luther, 131-133; in Trent
  decrees, 135; discussed, 137
Florus of Lyons, 33-35, 40, 44, 48-49